GANDHI THROUGH
WESTERN EYES

About the Author

HORACE ALEXANDER was born at Croydon, England in 1889. He grew up at Tunbridge Wells, in southeast England and was educated at the Quaker School, Bootham, in York, England, & later at King's College, Cambridge where he studied modern history. He has been an active Quaker throughout his life and was a conscientious objector during the First World War, but he was allowed to teach. In 1919 he was appointed lecturer in International Relations at the Quaker school of religion and social study, Woodbrooke, in Birmingham. This work was continued for over twenty years. He spent six months in India during a sabbatical year in 1927-8, where he was guided by Gandhi's English friend C.F. Andrews. He spent a week at Gandhi's ashram at Sabarmati, Gujarat and also stayed at Tagore's educational center, Santiniketan in Bengal.

When Gandhi visited England in 1931 for the Round Table Conference Horace Alexander spent part of each week with the Gandhi party in London. During the Second World War he again visited India with the Friends Ambulance Unit. He returned to India in 1949 & spent several years there in close cooperation with Gandhi and other leaders of Indian nationalism.

He has twice been married. His second wife is an American Quaker & for the past fifteen years their home has been near Philadelphia. Throughout his life he has enjoyed watching birds, and one of his published books is called *Seventy Years of Birdwatching*.

OTHER WORKS INCLUDE:
Indian Ferment
Consider India
Revival of Europe
Justice Among Nations
India Since Cripps

Gandhi through Western Eyes

HORACE ALEXANDER

NEW SOCIETY PUBLISHERS
Philadelphia, PA

© H. Alexander, 1969, 1984
Horace Alexander (1889)

ISBN: Hardcover 0-86571-045-7
Paperback 0-86571-044-9

New Society Publishers is a project of the New Society
Educational Foundation and a collective of Movement
for a New Society. Movement for a New Society (MNS)
is a network of small groups and individuals working
for fundamental social change through nonviolent action. This book expresses the opinion of the author, and
does not necessarily represent positions of MNS as a
whole. To learn more about MNS, write 4722 Baltimore
Avenue, Philadelphia, PA 19143

Printed in the U.S.A.
Published by New Society Publishers,
4722 Baltimore Avenue, Philadelphia, PA 19143

Contents

Preface

MAHATMA GANDHI died in January 1948. I complete this book in 1969. Twenty-one years is a long time in this century of revolutionary change. To those who are under thirty, Gandhi belongs to a forgotten generation. Soon we shall be celebrating his centenary. He is becoming a myth rather than a real man of flesh and blood. One purpose of the pages that follow is to try to save Gandhi from this fate.

Who was Gandhi? Why should we remember him? First, we may see him as the leader of India, their Moses, their George Washington, or what you will, the man who led the people of India out of British captivity into the promised land of political freedom. In India, Gandhi is still spoken of as the Father of the Nation. If one looks at him in broader perspective, he may be seen as the first man (or very nearly the first) in Asia or Africa who stood up to the white colonial overlords and asserted the human dignity of the dark-skinned peoples of the world. In this sense, he is to be seen as the pioneer of the great Afro-Asian awakening, which has led to the almost total disappearance, within twenty years, of "colonialism," in its older forms at least, from the map of the world.

But Gandhi does not belong only to India or only to any special section of humanity. He is, in a very special sense, a world figure, a man who belongs to us all, and who has something to say that all the world should attend to. In a unique way, he made himself the friend of all humanity. When the news of his death spread over the world, people in far off lands which he had never visited, people who had never seen him or heard his voice, wept in the streets. And these were the common people. They knew they had lost a personal friend. Why? One way in which he was unique was this: he never changed his way of life from the simplicity that he had adopted in early life. Even when he was world famous, he was still easily accessible to everybody. When, at the end of his life, he could have become Prime Minister or President of India, he took no office and continued to have no assured personal income. He identified himself with the poor as much as was humanly possible to the day of his death. Fame did not spoil him.

Nor did he ever begin to water down the principles he had early proclaimed as the right foundation for statecraft. He strove throughout his life to operate without violence or threat of violence. When India achieved independence, he still advocated the total disarmament of the country, without waiting for any other country to do the same. Common men throughout the world dread the oppression and violence implicit in the very existence of the modern nation state. They are familiar with statesmen who set out early in their careers to rid the world of war and tyranny and armaments, but who end up defending policies that depend for their existence on armed force and coercive authority. Gandhi, to the end, preferred the risks of anarchy to the kind of law and order that has to be upheld by a coercive government. Such life-long consistency is rare; and the man, who sticks to such radical convictions in spite of all the pulls of expediency, appeals to some very deep instinct in the human heart. He will not gain in votes of the multitude today, but he gains the love and devotion of millions through many generations.

Gandhi is not an easy man to place. To most Britishers, he looks very different from the picture that his name immediately evokes in the minds of most Indians. To most British people, especially those who were living in India or who were closely associated with India during his lifetime, he appears first and foremost as the political leader of what seemed to them an unreasonable, "disloyal" movement, which refused to work the reasonable reforms proposed from time to time by the British, and preferred appeals to mass emotion, thus arousing the passions of undisciplined millions, whereas the British believed that India could best be prepared for self-government by a process of political evolution. Such action as Gandhi led seemed to the British to be unwise and uncalled for. True, in his personal life he was something of a saint, and in politics he was clearly not influenced by personal ambition;

he could show a rare chivalry towards his opponents. But the ordinary Englishman finds it very hard to see him as the man of such towering spiritual personality as his fellow-Indians claim.

Then again, Americans, Europeans, Africans and other Asians may have ideas about him that are quite different from either the Indian or the British view. The impression he has made in circles where people are striving to break away from the hideous tyranny of political violence and counter-violence, which threatens quickly to destroy the whole world, is specially worth examining. In countries that are fairly aloof from the political controversies of Gandhi's lifetime, in which, inevitably, all British and Indian people were involved, there is a far greater interest in his philosophy of life, as revealed in his innumerable writings, than in this or that political action. In the past forty years I have read a great deal of "Gandhiana," coming from many different sources. In recent years especially, I have been amazed at the number of pure golden nuggets of penetrating human wisdom that these students of the human predicament continue to dig out of Gandhi's writings. Many have been collected together in Homer Jack's *The Gandhi Reader;* but there are many more to be found that are not included there. The appeal he makes is not primarily to the "clever" people. Whatever that overworked word "sophisticated" really means, Gandhi was not sophisticated. There was a rough directness about him that often shocked the bright boys from the West who came to see him. The New Testament records of Jesus that "the common people heard him gladly," not the graduates of Athens or Rome. So it was and still is with Gandhi. His appeal is wide and it is deep; but it is not to the clever elite who try to run the academic, the cultural and the political and economic life of the western world.

It will be seen that there are many difficulties that beset the man who attempts to write the story of Gandhi's life. Which life is it to be? The Indian, the British, the American or some other? Of course, it must be an amalgam of all these. But the story of his life is inevitably the story of his political activity, for he spent his life in politics. Yet the essence of the man was not to be found in his political activity. The things that made him "Mahatma" were there all the time, infusing his political activity no less than everything else that he did. One might say that his every act had an aroma about it, which made him the prophetic human being I believe he was. If you missed that quality, then you missed the true nature of the man altogether. It is hardly possible to bring that quality, that unique infusion, to life through the pages of a biography. So, if you read this book and leave off dissatisfied, as you should do, then go back to his writings, and see if the secret is revealed to you there.

If there is one expression which, more nearly than any other, expresses Gandhi's contribution to the world, it is the word "non-violence." This is a poor word, but what it seeks to express is rich. I hope the pages that follow will do something to illuminate Gandhi's non-violence. But his way of life was all of a piece; therefore, it is scarcely possible to disentangle his principles of action from his daily political activity. Gandhi was first and foremost a man of action. That does not mean that he was a superficial thinker, or that he allowed political expediency to rule his course of action. Far from it. But he believed that thought and action are not to be separated. It is idle, in Gandhi's view, for a man to talk about his "faith" unless he can be seen practising it. So, when anyone came to Gandhi and asked him to expound his philosophy of non-violence, he was apt to reply, in effect: "Come and watch me at work." Yet he never stopped thinking or trying new methods of expressing his convictions. He called his own autobiography, *The Story of my Experiments with Truth.* Truth was God to him. In this sense he was a scientist. When he was seized with a fresh hypothesis, which appeared to contain essential truth for man's life on earth, he started next morning to see how it worked in practice. This he would do with total disregard to his own comfort and convenience — sometimes, too, with little regard for the comfort of his friends and associates. Therefore, to understand his experiments in non-violence, it is important to study his whole life. This is not to disparage such an admirable systematic study of his methods as can be found in Dr Joan Bondurant's *Conquest of Violence.* Both this and Richard Gregg's classic, *The Power of Non-Violence*, should be studied by all who want to substitute sane methods of struggle for the madness of armed conflict.

There are already several excellent books about Gandhi's life and work. The books by C. F. Andrews, though written years before Gandhi's death, are still among the best studies of his life and thought. Among the shorter biographies, two are outstanding — those by Louis Fischer and B.R. Nanda. Nanda, as an Indian, has certain advantages. He never knew Gandhi personally; but he has mastered the mass of material remarkably; he is sufficiently detached to see Gandhi as he was, not just as a mythical figure; he is sufficiently Indian to appreciate fully the deep cultural source out of which the Mahatmaship of Gandhi grew. The composite biography by Polak, Brailsford and Pethick-Lawrence is also good, especially, to my mind, the middle section by Brailsford, which deals with the controversial years when Gandhi was making his mark in the Indian national movement. Pyarelal Nayar, Gandhi's former secretary, has been for years engaged on an "official" full-scale biography. He has now published two large volumes called *Mahatma Gandhi: The Last Phase*, and one dealing with the first twenty-one years of his life: *Mahatma Gandhi: The First Phase*; also a smaller book called *A Pilgrimage of Peace*, telling of Gandhi's visit to the North-West Frontier of India in 1938. These volumes, especially *The Last Phase*, are invaluable source material.

But, in the end, once a reader has a general picture of Gandhiji's life, he may learn more from reading extracts from his innumerable writings than from straightforward biography. The Navajivan Press in India has published a long series of volumes of his writings, under such titles as: *India of my Dreams*; *Rebuilding our Villages*; *Truth is God*; *My Religion*; *In Search of the Supreme*; *Christian Missions*; *True Education*; *Food Shortage and Agriculture*; *Women and Social Injustice*; *To the Students*; *Discourses on the Gita*; *Ashram Observances in Action*; and many more. The titles themselves indicate something of the range of his concern. Almost always he has something real to say on these topics; he speaks as one having authority, as one who has thought profoundly before he speaks. Most of these little books contain extracts from his writings covering thirty or forty years.

Is there any reason to add another biographical study? I believe there is. Gandhi appears to be one of those rare men whose stature will grow as the centuries pass. So I think it is of importance that a number of different first-hand portraits should survive, to show how he appeared to a number of different observers. None of us who knew him could see more than a limited part of his remarkable character. Each of us no doubt brings him down in some degree towards our own size or vision, however hard we try to avoid doing this. During his lifetime I recall that I would sometimes say to him: "You mean this, don't you?" And he would reply: "No, you have misunderstood me." Now he is not here to check what I have written, so I can only warn the reader not to assume that I have always got it right.

I first knew Gandhi in the spring of 1928, when I spent a week in his ashram near Ahmedabad. At that time he had recently completed his autobiography. He never attempted to carry his own story of his "experiments with truth" any further. So I have given more attention to the later years when I was in personal contact with him, than to the first sixty years. Moreover, there were a few brief weeks when I was close to him, day by day. These times include somé of the most dramatic or significant episodes in his later life, such as the days of the Round Table Conference in London (1931) and the days of the Cabinet Mission in India and the final withdrawal of British rule (summers of 1946 and '47). These periods I have written in much greater detail than the rest. The result is an unequal balance of events, but I think this is justified by the circumstances.

Just as I was concluding this Preface I found in the pages of that excellent weekly periodical *Manas* (February 16, 1966) the following paragraph, which expresses concisely what I have been struggling to say in the first part of this Preface. So I quote it:

There are some men whose achievements begin mainly in the world of imaginative synthesis and whose being, therefore, can be understood only by a corresponding use of the mind. In such cases, a lot of particulars about their personal lives may diminish their stature instead of adding to it. It is for this reason, no doubt, that thoughtful men often observe that myth contains more truth than history, since myths provide summations of meaning that are easily lost in the foliage of historical fact. So with Gandhi's life-work.

Another sentence from this article in *Manas* deserves quotation here. The writer says: "What are seen as 'oddities' by Gandhi's critics can almost always be found to embody a deep consistency with some basic principle of Indian philosophy, brought up to date and freshly applied to a contemporary situation." In other words, his sense of values, his sense of proportion, were often strikingly different from the prevailing world view of educated westerners. Whenever we meet in his life or thought something that is hard to understand, we may do well to consider, before impatiently rejecting it as non-sense, whether perhaps here Gandhi has something to say to us that we need to attend to. Especially, perhaps, in his tendency to mix together in his writings in *Harijan*, what look like trivial personal matters with discussions of great world issues, he is often deliberately asserting that the seemingly trivial things in human relations often contain the keys to big issues.

Perhaps I have warned the reader enough. We had better turn to the story of his life.

Preface to Second Edition

MAHATMA GANDHI was killed by a young Hindu in January 1948. It is hardly surprising that in 1980 most young people in Europe and North America had only a vague idea of who he was. They had heard his name. That was all. But in 1983 he came to life again. Millions of people went to the nearest cinema to see a film called "Gandhi." In the course of a few hours they discovered Gandhi for themselves. For many this discovery has meant something profound. I have seen for myself, and I have heard from many places, that when the film ended, the audience, or a large proportion of those who had seen the film, wanted to stay and be silent and think. They had seen something special, something different from the usual way of life. They had been enriched.

Those of us who had the exceptional good fortune to know Gandhi when he was alive, have been trying, with very little success, to interest people in him. Now, suddenly, we have a new opportunity. Can we build upon the foundation provided by Sir Richard Attenborough's film? We can try.

What is the message of the film? We see Gandhi fighting against what he saw as injustice, race prejudice, the arrogance of the colonial powers in Asia and Africa. But he refused to use any weapon that might hurt his opponent. Conflict must cause suffering; but he tried to make sure that the suffering should be endured by him and his fellow fighters, not by the "enemy." The Revolutionary army consisted of "Satyagrahis," men and women who relied on the power of truth to win the battle. Their weapons must be wholly non-violent. They must have no fear of the enemy, however powerful he might be. Total fearlessness is to be the nature of Gandhi and his followers.

All this is shown in the film; and it is true to the life that Gandhi lived in South Africa and in India. The film, which is rightly connected with Sir Richard Attenborough, was first propounded by Motilal Kothari in the early 1960's, and it was he who inspired Attenborough, as he, Attenborough, makes plain. Mr. Kothari was a member of the Indian High Commission in London; at the time my wife, who is American, and I were living at Swanage, on the south coast of England, and he soon brought us into his concern. When things began to move he abandoned his secure appointment, and gave all his time to the film. Alas, his health was poor, and he died young; he did not live to see the final result of his efforts, though his wife and son have sustained their interest, and have seen the remarkable portrait of Gandhi through the personality of Ben Kingsley.

I had known the Mahatma well for twenty years. I claim to be one of his ten thousand intimate friends and I could hardly believe that any western actor would be able to present Gandhi as he really was. He had a unique personality, simple, direct but always clear and strong. When I saw the film, the words and the manner were so true to the man that I had known that there were times when I thought we were listening to an old tape of the actual Gandhi. Perhaps only a half-Gujarati could so completely identify with the Mahatma. I have heard it suggested that the actor lacks the charisma of the real Mahatma. I am not sure that I agree. Did the true Gandhi have charisma? I rather think not. He allowed himself always to be on a level with the innumerable people that he met. He never put on airs. There was no sense of being reminded: Don't forget that I am a Mahatma? On the contrary: Do please forget my Mahatma-ship. I am a plain human being, just as you are.

Mr. Gandhi was the easiest man in all the world to meet and to know. He was ready for a laugh at any time. Here are two examples. During his visit to England for the Round Table Conference in 1931, he spent one of his weekends at Woodbrooke, the Quaker College where I was working at the time. I travelled with him and his staff by car from Nottingham, where he had made a call on the way from London. The Woodbrooke staff and students were assembled inside the front door (the weather was atrocious) whilst the Wardens, Henry and Lucy Cadbury, came out to meet us as we got out of the car. The first thing the people assembled inside heard was a loud laugh. Explanation: As soon as I introduced Mr. Gandhi to Mr. Cadbury, Mr. Gandhi said: "I ate your chocolates many years ago in South Africa." In Delhi, in the autumn of 1947, in the weeks after Independence Day and partition of India and Pakistan, when the

Hindus and Sikhs and Muslims were tearing each other to pieces in and around Delhi, I was talking to Mr. Gandhi one morning, when Mr. Nehru, the Prime Minister, suddenly arrived. I withdrew to the far side of the room. It was obvious that Mr. Nehru had come to get help in his desperate efforts to reestablish peace and good order. Within five minutes they were laughing together. What other help he got that day I do not know. He at least was reminded that, however harsh the situation, there is a redeeming joke not far away.

Mr. Gandhi was always quick to make friends. He loved people. One sometimes wondered if he ever met anyone whom he did not immediately like. Yes, perhaps those pompous political leaders who wanted to be recognized as important. He was inclined to pay more attention to some utterly non-political man or woman who visited him "under concern," as a Quaker might express it, than to some political leader from the West, who was determined to show him that he was all wrong.

He was easy to know; but that did not mean that he was easy to move. The life he lived had given him a quiet self-assurance that showed itself in all manner or matters, both small and large. His strength did not always show itself; but those who lived with him, even for a short time, soon discovered it. Acharya Kripalani, one of his first friends in India, after his return from South Africa, once told me that he had deliberately kept himself away from Gandhi's ashram (community). "All who live at the ashram," he said, "tend to be overpowered by the force of his character." Having quoted Kripalani on the danger of becoming a mere echo of Gandhi if you lived in his ashram for any length of time, it seems appropriate to quote him again in a way that shows how his associates relied on him. One day, a year or two after Gandhi's death, I happened to find myself, along with Kripalani, on the platform of some meeting that was slow to begin. In India, chairs are not normally provided for those who sit on the platform. They sit on the ground, probably raised a little above the ground used by the audience; and a few cushions are provided for them to rest against if they need such support. Kripalani drew one of these cushions to his side, and commented: "I always like some support to rest on. I used to get support from Gandhiji. Now I get it from this cushion."

Such casual comments might be found among all Gandhi's close colleagues. Unfortunately, the film does not bring out the independent thought and action of these colleagues. The portrayal of his colleagues,

especially perhaps Jawaharlal Nehru, seems to me to be the most
unsatisfactory feature of the film. British officialdom, from some of
the Viceroys down, was fond of declaring that Gandhi's close
associates were all just pale copies of Gandhi himself. Nothing could
be further from the truth. Gandhi never surrounded himself with "yes
men." To gain his respect, it was almost essential that you should
show yourself to be at some point sharply critical of him. One of the
young men who had listened to some of the intimate talks of the
leaders once told me with delight how he had listened to Mr.
Rajagopalachari explaining to Mr. Gandhi how he had gone quite
wrong in some public statement about the nature of non-violence. No
one who knew Vallabhai Patel could see him as a pale copy of any
other man. When, at the end of the long negotiations with the British
Cabinet Mission, Mr. Gandhi, who at first welcomed the British
proposals as "the best the British could do, " then advised the
Congress Working Committee to reject them, Patel utterly refused
to follow him. Some of Mrs. Naidu's famous witticisms about the
expense of keeping the Mahatma in poverty hardly suggest a woman
who had surrendered her independence of mind. Mr. Nehru, in every
speech he made, or every letter he wrote, was so unlike the Mahatma
that the outside world was apt to ask: How could two such different
minds ever live together? But they did. Gandhi and his colleagues may
well be seen as the Founding Fathers of free India. They did not
challenge one another to fight duels; but there was every type of
political outlook amongst them. One of the most remarkable of the
Mahatma's qualities was his ability to get each of these strangely mixed
human beings to accept one another.

The strength of Mahatma Gandhi's personality cannot be missed
by those who see the film. News has been published of an American
girl, who resigned from the American Navy after seeing the film. What
Gandhi told her was that she must have nothing to do with this whole
killing business. When last reported, she still was holding out against
the American Navy's efforts to break her. It is likely that other young
people will have their lives changed by the film.

But of course there are those who reject the Gandhi of the film
as they rejected the real Gandhi. The film deliberately confines itself
to the political life of Gandhi, but he broke ground in many other
aspects of life, including sex. There are always some diseased people
around who will find that the world's heroes are less than heroes in
their sex lives. So it is with Gandhi. It happens that, at the time when

I walked for a couple of days with Gandhi in Noakhali, he was sharing his bed with the great niece who was looking after his personal well-being. He asked me to give him my opinion, "as a Christian" of what he was doing. So we spent an hour or so discussing it, and we returned to the subject the next day. Afterwards he wrote to tell me why he had given it up. The letter telling me of this is published in full, together with his other letters written to me from time to time, in an appendix. Let me briefly tell the story as he told it to me.

His great niece had assured him that she had no sexual feeling toward him. He was, to her, just like her mother (who had died). Now, as it happened, during those months he walked through rural Bengal, striving to restore communal harmony in an area where the Muslim majority had driven the Hindu minority from their homes, he was very conscious of the fact that most of the villages where he stayed for the night had no such facility as guest rooms. Each village had difficulty in arranging accommodation for Mr. Gandhi and his party. He had to restrict the press to (I believe) one man at a time. In my case, although he had urged me to come as his guest, I was aware that my presence created difficulties, so I only stayed for two nights. For a time he and his great niece had two beds in one room. Then he arranged that they should share a single bed. This would test her declaration. If the girl was sexually excited, he would, of course, be obliged to revert to the two beds. When I was with him, all was going well; and he was almost lyrical in his assertion that, if they found it possible to sleep side by side, it would be an important discovery for mankind. He wished me to understand that it would be a test for the girl, rather than for himself. He had trained himself to be free from sexual demands many years earlier. This I readily believed. It went with his ability to go to sleep with no delay at any time. But the fact of his sharing his bed with the girl (there was only one girl involved, not several, as some of the journalists said) was published to the press, leading to hostile comment. Several of his intimate colleagues in the leadership of the Indian National Congress wrote to him begging him to abandon this "experiment with truth." There were enough agonizing controversial issues facing India just then. Was it really necessary for him to add to them? But he did not easily give way. Issues of personal conduct had always seemed to him quite as important as any political issue, as the pages of his weekly paper *Harijan* show. It was one of his less "political" friends, A. V. Thakkar, who begged the girl, Manu, to end the experiment, and this led to its abandonment.

I think it almost certain that I was the only non-Indian whom he told about it and with whom he had a frank discussion; so it seems appropriate to refer to the matter here. He only shared his bed with one girl, not with several; there were special, extraordinary reasons for doing it just there and then.

Anyone who is prepared to study Gandhi seriously should at least read his book, *Hind Swaraj,* to see how and why he rejects the very basis of modern western culture. I must confess that when I first read it, long after I had met Gandhi and read a great deal of his weekly writings in *Young India* and *Harijan,* I thought that he would surely now reject some of the positions he there defends. But I was wrong. To his dying day, he accepted it all. And the western way of life seems to be leading the world to very strange and alarming conclusions. Perhaps the time is due for paying closer attention to the wisdom of Gandhi.

If we are prepared to take him seriously, we cannot do better than begin with his utter fearlessness. He believed that if one man attacked another, whatever the visible result of his action, even if it leads to the death of the victim of the attack, it is the aggressor, the man who commits the crime, who is the real sufferer. And he applied this not only in the case of individuals but also in international relations. When India became free, and was divided into the two States of India and Pakistan, he would have liked to see India disarm, without fear of what Pakistan might do. It may well be that, in such a situation, Pakistan would have sent armed force, not only to capture Kashmir, but also to seize west Bengal including Calcutta and parts of Uttar Pradesh, including Lucknow with its strong Islamic traditions. Then what would Gandhi do? He would lead the people in non-violent resistance to the invader. He knew that India was not ready for this; so he did not press his ideas about disarmament, although his colleagues, Patel, Nehru and the rest, knew that he still believed in them, as essential parts of his convictions about total non-violence. Indeed, when Kashmir was invaded he openly supported Indian military resistance. He had always held that fighting with the weapons you believe in is far better than running away.

As he refused to act out of fear of Pakistan, he would no doubt have advised the citizens of America and Russia to throw away all fear of the other super-power. If every American could learn to believe: "We have nothing to fear from the Russian; what can man do unto me?'' and if every Russian would say: ''We have nothing to fear from the Americans; what can man do unto me?'' our world, overburdened by the load of useless and diabolical armaments, might soon find the way to a world of justice and harmony. It is obvious that the world as it is today would reject such ideas as idle dreaming. But it is necessary to point out that the life Gandhi invites us to share with him can only be discovered by those who are willing to begin again from the foundations. If total fearlessness is to be our aim, we must study thoroughly the life of the man who has already arrived at that goal.

Not many of us will become Gandhis; but there is no reason why we should not learn from him.

A year or two after Gandhi's death, the right wing of the Hindu Mahasabha, known in India as the R.S.S., was openly preaching death to the followers of Gandhi. A small boy who was attending a school in Delhi, came home from school one day and said to his father: ''I shall have to kill you some time, Daddy.'' ''Why must you kill me?'' asked the father. ''Because you are a follower of Gandhi,'' said the boy, ''our teacher has been telling us that all Gandhi's followers must be killed.'' The situation became so menacing that some of the leaders were arrested. Sardar Patel, the Home Minister, told me: ''We do not like arresting these men. Gandhiji would not have done it. But we have not his courage. We are afraid of what may happen if we leave them at large.'' Absolute fearlessness may be beyond what most of us can achieve. But we can at least make serious efforts to banish some of our fears.

1983

1

Youth: Life in South Africa
(1869-1914)

MOHANDAS KARAMCHAND GANDHI was born at Porbandar on 2 October 1869. Porbandar is in the part of India known as Kathiawad, on the Arabian Sea. When Gandhi was born, no one had thought of Pakistan, but today Porbandar is on the western edge of India, with Pakistan and the desert beyond. Even in the nineteenth century, it was remote from any great city. Kathiawad was ruled by a number of Indian princes who had British advisers. It was not under direct British administration. There must have been very few white men to be seen in the streets of Porbandar when Gandhi was a boy. To be sure, he knew that India was not an independent country; he knew that the British were in control; but he did not grow up in the midst of a surging national movement for liberation, to which eager young men would naturally surrender themselves. Kathiawad might be described as a backwater, where most things happened very much as they had for hundreds of years.

Mohandas' father was the Chief Minister of the small State. He and his brothers lived in a large family-home, and Mohandas grew up as one of a large family of cousins. He also had two elder brothers and an elder sister, as well as two half-sisters from his father's earlier wife who had died. His father was an elderly man when Mohan was born, and he died soon after his youngest son grew up. There was no family occupation for the youngest son to fit into; so he resolved, with the encouragement of his elder brother, to go to England and take legal training. This was not an easy thing to do. It involved heavy expenditure for the family. No

other member of the family had gone abroad for education. His
mother and other senior members of the family believed that young
men who went abroad fell a prey to evil influences. In any case,
the Gandhi family were orthodox Hindus, of the *baniya* (trading)
caste; going abroad meant breaking the caste rules. In spite of
all this, Mohan decided to go; already he showed the strength
of character that found a way through all obstacles. This was
remarkable, for he was a shy, timid, awkward young man, with
a poor physique and no outward signs of strength or force of
character.

At the age of nineteen, leaving behind him his beloved mother,
his young wife, and an infant boy, Mohan set off by ship to England.
He had promised his mother that he would touch no meat or wine
while he was away from home. On board ship, no vegetarian meals
were served. So for several weeks the young man lived on the fruit
and sweets he had brought with him. Once again, his strong will
is visible, perhaps also, if we look at him in terms of his own later
life, his extraordinary devotion to truth. Vegetarianism was to him
a family tradition, not a personal conviction. He had given a
promise to his mother. But had not many other young Indians
gone to England bound by similar vows? Most of the others had
presumably persuaded themselves that their mothers would not
want them to starve; so the vow had been abandoned. Not so
the young Gandhi. To him a vow to his mother was a matter of
life and death. Whatever difficulty he had to face, he must go
through with it.

Then, one day, as he was walking the streets of London, he came
upon a vegetarian restaurant in Farringdon Street. This was one
of the decisive moments of his life. Not only did he enjoy the first
good meal since he left India; he bought a copy of Henry Salt's
Plea for Vegetarianism. He became a convert to the idea of
vegetarianism. He joined the London Vegetarian Society. Soon
he was on its committee. He wrote articles for the journal,
Vegetarian, about life in India. He began to be a man with a
mission. As Nanda puts it:

With the zeal of a new convert he devoured books on dietetics,
developed an interest in cooking, outgrew the taste for condi-
ments, and came to the sensible conclusion that the seat of taste

is not in the tongue but in the mind. The control of the palate was one of the first steps in that discipline which was to culminate years later in total sublimation. The dietary experiments, dictated by considerations of health and economy, were to become a part of his religious and spiritual evolution....

There was a long and hard but sure road which led from Farringdon Street in London to the Phoenix and Tolstoy Settlements in South Africa, and to the Sabarmati and Sevagram ashrams in India.[1]

One other aspect of his life in London is worth attention. Once he had made up his mind about the way he was to live, not only did he economise in every possible way, but also decided to move from his lodgings frequently, so that he might get closely acquainted with as much of London as possible. It was not that he quarrelled with his landladies. On the contrary, he made lasting friendships with some of them. One of them came to see him many years later when he was in London for the Round Table Conference of 1931. As it happened, I was with him that morning and we travelled together by car from the Kingsley Hall settlement in Bow to Gandhi's office in Knightsbridge. Much of the way he talked with his landlady of forty years back about her family and personal circumstances. During those years in London, 1889 and 1890, young Mohan walked the streets day by day to save bus and tram fares and also, surely, because he was a born explorer, an explorer of many things. London streets to him meant human beings and the way they live. One afternoon, in the late autumn of 1931, I was driving with him and his secretary, Mahadev Desai, across London to Kingsley Hall, Bow, where he spent the nights as the guest of Miss Muriel Lester. For some reason we drove by an unusual route, and so we passed through Smithfield where all the butchers' shops were gaily decorated for Christmas. Mahadev Desai, who was new to London, was horrified by the sight of carcases hanging in the shops, garlanded with bright-coloured paper. But Gandhi's comment was quite different: "I walked along all these streets when I was a student. I knew it all." No wonder that when the bombs began to fall on London in 1940,

---

[1]The significance of these settlements and ashrams is explained later.

he cried out with agony.   He was thinking not so much in terms
of "England" but rather of all those humble human beings whose
homes he knew.

Most of the thousands of foreign students who came to London
every year no doubt made a point of visiting the British Museum,
Westminster Abbey, and other famous and beautiful places; has
any other spent his spare time month after month walking the drab
streets of eastern London?   In most respects, the young Gandhi
must have appeared to be an ordinary and quite unimpressive
young man.   But already he was showing some exceptional
qualities.

In 1891 Gandhi returned to India.   He notes in his autobiography
that the Arabian Sea was rough but that he was one of the very few
passengers who enjoyed it all and he regularly took his meals in the
dining-saloon.   When he arrived in Bombay, his brother told him of
the death of his mother some time before.   This was a great blow to
the young man.   There can be little doubt that much of his character,
his strong determination, his gentleness, his religious tendencies, his
devotion to prayer, even though they were not yet fully in evidence,
had been implanted by his mother.   And it seems not unlikely
that, when in his later life he relied on women to be his strongest
soldiers in his satyagraha campaigns in India, he saw in them the
dauntless faith and capacity for self-discipline and sacrifice which
he had seen in her.

His elder brother, who had done so much to help Mohan through
his English years of study, naturally hoped soon to see him earning
good money as a result of his qualifications as an English-trained
barrister.   But he was doomed to disappointment.   Mohan's
qualifications were of little use in the small provincial courts of his
home State of Rajkot.   Knowledge of the local law was needed
there, and he did not possess it.   So he migrated to Bombay.
Here too he had to study Indian law before he could get briefs
and defend clients in the courts.   When at last he did undertake a
case, he was quite unable to utter a word when his turn to cross-
examine came.   He returned the fee, and in despair he tried to get
a teaching job.   As he was always very fond of children and of
teaching, he would probably have made a good teacher.   But he
had no Indian university degree, and his London matriculation
and his good knowledge of English were no adequate substitute

in the eyes of the headmaster whom he approached. So nothing came of that.

After six months in Bombay, he returned again to Rajkot, where he helped his brother, himself a lawyer, by drafting applications and memorials. Though at this stage in his life he had insufficient self-confidence to plead in open court, at least he was already fluent and competent with his pen. However, this was not very lucrative and, what was worse, he came in conflict with the British Political Agent who presided in the local court. So, when his brother received a letter from an Indian businessman in South Africa, asking if the younger brother would help his firm with a legal case there, the attraction of a new world to explore and possible new openings were sufficient for him, and in 1893 he set off for South Africa, where he expected to spend one year. He arrived there an unknown, impecunious, unsuccessful, young Indian lawyer. More than twenty years later he finally left South Africa for India, a man who had achieved fame far beyond the boundaries of South Africa and India.

The South Africa that Gandhi first saw in 1893 was not a single political unit. The Union of South Africa only came into being after the Boer War which was fought from 1899 to 1901. In 1893, the two southern provinces, Natal and the Cape Colony, were parts of the British Empire, ruled from London. To the north were the two independent Boer Republics—the Orange Free State and the Transvaal. Nevertheless, there were close connections between the four States. Gandhi arrived at Durban, chief town of Natal, and it was here that his employer, Abdulla Sheth, lived and carried on his business. But the case in which Gandhi was to represent him was to be heard in Pretoria, the capital of the Transvaal.

His first few days spent in Durban were sufficient to show Gandhi that he had come to a land of race prejudice. Already in India he had had an experience with the British Resident in Rajkot which seemed like a personal insult tinged with racial arrogance; but in South Africa he soon learnt that every coloured man was liable to suffer constant insults from the white population, unless he was prepared silently to submit and never attempt to assert a position of equality. When Abdulla Sheth took him to the Durban law courts to give him an opportunity to see them at work, the presiding magistrate ordered him to take off his turban. This he refused to do, so he left the court.

In the middle of the nineteenth century, when there was a need for unskilled labour in South Africa in order to develop mines, mills, and factories, as most of the local Africans were unwilling to leave the land and work as wage-earners, the British Government organised indentured labour from India. Thousands of poor Indians, chiefly from the south of India, had thus migrated to South Africa and, at the end of their period of indenture, they remained in South Africa as free labourers and their families grew up there, having never known India. These Indians were called "coolies," which simply means "manual labourers." In course of time, Indian businessmen and merchants followed. Some of these managed to get themselves accepted as "Arabs" or "Persians." But, if they were identified with the Indian community, they were all called "coolies." Thus, Gandhi, barrister of the Inner Temple in London, found himself called a "coolie lawyer."

Within a few days he proceeded to Pretoria to take up work on the case in the courts there. This was a long and difficult journey, partly by train and partly by bus. His employer had bought him a first-class ticket. In the evening, at Maritzburg, capital town of Natal, he was ordered out of his compartment. He refused to move. Finally, a police constable was brought, who forced him out of the compartment. He refused, however, to enter the "van compartment," and preferred to spend the whole night shivering on the cold platform, wrestling with this problem: to stay and fight colour prejudice, or return to India. He made up his mind to stay and fight it out.

Even before the end of this eventful journey, he had to fight his second battle. From Charlestown to Johannesburg there was no train, so he had to travel by stage-coach, with a night's stop at Standerton. He had a ticket for the inside of the bus, but the conductor would not allow a "coolie" to sit inside and ordered him to sit by the coachman. This he agreed to do but when, after a stop, the conductor wanted to sit by the driver and ordered Gandhi to sit on the footboard at his feet, he refused and held on tight to the brass rails while the conductor began to belabour him. Finally, the passengers intervened and took his part, and the conductor had to give way. Thus, the timid young lawyer won his first non-violent battle against insolent might.

There are always people who love to overdramatise things and who suggest that, if Gandhi had not been provoked by these insults, he might have remained a loyal subject of the British Crown to the day of his death. This is manifestly absurd. In his autobiography he explains how every Indian he met told him of similar experiences that they had constantly to suffer. Sooner or later, Gandhi, by remaining in South Africa, was bound to suffer in this way. The difference to be noted is that, apparently from the very beginning, he made up his mind that, for the sake of not just his own prestige, but for the vindication of justice between man and man, it was his duty to resist. And also, at a very early stage, he had realised that the way to fight successfully was to repay the bully and the arrogant man, not in their own coin, but with the treatment he demanded from them. Thus, at the time of these first incidents, although he wrote letters to the newspapers and invited the public of South Africa to attend to what was happening, he refused to prosecute the offenders.

Gandhi's part in the law-suit that had brought him to South Africa revealed some of the qualities that were to remain with him throughout his public life. As he studied the case, he not only concluded that his client was in the right but, more important, that both he and the rival firm were ruining themselves with the expense of a long and tortuous litigation. So, with difficulty, he persuaded both firms to agree to a settlement out of court. The arbitrator decided in favour of Abdulla. Gandhi then persuaded Abdulla to accept payment by instalments. Looking back on this, he wrote later: "I had learnt the true practice of law. I had learnt to find the better side of human nature and to enter men's hearts. I realized that the true function of a lawyer was to unite parties riven asunder."

The time came for him to return home. But, just as he was making his plans to leave, news came that the Natal Government was contemplating fresh legislation to discriminate against Indians. While he had been in Pretoria, Gandhi had already tried to unite the Transvaal Indians in the efforts for their own protection against white dominance. Now, the Natal Indians persuaded him to stay for a month to lead a fight against the new legislation. He agreed to stay on, and his farewell party became a committee from which ultimately sprang into being the Natal Indian Congress.

In India, the Indian National Congress, which ultimately became a powerful force representing India's popular movement for political freedom, was in the 1890s little more than an annual meeting (or congress, in fact) where some hundreds of the Indian intelligentsia met to pass resolutions demanding political reforms from the British Government in India. British officials had some justification for treating it as an assembly that had no real contact with the masses. But Gandhi had never attended a session of the Congress in India. He had the highest regard for the then President of the Congress, Dadabhai Naoroji of Bombay; so to him it seemed the natural and appropriate thing to call the newly created body that was to represent the Indians of Natal in their struggle for political rights, the Natal Indian Congress. Without regard to the organisation or functioning of the parent body in India he proceeded to organise the Natal Congress along the lines that seemed appropriate to their circumstances.

In the first place, he needed to weld a divided group into some kind of unity. There were Muslim merchants and their Hindu and Parsi clerks from Bombay, semi-slave indentured labourers from Madras, and Natal-born Indian Christians no longer bound by the stringent terms of indentured labour. These groups had neither language nor religion, nor traditional custom, nor social position in common—nothing, indeed, save their common disabilities, their brown skins (and even at that point there must have been a great contrast between the pale-skinned Parsis and the dark-skinned Madrasis) and a common descent from the great land of India. Gandhi, with his characteristic selfless devotion, inexhaustible energy, and equal regard for every sort of human being, in a surprisingly short time, did in fact weld these groups into a single unit with a strong sense of common purpose. In December 1894, a petition signed by five hundred representative Indians was presented to the Legislative Assembly of Natal. When that proved futile in preventing the passage of the obnoxious legislation, a petition was prepared, which was signed by about ten thousand Indians, almost the total population of free Indians in Natal, appealing to the Colonial Secretary in London not to sanction the bill. The preparation of this petition involved an immense amount of work; no one was allowed to sign who had not shown that he really understood what it meant. A thousand copies were printed and sent to politicians and newspapers. Gandhi took no salary as Secretary of the Congress. He was always meticulously careful about the use of funds. In his preparation of the case to be presented, he was always scrupulous to avoid exaggeration in stating his own case, and generous in recognising the best motives in his adversary. This first effort was in some degree successful. The Colonial Office in London vetoed the Natal Bill on the ground that it discriminated against the inhabitants of another part of the British Empire. However, the Natal Legislature, which was purely European, passed a new bill, the effect of which was to keep the Indians disfranchised, although it was not nakedly a colour-bar bill. All this took time. Gandhi was now established as a practising lawyer in South Africa and was giving all his spare time to the cause of the Indian community.[2] In 1896, as he could see no early end to the work, he returned to India to make arrangements for bringing his family to South Africa.

While he was in India, he journeyed around the country, meeting many of the Indian political leaders, and publishing reports of the disabilities of the Indians in South Africa. What he published was as scrupulously fair as his writings always were. But a press cable to South Africa stated: "A pamphlet published in India declares that the Indians in Natal are robbed and assaulted and treated like beasts and are unable to obtain redress." When this was published in the South African papers, naturally there was great indignation and the Europeans of Natal resolved that they would not allow Gandhi to return. When it was known that two shiploads of Indians, including Gandhi and his family, had arrived outside Durban harbour, efforts were made to prevent them from landing. They were kept in "quarantine" in the harbour for over three weeks. However, Gandhi persuaded his compatriots not to give way to threats and, finally, when he had been able to convince the leading people of Natal that the Reuter cable from India was a falsehood, the Indians were allowed to land.

Although the Natal political leaders had by now realised their mistake, some young hotheads, whose passions had been aroused, were not so readily appeased. Gandhi himself landed from the ship in the company of a European friend, and separately from his

[2]It is believed that for some years Gandhi was earning as much as £5,000 to £6,000 a year.

family.   He was soon recognised by some young men who managed
to separate him from his friend and attacked him with brickbats
and rotten eggs. He might well have been killed, had not a European
lady, Mrs Alexander, wife of the Superintendent of Police, appeared
on the scene.   She walked beside him, holding her sunshade over
him to protect him from the mob, until police arrived and brought
him to safety.

The Secretary of State in London proposed that the miscreants
be duly prosecuted.   But Gandhi refused to prosecute the young
men, whose guilt, in his view, was much less than that of certain
members of the Natal Government who had started the agitation
against him.   The *Natal Mercury*, which represented the European
point of view, after reading Gandhi's Indian pamphlet, confessed
that it was a perfectly fair statement from the Indian point of view,
and that the "Reuter cable is a gross exaggeration of Mr. Gandhi's
statement."

When the Boer War broke out in 1899, Gandhi was convinced
that the Indians in Natal could not simply stand aside saying that
the war was no concern of theirs.   He did not judge that the British
had a better case in the war than the Boers.   Indeed, if anything,
he took the opposite view.   But at this time of his life he considered
that the British Empire was a good thing.   More important, the
Indian community in Natal was demanding civil and political
rights in that country; so, when the country was in peril owing to
war, they must show that they recognised a duty to it and were not
only concerned for their own rights.   Accordingly, on behalf of the
Indians, he offered help.   At first this offer was rejected with
something like contempt.   But, when things went badly for the
British, the offer was accepted and an Indian Ambulance Corps was
organised with Gandhi himself as the real leader, though a British
missionary doctor was appointed Superintendent.   The British
obviously believed that the Indians would not be much good, and
they were not expected to work on the field of battle.   But in fact
they did so on several occasions.   They showed themselves well
disciplined and tireless, and Gandhi received a decoration from
the British Government.

After the Boer War, late in 1901, Gandhi returned to India.   For
the first time he attended a session of the Indian National Congress
which met in Calcutta.   At this time he was no "Mahatma" in the

eyes of his fellow-countrymen; so, observing the lack of proper organisation and decent sanitation, he set himself quietly to put these things in order. He was able to get the Congress to pass a resolution in support of the claims of Indians in South Africa. G.K. Gokhale, already an outstanding leader of Indian nationalism, although a comparatively young man, was deeply impressed with Gandhi's integrity, dedication, and moderation, and a firm friendship grew up between these two men. Gokhale had hoped to get Gandhi into Indian political life. Neither at that time realised how many more years must be given by him to South Africa.

He returned to South Africa in December 1902 in response to a fresh cable from the Indian community. After the annexation by the British of the Orange Free State and the Transvaal, the Colonial Secretary, Joseph Chamberlain, visited South Africa. The whole future government of the country was under review. The Indians sought an opportunity to present their case to Chamberlain, but he advised them that the four territories, though now to be united under the British Crown, were to all intents and purposes self-governing and they must come to terms with the white colonists, whether Boer or Briton. Soon it became clear that annexation by Britain was not going to help the Indians at all. The British colonists in South Africa were chiefly concerned to establish their position in relation to the Boers. For many years to come, the uneasy relationship of Briton and Boer was to be the main consideration of both these white communities. Though in principle the British colonists were less outspoken in their racial intolerance than the Boers, in practice there was little to choose. Dark-skinned Africans and brown-skinned Indians were still denied political or social equality.

The first test came in the Transvaal, where a new Indian Registration Ordinance was enacted in the year 1906. Under this measure every Indian, including children over eight years of age, was required to give finger-prints on a registration form, which he or she must always carry. Gandhi and his fellow Indians resolved that, come what may, they could not obey such a humiliating law. Death would be better than submission. At a meeting held in Johannesburg on 11 September 1906, "packed from floor to ceiling," after being warned by Gandhi of the possible consequence of defiance, the whole meeting rose up and with raised hands undertook a solemn oath, with God as witness, not to submit to the new Ordinance. Thus began Gandhi's life of civil disobedience. When the vow was taken, he did not yet see how it could be implemented, though he was aware that any action must be wholly non-violent. The measures shortly taken thereafter were in the early days called "passive resistance." Gandhi did not care for this expression, as it suggested something much less positive than the kind of action he envisaged. Before long he invited the readers of *Indian Opinion*, his weekly journal, to suggest some more fitting name. Thus came into being the expression "satyagraha," which is variously translated as "soul force" or "truth force." In any case what it really signifies is the mighty power of the undaunted human spirit as opposed to the power of weapons or of money.

A year or two later, when Rev. J. J. Doke, Baptist Minister and missionary in South Africa, and his first biographer, asked Gandhi how he had learnt these ideas, he insisted that he had found them first of all in the New Testament; and it was only later that he found that they were also implicit in the Bhagavad Gita, that great Hindu scripture which to Gandhi in his later years was his greatest inspiration. Nevertheless, it is clear that, when he found the teaching of returning good for evil in the Sermon on the Mount, his mind was ready for it; even in his childhood, he had been impressed by a Gujarati poem which taught that real beauty consists in doing good against evil. By 1906, he was also under the influence of Tolstoy. He first read Thoreau's famous essay on civil disobedience in 1907.

Indians were to register under the new law, known as the "Black Act," by 31 July 1907. So few had done this that the date was extended to 30 November. Even so, only 511 registered out of a total population of about 13,000. And this in spite of explicit warnings from the Transvaal Government that those who refused to register would be very severely dealt with. The Government perhaps thought that, once Gandhi the "agitator" had been punished, the resistance would peter out. Nothing of the sort happened. He was arrested and sentenced to two months' imprisonment. At once, others were courting arrest. Soon there were 155 in the gaol which had only room for fifty. The Indian community began to call the prison "King Edward's Hotel."

The name, "King Edward's Hotel," illustrates the way in which the Indian community saw the country they were living in. To them the whole of South Africa, including the Transvaal, was part of the British Empire—that is to say, part of the Empire of King Edward VII. And so, indeed, it was. Scarcely four years had elapsed since the end of the cruel and bitter war between Boer and Briton, which had ended in the annexation to the British Empire of the two Boer Republics—the Transvaal and the Orange Free State. Yet, already, the Transvaal, owing largely to the generous and imaginative statesmanship of Sir Henry Campbell-Bannerman, was practically self-governing again, and its leading statesmen were two of the defeated Boer Generals, Botha and Smuts. The way was already opened for the establishment, a few years later, of the Union of South Africa, which for fifty years was to be a wholly self-governing member of the British Commonwealth. It was largely due to the influence of General Smuts that the word "Empire" was changed to "Commonwealth." The time came when this same General Smuts, in his youth one of the most determined fighters against the British, was a member of the British War Cabinet. So far as he was concerned, the wound of that despicable war was totally healed. But all this was in the future. At this moment, when Gandhi found himself fighting non-violently against Smuts, Gandhi and the Indian problem appeared to the South African leaders in the form of a maddening distraction from the huge task of building again a country that had been devastated by war—a country, moreover, where to the Boer leaders the first problem was to come to terms in everyday life with the large population of English-speaking residents, former migrants from Britain, who composed the majority of the white population of the Cape and Natal; and the secondary problem, if indeed it was not equally important in their eyes, was the relationship of the white government with the majority of the population which was neither Boer nor British nor Indian. In biographies of Gandhi, it is natural that attention should be concentrated on the grievances of the Indian population; but it is unfair to Smuts to forget the background against which he was working. Gandhi, perhaps, was one of the few Indians in South Africa at that time who did not forget it. And partly on that account, in spite of their sharp conflicts, Gandhi and Smuts did in the end discover each other as human beings.

Moreover, the new Boer Government did not start with a clean slate. The British authorities, immediately after the end of the Boer War, had, as we have already observed, undertaken strong measures to keep the Indian community in a condition of subjection. So that what Gandhi and his compatriots were demanding was that Botha and Smuts should immediately reverse engines. The drama developed rapidly.

Smuts agreed to meet Gandhi after his release from his first jail sentence. They met, and they exchanged letters. What they said at their meeting is not known, for the two men had different recollections. Gandhi believed that Smuts had agreed to repeal the Black Act, provided the Indians agreed to register voluntarily. But, in his letter, what Gandhi wrote was: "We recognise that it is not possible during the Parliamentary recess to repeal the Act, and we have noted your repeated public declarations that there is no likelihood of the Act being repealed." Smuts' secretary, in his reply, promised to "lay the matter before Parliament at its next session." It looks from this as if Gandhi was not expecting an immediate repeal of the Act; but also that he had reason to believe something would be done in the coming session that would meet the Indian demand. It is difficult to see how that demand could be met without repeal.

Anyhow, Gandhi assured his fellow-Indians that, if they voluntarily registered, the Act would be repealed. The prisoners were all released and Gandhi declared that he would be the first to register. Some of the Indians believed that he had been tricked, or bought. One Pathan from the north-west frontier of India, a man of powerful physique, vowed that he would kill any Indian who registered. When Gandhi, ignoring this threat, led the way to the place of registration, some of the Pathans waylaid him and very nearly killed him. He was nursed back to health in the house of the Dokes, but even before the surgeon arrived he insisted on signing the Register. It is recorded that the Chief Registrar, who was no friend of the Indians, had tears in his eyes as he took Gandhi's signature.

But the repeal did not come. Smuts declared that it was impossible. Accordingly, the Indians, led by Gandhi, believing that this was a breach of faith, met for a fresh public ceremony. This time they burnt their registration forms which under the law they were obliged to carry on their persons. At this ceremony,

Mir Alam, the Pathan who had tried to murder Gandhi, took his hand and the two men threw their registrations on to the bonfire simultaneously. Gandhi declared publicly that he bore no ill-will towards Mir Alam, and this was no idle boast, for he had tried to save him from prosecution and a prison sentence. The public burning of the registration forms did not automatically take the Indians back to jail, but they were soon courting arrest again, by refusing to obey a number of discriminatory measures. This time they were given hard labour; and hard it certainly was. In October 1908, Gandhi himself was back in jail. As Nanda puts it: "At seven in the morning he was one of a gang of prisoners, led by a relentless overseer, which dug hard ground with spades. As the day wore on, with his back bent and hands blistered, Gandhi was seen cheering up his companions, many of whom all but broke under the strain." One eighteen-year-old boy, taken out daily to work in the early winter morning, died of pneumonia—satyagraha's first martyr, first of a long line.

Reading the Bhagavad Gita and the works of Tolstoy and Thoreau helped Gandhi to endure this hard life.

The braver men continued in and out of jail as the months and years went by. But the Indians of South Africa were as human as the rest of humanity and, as time went on, some began to drop out of the struggle, especially the wealthier members, whose businesses were being ruined. Gandhi's own savings from his successful legal practice were being eaten up and, as he was giving his whole time to the struggle, he had few if any new cases. Generous donations came from wealthy men in India. But these in turn gave out, and it seemed as if the weekly *Indian Opinion* would soon be bankrupt. However, a German architect, Kallenbach, a man of property, came to the rescue. Kallenbach was already actively associated with Gandhi. He now offered him an estate of 1,100 acres, containing about a thousand fruit trees. Here the Gandhi family and several others settled and lived a Tolstoyan life on what was called Tolstoy Farm. The total number of people living there was well over fifty and it included Indians of all the chief religions and of many provinces and languages: Hindus, Muslims, Parsis, Christians. Those who, later in his life when he was leading the national movement in India, tried to make out that Gandhi could only represent the

Hindus of India, and that he had little following outside his own Gujarati province, evidently knew nothing of his life in South Africa.

The Tolstoy Farm community was as nearly self-supporting as it could be—not out of a desire to escape from the world, but because the economic pressures of the South African Government and white community forced them to live this way. Nevertheless, Gandhi himself, and no doubt many of the others, too, found this way of life most attractive. He himself has written that his "faith and courage were at their highest on Tolstoy Farm."

The year 1911 brought a measure of relief to the Indians in South Africa. Partly this was the result of their own constancy in the struggle, but mainly it seems to have been due to outside pressures, both from India and from Britain. At the end of May that year, the satyagrahi prisoners were released; the bar on the entry of Indians into the Transvaal was lifted; instead, all would-be entrants there now required to pass a severe educational test.

In the following year, Gokhale, who as a member of the Viceroy's executive council in India had continued to press the Imperial British Government to put pressure on the Government of South Africa, paid a visit to South Africa. He was received as a State guest and was provided with a saloon compartment for all his railway journeys—quite a contrast to the treatment meted out to the "coolie lawyer" who landed in South Africa in 1893. Indeed, the very fact that the South African Government was prepared to do such honour to anyman of the "coolie race" was an eye-opener to many white South Africans.

At the end of his visit, Gokhale assured Gandhi that he had been promised that the "Black Act will be repealed. The racial bar will be removed from the emigration law. The £3 tax will be abolished." Gandhi did not believe that these promises would be fulfilled, nor were they. Soon afterwards a judicial decision, for which the Government could not be blamed, added to the indignation of the Indians. This was a ruling that only Christian marriages, duly registered, were legally valid in South Africa. Thus, at a blow, all the children of Hindu, Muslim, and Parsi marriages were declared illegitimate. The £3 tax was levied on all the formerly indentured labourers in the State of Natal. Thus, the breach of the promise to Gokhale for its abolition brought the Indian labourers into Gandhi's arms (he had done his utmost to improve their conditions of labour for many years); while the judicial ruling roused the indignation of all the Indian women. So, for the next and final satyagraha, the whole Indian community of South Africa was united as never before.

What proved to be the final and decisive satyagraha began with marches of Indian women across the borders between the Transvaal and the State of Natal. By law, no Indian was allowed to cross from one State to the other without a permit. At first the authorities turned a blind eye to this; but the women were determined to get themselves arrested, so they continued to cross until the Government did arrest them. When it did so, the Indian workers in some Natal mines resolved to go on strike. Such a thing had never happened before and the employers were furious. In order to force them back to work, they cut off their water and other supplies. Thereupon the workers, after a conference with Gandhi, decided to leave their homes and march into the Transvaal, some thirty-five miles away. But what was to happen to them when they got there, supposing the Government left them at liberty? The ever-fertile mind of Kallenbach evolved a plan for bringing them to Tolstoy Farm, helping them to build mud huts, and setting them to work on the land.

So the marchers, men, women, and children, over two thousand in all, mostly illiterate people who had lived lives of subjection, set off on this amazing march into the unknown, inspired by faith in Gandhi, the leader who always warned them not to act unless they were prepared to undergo suffering and privation. Indian businessmen looked after them at their first halt. Gandhi himself, in his usual way, organised sanitary and other essential arrangements. When he was suddenly arrested, the march remained perfectly orderly. He was released again, and then again arrested. Finally, all the responsible, educated leaders were arrested. Still the army of satyagrahis held together. Hence the Government arrested all the men and condemned them to hard labour, to be carried out in the mines where they had struck work. Their treatment at the mines was so brutal that sympathetic strikes broke out amongst most of the other Indian labourers in Natal. They too were brutally handled. At one place the police shot them down, killing several and wounding others.

News of these things spread to India where Gokhale did his utmost to rouse opinion. Then Lord Hardinge, the British Viceroy in India, without consulting the British Government to which he was directly responsible, in a public speech at Madras openly denounced the South African Government and expressed support for the Indian satyagrahis. At first it was thought that the British Government might recall him, as public disapproval by the head of one Empire Government of a "sister Dominion" was highly irregular. But Lord Hardinge refused to recant; the British Government did not disavow him; and it was the South African Union Government that was obliged to change its policy which had been shown up to the world as an odious tyranny. This was too much for General Smuts. He appointed a commission to investigate the facts, though they were not in doubt. The Government then proceeded to abolish the £3 tax; it eventually abolished the Black Act which had been the cause of the earliest troubles; non-Christian marriages were accepted under the law; and, finally, all the Indian satyagraha prisoners were released.

In his autobiography, Gandhi tells the story of what Smuts' secretary said to him about this time:

> I do not like your people, and do not care to assist them at all. But what am I to do? You help us in our days of need. How can we lay hands on you? I often wish you took to violence like the English strikers, and then we would know at once how to dispose of you. But you will not injure even the enemy. You desire victory by self-suffering alone, and never transgress your self-imposed limits of courtesy and chivalry. And that is what reduces us to sheer helplessness.

And Gandhi adds: "General Smuts also gave expression to similar sentiments."

At the critical moment, when one of the main strikes in Natal was about to start, the Union Government was involved in serious trouble with the white railway workers. To some of the Indians this seemed to give them a magnificent opportunity of forcing concessions from the Government. But Gandhi insisted that this was not the way of true satyagraha. When the opponent was in trouble that was unrelated to the matter at issue, far from taking advantage of his predicament, satyagrahis would wait for a more appropriate time. No wonder Smuts and his colleagues learnt to respect Gandhi and his colleagues even when they did not love them. This was in fact not the only occasion when Gandhi persuaded his compatriots to show special consideration to their opponents. Their refusal to proceed at the time of the railwaymen's strike came at the critical moment when the South African Government was under fire from Lord Hardinge and presumably to some extent from London. Probably it influenced Smuts more than the outside pressures.

It has regretfully to be recorded that this victory for satyagraha did not endure. The South African Government had been shamed into reform; it had not resolved to reform as a result of any change of heart. The great majority of white South Africans have remained hostile to the claims of their Indian fellow-nationals to receive legal or social equality. Full citizenship has never been conceded. But at least the eight-year campaign had shown what amazing self-discipline and courage can be displayed by simple, unlettered men and women under inspired leadership. Moreover, it had led to a curiously close relationship of mutual regard between two of the outstanding men of their time, Gandhi and Smuts.

What did each man really think of the other? When Gandhi died, Smuts declared: "A prince among men has passed away and we grieve with India in her irreparable loss." However, when Gandhi left South Africa in 1914 Smuts wrote: "The saint has left our shores, I sincerely hope for ever." Moreover, in the last year of the Second World War, when the Government of Britain was holding Gandhi in jail for his leadership of the "Quit India" movement, a friend of mine with whom Smuts was staying asked him if he would find time to see me, as I had recently returned from India where I had been in touch with Gandhi. By way of reply he got a passionate outburst against Gandhi's disastrous policies.

A much fuller estimate is to be found in Smuts' contribution to the volume, *Essays and Reflections on his (Gandhi's) Life and Work*, published in 1939. Smuts wrote that Gandhi's activities in South Africa

show that while he was prepared to go all out for the causes which he championed, he never forgot the human background of

the situation, never lost his temper or succumbed to hate, and
preserved his gentle humour even in the most trying situations.
His manner and spirit even then, as well as later, contrasted
markedly with the ruthless and brutal forcefulness which is the
vogue in our day....

Men like him redeem us all from a sense of commonplaceness
and futility, and are an inspiration to us not to be weary in well-
doing.

He also candidly says: "I must frankly admit that his activities at
that time were very trying to me." Obviously, Smuts' admiration
of his opponent could not be unqualified. Presumably, this was
also true of Gandhi's respect for Smuts. But it is to the credit
of both men that though they fought each other politically for
years, and though each was inclined to suspect the other of
sharp practice on occasion, yet each saw the greatness in the
other.

2

Gandhi Reforms the Indian National Congress (1915-1922)

GANDHI arrived back in India on 9 January 1915. What was his life in India to be? His mentor, G.K. Gokhale, advised him not to plunge into Indian politics for a year. He agreed. Gokhale wanted him to join the Servants of India Society. This Society had been founded by Gokhale a few years before and consisted of men who lived at a subsistence level and who gave their time to the service of their country through various forms of social service, by assisting industrial workers, by helping aboriginals, and in a number of other ways. The Society still carries on its remarkable work. But some of the members doubted whether Gandhi would fit into the pattern of their life and work. In the end, he did not join.

While Gandhi was at work in South Africa, he had been helped for a time by two young English men, Charles Andrews and William Pearson. Andrews began his life in India as a missionary. He taught in the Anglican college, St. Stephens, in Delhi. But he soon learnt that some of his Hindu and Muslim neighbours in Delhi were at least as profound in their religious life and insights as any Christian he had known. His outlook on life and religion changed. When he read of the needs of the Indians in South Africa he obtained leave from St. Stephens to go to South Africa and help. Willie Pearson, already working with Rabindranath Tagore at Shantiniketan, also went there. Soon afterwards, C.F. Andrews too made his home in Shantiniketan. They persuaded Tagore to invite Gandhi and his family on their arrival from South Africa to come first to Shantiniketan, which they did. It was a brief stay, so far as

Gandhi himself was concerned, but some of his family and other members of the South African ashram spent a much longer time in Shantiniketan.

Within a day or two of his arrival, Gandhi suggested to the teachers and students that they might do all the cooking for themselves; the food would be more hygienic and the boys would learn the virtue of self-help. The teachers were divided, but the boys were enthusiastic—in the first place at least. Tagore raised no objection and told the boys that "the experiment contains the key to swaraj" (self-rule or home rule for the country). Willie Pearson showed himself most enthusiastic and hard working. When the boys began to tire, as they soon did, he provided the determination that helped to keep them at it. But it must be confessed that the experiment only lasted forty days. After that the professional cooks returned. It is not recorded whether the health of the community went up or down before or after. But *swaraj* certainly tarried.

Gandhi had only been at Shantiniketan for a week when the tragic news reached him of the sudden death of Gokhale. He went at once to Poona, the home of Gokhale. "Launching on the stormy seas of Indian public life I was in need of a sure pilot. I had had one in Gokhale and had felt secure in his keeping. Now that he was gone, I was thrown on my own resources." It is idle to speculate what difference there might have been in the course of the next ten years if Gokhale had lived. Would he have approved of Gandhi's first efforts at satyagraha in India, his first direct attacks on the system of British Government? It is impossible to say.

During 1915, the Kumbh Mela, one of the greatest religious pilgrimages of India, was due to take place at Hardwar, a town on the sacred river Ganges (more correctly, Ganga), where the river flows from the Himalayan gorges out into the plains of India. This great pilgrimage takes place once in twelve years. In 1915 some two million people are believed to have attended. Many of them would arrive on foot, having walked hundreds of miles from their homes. Gandhi had seen little of this side of Hindu religious life and, although he was not attracted to Hardwar with the single-minded devotion of a pilgrim, he resolved to go there and see for himself what took place. It is clear from the account of his experience that he disliked many aspects of the *mela*, though he recognised that "countless people amongst them [the pilgrims] had gone there to earn merit, and for self-purification." He adds the comment: "It is difficult, if not impossible, to say to what extent this kind of faith uplifts the soul."

Following his experience of mixing with the pilgrims—many of whom, incidentally, flocked around him to obtain his *darshan,* an untranslatable word which in effect may here be translated as his blessing—he spent a night in deep thought, and by morning he had made up his mind to take a vow which he was to keep for many years. "I decided to limit the articles of my diet and to have my final meal before sunset.... I pledged myself never whilst in India to eat after dark." When, some years later, he wrote his auto-biography, *The Story of My Experiments with Truth* (here was one of these experiments), he wrote of this vow: "I have been under these vows for thirteen years. They have subjected me to a severe test, but I am able to testify that they have also served as a shield. I am of opinion that they have added a few years to my life and saved me from many an illness."

He also notes: "My life is based on disciplinary resolutions." This was not the first vow he had taken, nor by any means the last. He had great faith in vows, and no doubt they often strengthened his will in undertaking difficult enterprises and in standing firm in the face of trials. Some years before, when he was first undertaking his experiments in non-violence in South Africa, he wrote to Leo Tolstoy to ask his blessings in what he was attempting. Tolstoy was greatly impressed and said so publicly. The exchange of correspondence between these two great advocates of non-violence shows how much Gandhi learnt from Tolstoy. But, in the matter of vows, he seems to have remained throughout his life in total opposition to the Tolstoyan position. For, to Tolstoy, every vow was equivalent to a surrender of one's judgment in regard to future situations. The wise man, in Tolstoy's view, would never give away control of his future actions. Gandhi thought otherwise and lived by vows which he kept with utmost strictness.

During this "probationary" period, when Gandhi was seeing India at first hand, one of his important discoveries was the plight of third class passengers on the railways. He was not yet a famous "Mahatma"; so if he travelled in the garb of the poor, as in fact he did from this time on, the railway officials did not know him for anything but one more of the voiceless millions of Indian villagers. In his autobiography he gives some details of his experiences, and he sums it up in these words:

> My experience is that the officials, instead of looking upon third class passengers as fellowmen, regard them as so many sheep. They talk to them contemptuously, and brook no reply or argument. The third class passenger has to obey the official as though he were his servant, and the latter may with impunity belabour and blackmail him, and book him his ticket only after putting him to the greatest possible inconvenience, including often missing the train. All this I have seen with my own eyes. No reform is possible unless some of the educated and the rich voluntarily accept the status of the poor, and instead of taking avoidable hardships, discourtesies and injustice as a matter of course, fight for their removal.

Probably it would be easy to find country stations in India where even today these abuses occur, but they are much less general than they were, and this is largely because, once Gandhi had aroused the enthusiastic support of numbers of young men for his political and social mission, many of them did begin to travel third class—a very few, to their honour, still do, even after many years of independence —and they have shamed the railway officials into better behaviour. Today there are even a few one-class-only trains that run long distances across the Indian subcontinent.

One of Gandhi's earliest journeys on his return to India was to his old home area of Rajkot. All third class passengers were forced to undergo medical examination at a certain railway station on the way from Bombay. There had been an outbreak of bubonic plague, so the establishment of this cordon was reasonable. But it was continued unnecessarily and was enforced with great hardship. A local tailor begged Gandhi to take up the matter. Gandhi asked him and his neighbours if they were prepared to offer satyagraha against the government if they could not get any easy redress. They gave serious consideration to his proposal and said they were ready. Gandhi was delighted. But, when he discussed the whole matter with the secretary of the Governor of Bombay, the secretary suggested that he was thus holding out a threat. Gandhi did not see it that way. He was concerned to make sure that the objectors were serious in their intentions, that their objection was not transitory or frivolous, and the way to test this was to find out whether they were willing to suffer for their convictions, if necessary by going to prison. Again and again in his political career in India, Gandhi found himself saying to the government: "We feel so deeply about this matter that if you cannot see your way to make some concession, we may feel obliged to defy you by peaceful means." Thereupon the government would retort: "You are threatening us. How can you expect us to give way to threats?" Perhaps it is characteristic of Gandhi's fair-mindedness that, in recounting this first example of what became a frequent pattern of action and reaction between him and the government, he calls his chapter: "Was it a Threat?"

During all his later years in South Africa, Gandhi had lived in an "ashram," that is to say a community of men, women, and children bound together by common vows and common work and a common purpose. Some twenty members of the Phoenix ashram, most of them boys, joined him in India, and he was resolved, from the beginning, to found a new ashram somewhere in India for these colleagues from South Africa and for others who might be attracted. For a time they were all housed in Shantiniketan and, in the frequent absence of Gandhi himself, the community was under the guidance of his kinsman, Maganlal Gandhi, who had been one of his most trusted lieutenants for many years.

Before long, this little community found a place to live together close to the city of Ahmedabad, near the west coast of India, in the part known as Gujerat, where the people spoke the language of his family, i.e. Gujerati. Gokhale had promised to finance his ashram, but Gokhale was dead, so he had to rely on the charity of others who knew his reputation but who hardly knew him as a man.

Very soon a crisis arose. Amritlal Thakkar, a member of the Servants of India Society, one who spent his whole life assisting the outcastes and the despised tribal people of the jungly hill-tracts of India, came to Gandhi and told him that a family of outcastes or Untouchables wished to join the ashram and were prepared to abide by the ashram vows. Gandhi had from his boyhood regarded the refusal of high-caste Hindu to mix with Untouchables as foolish and wrong. So he gladly consented to receive the family. But he

soon found that the mixing of religious communities and of caste
and outcaste, which had been easy enough in the peculiar conditions
of South Africa, was not so simple in India. Among those who
objected were his own wife and Maganlal. Their objections were
overcome, but the next difficulty was that funds for the ashram
dried up. Gandhi decided that the whole company must move to
the untouchable part of Ahmedabad city and live by manual
labour. However, before this move could take place, one day an
Ahmedabad businessman rode up in his car and said he would like
to help if his help were required. Gandhi had met this man once
before. He asked no questions, but promised to come again the
next day. He came, bringing Rs 13,000 in currency notes, enough
to keep the ashram going for a year. This unknown friend proved
to be Ambalal Sarabhai, owner of big cloth mills. His wife became
an ardent follower of Gandhi, and younger members of the family
have given their lives in public service. But before long Gandhi
was to find himself supporting the workers of the Sarabhai mills
in a strike against their employer. Yet the good personal relations
between the two men were not broken.

The ashram by the Sabarmati river was called the Satyagraha
Ashram. Satyagraha means the power of truth, so it was natural
that the first vow should be a vow of truthfulness. This was not
rigidly interpreted. Every man, said Gandhi, has his own vision of
truth and he must follow that, not the vision handed on by another.
Next, all must follow the way of non-violence. Again, this was not
followed as a rigid rule of conduct, but rather as a general direction
that each must strive to live by: non-violence in thought, word,
and deed, the inner non-violence being the most essential. The
third vow was chastity. Here, again, such a vow would be differently
interpreted by each member. When I visited the ashram in 1928
a number of children were there. Gandhi loved children and they
loved him. He would not have been happy in a community without
children. The vow of non-stealing was so interpreted as to mean that
no member ought to possess anything he could fairly live without.
If he kept things he did not really need, he was a thief. Again, the
decision as to what each needed was his own. But Gandhi
stripped himself of almost all personal possessions. Members were
also required to take a vow to fight against all forms of untouchability, and they must resolve to learn to be fearless, especially in

all struggles that might develop against the authority of the government or indeed any other authority, such as orthodox Hinduism.

Ashram life began with a very early community prayer, when most of the chants were familiar Hindu hymns or recitations; there was a recitation from the Bhagavad Gita and at least one Muslim prayer was included. From time to time prayers from the Christian tradition or from other faiths were also included. Some members of the ashram were devoutly religious; others were of more sceptical mind. The day ended with a second corporate prayer.

Quite unexpectedly, the first demand for public action that came to Gandhi and to which he responded was to assist the peasants of a remote district in Bihar Province (Champaran) to resist the oppression of their landlords who were in most cases British. These men had for a hundred years grown indigo for the world market and the peasants were under obligation to grow indigo on three-twentieths of their land each year. This system had led to many abuses and, as the planters had much influence with the government, there was no redress for the peasants. By the time Gandhi came into the picture, German synthetic indigo had already nearly destroyed the Champaran indigo market. It was a dying industry. But that did not make the lot of the peasants less grievous. Probably, it made it worse.

Gandhi hardly knew where Champaran district was; he knew nothing of the indigo trade. So he was most reluctant to get involved. But a persistent man, Rajkumar Shukla, who had himself suffered as a peasant, followed Gandhi from place to place round the country until in the end he agreed to go to Champaran and see for himself.

Once on the spot, he realised that nothing but a very thorough enquiry would lead to any reform. He thereupon set about travelling from village to village with the help of some local men, one of whom, Dr Rajendra Prasad, was destined to be the first President of free India. Wherever he went, he invited the peasants to come and state their cases. The local officials got alarmed and ordered him to leave the district immediately. This he refused to do. So he was arrested and brought to court, where he explained, in typical Gandhi fashion, that he was not carelessly defying government: "I have disregarded the order served upon me, not for want of respect for lawful authority, but in obedience to the higher law of our being—the voice of conscience." He made it clear that he had no intention of stirring up any violent commotion; however, having promised to enquire into the facts, he could not but complete his enquiry before he left.

It soon appeared that the order to leave had been served upon him without reference to higher government authority. The government knew that in dealing with Gandhi they were dealing with no ordinary man, and that he could not be easily frightened away from a task he had undertaken. So he was allowed to continue his work. Members of the Criminal Investigation Department kept close to him in all that he did. Gandhi welcomed their presence, as it gave them the opportunity to see how he conducted his enquiry, and their presence tended to prevent the witnesses from overstating their case.

In due course the government itself realised that it must take the matter seriously. It appointed a committee of its own and invited Gandhi to be a member. He agreed to this. Although it was a composite committee, with officialdom predominant and the planters represented, the Governor of Bihar, Sir Edward Gait, persuaded it to present a unanimous report. The old *tinkathia* system, the system of enforcing the farming of indigo, was abolished, and so were other illegal exactions which had become customary. Illegal recoveries which had been extorted were to be refunded up to twenty-five per cent. Some of Gandhi's friends protested that he should have held out for full refund. But he took the view that moral victory was the essential thing. The peasants had learnt to shed their fear. The power of the planters was broken. Within a few years most of them abandoned their estates and left the district.

But Gandhi was not satisfied with his own work in Champaran. He had very soon seen that the peasants suffered not only from abject poverty but also from ignorance of simple hygiene and other foundations of a good life. He induced several experienced social workers, including one of the members of the Servants of India Society, Dr Dev, to join him in Champaran, and they set up medical clinics and other social centres. To some extent the village people welcomed this, but it was often hard going. Unfortunately, Gandhi himself was soon called away to other essential work; the remaining outside volunteers soon withdrew, and although he had promised himself that he would return to carry on the work, he was never able to do so. Nor were local workers available who had the necessary patience and persistence to see that the work was firmly established.

The following experience, as recounted by Gandhi himself, will illustrate the abject poverty in some of the villages:

> I happened to visit a small village where I found some of the women dressed very dirtily. So I told Mrs Gandhi to ask them why they did not wash their clothes. She spoke to them. One of the women took her into her hut and said: "Look now, there is no box nor cupboard containing other clothes. The sari I am wearing is the only one I have. How am I to wash it? Tell Mahatmaji to get me another sari, and I shall then promise to bathe and put on clean clothes every day...."
>
> In countless cottages in India people live without any furniture, and without a change of clothes, merely with a rag to cover their shame.

Two more appeals for help came to him while he was still winding up the work with the committee in Bihar. Both were from his own part of India, where he felt a special obligation to help if he could.

From Ahmedabad itself came an appeal from the sister of the mill-owner, Ambalal Sarabhai, saying that the wages in her brother's mill were far too low and the workers wanted Gandhi's advice on how to act. He recommended arbitration of their claim for a wage increase, but the employers refused this and expressed their strong disapproval of Gandhi's intervention. As he was devoted to the whole family of the Sarabhais, he was reluctant to intervene, but he also felt obliged to advise the workers that, if they felt convinced of the justice of their case, they must go on strike and refuse to yield till their claims were met. They should never resort to violence, they must not molest blackleg workers, and they must try to keep alive by undertaking some other honest labour.

All went well for a fortnight. Then they began to weaken and also to threaten the blacklegs. Gandhi was at his wit's end. This decline in their behaviour appalled him. Suddenly he decided

that he must refrain from all food until the workers became disciplined again ·and went through with their resolve. Although he
intended this as a stimulus to the workers, it was inevitably seen
by the employers as a measure of coercion against them. They
were very angry. However, the workers became disciplined; work
was found for them at the new Satyagraha Ashram, where sand was
needed for the foundations of a new weaving school. So all the
workers began to carry sand, led by the sister of the mill-owner,
Anasuyabehn Sarabhai. After three days the mill-owners capitulated and an arbitrator was appointed. There was a presentation
of sweets by the employers to all the workers—which turned
into a bit of a scramble, as all the local beggars got wind of it and
came to join in the festivities. However, peace was restored, and
the Commissioner, a British official, who presided over the meeting
to celebrate the settlement, advised the workers always to follow
Gandhi's advice. Within a few weeks he found reason to change
his mind about Gandhi.

Almost immediately after this, Gandhi was called to help the
peasants in the district of Kheda, near Ahmedabad, where the crops
had failed. According to the government regulation, when, owing
to flood or drought, the crop in a district was less than four annas
(which means less than a quarter of a full crop; sixteen annas
equal one rupee), then their revenue should be remitted for the year.
The officials declared that the Kheda crop was above four annas.
The peasants declared that it was less. Gandhi persuaded the
peasants to enter into a solemn agreement not to pay but to incur
any penalty for non-payment that the government might enforce.
Even those who could pay agreed to refuse to pay in order to stand
beside those who could only pay by borrowing from moneylenders.

The government was relentless. In the end the peasants began to
waver. However, they had demonstrated their strength, and the
government agreed to remit the revenue of the poorer peasants;
the wealthier paid. In general, the local people felt that a great
victory had been won. But it had not satisfied Gandhi who expected
true satyagrahis to stand firm in spite of suffering.

Some of his own comments are characteristic of his aims and
methods: "The main thing," he wrote, "was to rid the agriculturists
of their fear by making them realise that the officials were not the
masters, but the servants of the people, inasmuch as they received

their salaries from the taxpayer." Fearlessness they learnt, but not civility. "Experience has taught me," he added, "that civility is the most difficult part of satyagraha. Civility does not here mean the mere outward gentleness of speech cultivated for the occasion, but an inborn gentleness and desire to do the opponent good."

Although Gandhi was not happy about the outcome of this satyagraha, yet he recognised that it marked "the beginning of an awakening among the peasants of Gujarat, the beginning of their true political education."

This has taken us well beyond the probationary year that Gokhale had advised. With Gandhi it was impossible to separate one kind of public action from another. Already he was helping needy, dumb peasants and workers to fight battles against landlords, employers, and the government, to obtain redress of their wrongs. To Gandhi this was the very essence of the demand for swaraj—self-rule or home-rule for the country as a whole. Hitherto, the Indian National Congress, the name given to the organisation that was working for political freedom, had been chiefly concerned with decreasing the power of the British and acquiring additional political rights for Indians. Most of the leaders of the Congress were themselves rich men, landlords, lawyers, city dwellers, and the British officials complained that they knew less about the needs of the millions of silent, illiterate villagers than the British officials whose job it was to have contact with the people. Whatever measure of truth there may have been in this, Gandhi quickly changed it. Not only did he himself spend his time and strength in helping the rural masses to fight their battles and to discover their own strength, but also insisted that the Congress at its annual sessions and also in its activity throughout the year should bear the hapless millions in mind. At a later stage he declared that he was not interested in substituting exploitation of the masses by brown men for exploitation by white men. He wanted the whole system of government changed in the interest of the primary producer who carried all the rest on his back. India must become strong by conquering her own weaknesses. This meant abolishing untouchability and other caste abuses; it meant bringing hygiene and true education to the villages; it meant better care for the masses of half-starved cattle; it meant bringing women into public life and giving them a part in the upbuilding of the new India; it meant that the several religious communities must learn mutual respect and understanding; it meant fighting against poverty in all its manifestations. The India of his dreams was an India of prosperous, largely self-contained villages, where all communities should live in mutual respect and harmony.

Before we "launch on the stormy seas of Indian public life" with Gandhi, it will be useful to look at the idea of Indian freedom as he had expressed it in a booklet called *Hind Swaraj* (Indian self-rule) which he had written in 1909. In that year, he visited England in connection with his work for the Indian community in South Africa and, while he was in London, he had many talks with Indian students about the Indian desire for independence from the British. These students were all eager to throw off the yoke of British Government, but all that they wanted was to substitute Indian Government for British Government. As far as the content of self-rule was concerned, they were all for adopting Western forms of life—political, social, and economic. They wanted India to be a copy of the latest fashions in the West. Gandhi had quite another point of view. He had come to regard the Western way of life with distaste. He believed that the essential values of India's ancient civilisation were far superior to modern Western civilisation; so the swaraj he wanted was not in any way a copy of the West. Thus, his *Hind Swaraj* took the form of a dialogue between himself and a reader who represented the typical Indian student in London at that time.

It is not easy to summarise this pamphlet and yet do justice to it. There is plenty of strong meat in it. Gandhi accused the English of making money their god. He declared that he would prefer to have Indian "thugs" to deal with than live as a coward under the imposed *Pax Britannica*. He believed that the railways and other machinery introduced by the British only added to the slavery of the people. The educated Indians, especially the lawyers and the doctors, were only helping the British to sustain their government. They were an additional burden on the backs of the people. He did not prefer the tyranny of Indian princes to the tyranny of the British:

> If I have the power, I should resist the tyranny of Indian princes just as much as that of the English. By patriotism I mean the welfare of the whole people and, if I could secure it at the hands

of the English, I should bow my head to them. If any Englishman dedicated his life to securing the freedom of India, resisting tyranny and serving the land, I should welcome that Englishman as an Indian.

The Reader was made to suggest, as no doubt most young Indians at that time did believe, that the English could only be driven out by the sword, India perhaps losing a quarter of a million men in the process. Retorted Gandhi:

That is to say, you want to make the holy land of India unholy. Do you not tremble to think of freeing India by assassination? The millions of India do not desire it. Those who are intoxicated by the wretched modern civilization think these things. Those who will rise to power by murder will certainly not make the nation happy.

There followed two chapters on Brute Force and on Passive Resistance, or, as it was soon to be more correctly called, Satyagraha. The guiding principle was that "your belief that there is no connection between the means and the end is a great mistake . . . there is just the same inviolable connection between the means and the end as there is between the seed and the tree."

The Indian poet, Tulsidas, was quoted: "Of religion, pity or love is the root, as egotism of the body. Therefore, we should not abandon pity so long as we are alive."

Gandhi himself declared, as he continued to do again and again throughout his life:

Passive resistance, that is soul-force, is matchless. It is superior to the force of arms.... Physical force men are strangers to the courage that is requisite in a passive resister.... Even a man weak in body is capable of offering this resistance. One man can offer it just as well as millions. Both men and women can indulge in it.... Control over the mind is alone necessary, and when that is attained, man is free like the king of the forest and his very glance withers the enemy.

There is much else in this booklet, including a wholehearted denunciation of machinery. Gokhale found it a muddle-headed

and raw piece of writing and prophesied that its author would soon
modify much that he had written.   However, when it was republish-
ed in 1938, Gandhi declared that there was hardly a word that he
wished to change.   It may well be accepted as the main text of
the Gandhian revolution, the revolution based on truth and non-
violence and aiming at the welfare of all, not just the majority or
just one class, and it stands therefore to the Gandhian way of life
as the 1848 Manifesto stood to the whole Communist movement.

Such was the man who plunged into Indian national politics in
the years 1916 and 1917, bringing a totally new orientation to the
Indian National Congress.   All propositions must be judged by
new standards.   Were they promoting the welfare of the masses?
Were they genuinely non-violent?   Were they open, honest, and
truthful?

It is not necessary to give here the detailed picture of Indian
politics during the next few years.   But enough must be said to show
how Gandhi's attitude developed and changed up to the time of his
imprisonment in 1921.

As late as 1915, in a speech, at Madras, Gandhi had pronounced:

It gives me the greatest pleasure this evening to redeclare my
loyalty to the British Empire.... I discovered that the British
Empire had certain ideals with which I have fallen in love and
one of these ideals is that every subject of the British Empire has
the freest scope for his energies and honour and whatever he thinks
is due to his conscience.

Such words may startle those who only think of Gandhi as the
leader of Indian nationalism and even seem to contradict what we
have just seen of his fundamental outlook as he expounded it a few
years before in his *Hind Swaraj*.   The fact is that he was very
conscious of many blemishes in British administration, both in
South Africa and in India; but it seemed to him to be true that the
British were sincerely trying, throughout their empire, to accept
the principle of equal justice for all men, of human rights for all,
and of liberty of conscience—rights which were then and are still
today quite openly denied in many parts of the world.   That
they often failed to live up to their own principles was no doubt
true, but that, as he knew, is an almost universal human failing.   It

did not mean that the principles were bogus or that all the British were a lot of hypocrites. So far, in spite of disappointments, he was prepared to believe the best.

Again, as in South Africa, so in India, he was unwilling to take advantage of the other man's difficulties. Some Indian leaders took the view that the British might well be squeezed when they were in danger from the German foe in Europe. Not so Gandhi. He believed on principle that this was a morally unsound attitude to take; moreover, he still had faith that, if the Indians helped the British in their time of stress and danger, they would find a reward of trust and confidence, bringing with it a generous measure of self-government, when the war was over. So, while the war lasted, although he was prepared to act on behalf of the harassed villagers in Bihar or Gujerat, he accepted the British Government and even proved his good faith by undertaking a recruiting campaign in the very area where he had helped the peasants to defy the government tax assessment. However, he soon discovered that the peasants who had followed his lead so loyally a few months earlier were not at all inclined to fight even at his behest for the British Government in remote lands. The campaign, indeed, so undermined his health that he very nearly died and probably would have if he had not been rescued by a man who had faith in ice treatment. He had already given a last message to India that "she will find her salvation through non-violence, and through non-violence alone India will contribute to the salvation of the world." However, he did not die in 1918. He had nearly thirty more years to live, but, when the time came, his last message was in effect the same.

In the years 1919 and 1920, three main developments led to the final alienation of Gandhi from the system of government the British had brought to India. These were the Punjab atrocities, the treaty imposed by the victorious allies on Turkey, and the so-called Rowlatt Act. Each of these must be briefly explained.

Following the war, Indian opinion was excited in varying degrees in the several parts of the huge country. In the north-western province, the Punjab, many soldiers had been recruited to fight the Germans in Europe and the Turks in the Middle East and, after these men returned home, their wartime experiences brought new ideas to the towns and villages. Many of them were Muslims who were readily persuaded by the leaders of what was called the

Khilafat movement that the demolition of the Turkish Empire
was a blow struck at Islam.   British officials in the Punjab seemed
to have convinced themselves that an open revolt was being
prepared.   Actually, there was no truth in this.   In early April
1919, in the large town of Amritsar, after local leaders had been
arrested, a crowd ran amuck; they burnt the town-hall and the post-
office and injured some Europeans including two women.   There
had been isolated murders of Europeans elsewhere.   All public
meetings were prohibited.   Many people certainly did not know of
this ban.   13 April was a day of religious festival and large crowds,
entirely unarmed, assembled in a square called the Jallianwalla Bagh,
a place from which there was no large exit.   A certain General Dyer
marched troops into the square and ordered them to fire on the
crowd.   Some four hundred people were massacred and over one
thousand were injured.   Needless to say, the whole of India was
shocked and staggered.   It is perhaps amazing that any Indian still
remained loyal to the British connection.   Yet they did.   Even
Gandhi seems to have been more shocked by the inadequacy of the
punishments meted out to the main culprits and by the tone of
the Hunter Commission of Enquiry than by the deed itself.   The
deed, like other gross injustices, might have been the aberration
of one man or of a few misguided British "patriots"; but the
action taken by the Commission and the administration afterwards
demonstrated to Gandhi that the whole system of government
was fundamentally based on violence.   Although Gandhi had
recognised this in *Hind Swaraj*, it was now proved beyond
any question.

The treaty imposed on Turkey is a much more complex matter,
which can only be summarised here.   Up to 1914, the British
had prided themselves that most of the Muslim minority in India
accepted the British Raj.   But, during the war, new movements
gathered strength among Indian Muslims, especially the so-called
Khilafat movement which declared that the Caliphate, representing the religio-temporal power of Islam residing in the person
of the Sultan of Turkey, was an essential bulwark of Islam.
They insisted that nothing must be done by the victorious allies
to weaken this theocratic power.   The leaders of this movement
were two brothers, Shaukat Ali and Muhammad Ali.   Gandhi
became a close friend of the Alis, especially of the younger brother,

Muhammad Ali, who was by far the abler man and probably the more sincere in his religious convictions. To Gandhi, the religious convictions of any man were sacred, and were to be respected by the government. For a time the alliance between Gandhi and the Ali brothers brought the Hindu and Muslim communities of India closer to each other than at any other time. The Indian Government interned the Ali brothers and Gandhi continually appealed for their release. Although the government gave vague reassurances, when the treaty with Turkey became public, it was clear that the old Turkish Empire was totally dismembered. What perhaps was not clear to Gandhi or his Indian colleagues at the time was that this was in fact an act of emancipation for the Arabs of the Middle East. Moreover, the new Turkey, which arose from the ashes of the old, declared itself a secular State and proceeded to abolish the Khilafat, with hardly a murmur from most Islamic countries. In fact, the whole Khilafat movement in India appeared to have been unrealistic and, to judge from the later story of the Ali brothers who by 1925 were almost wholly alienated from Gandhi, it was something of a cloak for a new Pan-Islamic movement which dreamed of a new empire of Islam stretching from West Africa to Indonesia.

All that we are concerned with here is that Gandhi was inclined to convict the British Government in India of bad faith in its attitude to Turkey and to the Khilafat.

Finally, although the British Government proposed political reforms, giving away a substantial measure of self-government and the beginnings of a democratic franchise to the several provinces of British India—proposals which in the first place Gandhi welcomed —at the same time, and indeed before these political reforms could be brought into effect, a measure was rapidly pushed through the Indian central legislature (which had an official majority) giving the officials, which of course meant in effect the British, extraordinary powers to deal with all kinds of lawlessness and disaffection. As Gandhi saw it, India had been patiently waiting for bread and had received instead a stone.

From this time on, instead of seeing tyrannous acts by British officials as the aberrations of individuals who were violating an essentially benevolent system, he saw the whole British system as diabolical, though he was still willing to believe that individual

British Viceroys or other officials could be approached as men who
might to some extent redeem a Satanic system.

By 1920, Gandhi was convinced that the sooner the British left
the better it would be for India. He also believed that they must
be induced to leave, not by armed rebellion, still less by acts
of terrorism, nor yet would they be persuaded to hand over power
by parliamentary methods of persuasion and agitation. Non-
violent direct action, the mass disobedience of law, was to be the
remedy. This would not only drive them out of the country, but
also convince them that India was fit and disciplined enough
to govern herself. If the people of India would accept discipline,
and unite to act non-violently, he promised that swaraj could be
obtained within one year. He did not define swaraj; when he came
near to define it, it was clear that he was not thinking only, perhaps
not primarily, of a system of government. He had a much broader
perspective in his mind, difficult not only for the British but even
for his colleagues in the leadership of the Indian National Congress
to understand. First, therefore, he had to convince them that this
was the right road to follow, and this was no easy task.

A special session of the Indian National Congress was held at
Calcutta in September 1920 to consider Gandhi's plan of progressive
non-violent non-cooperation with the government. He had been
touring all over India, expounding his ideas, and had stirred the
common people in a way that no Indian political leader had done
hitherto. His resolution was to the effect that

> there can be no contentment in India without the redress of the
> two wrongs [the Khilafat and the Punjab] and that the only
> effectual means to vindicate national honour and to prevent a
> repetition of similar wrongs in future is the establishment of
> Swarajya [self-government]. The Congress is further of opinion
> that there is no course left open for the people of India, but to
> approve of and adopt the policy of progressive non-violent
> non-cooperation until the said wrongs are righted and Swarajya
> is established.

The language is mild, but the intention to launch an open, though
non-violent, rebellion against the government is clear.

Most of the old Congress leaders, however, were by no means

converted to the Gandhian method of action. They believed that more would be achieved by contesting elections to the new provincial councils and then attacking the government by obstructive tactics in these councils. However, when it came to the vote, 1,855 members voted for the resolution, and only 873 against. This was the first time that Gandhi had put his new type of action to the test in an open Congress session. His victory was no doubt due largely to the fact that he had roused mass emotions of a kind hitherto unknown in India. He used his success with characteristic moderation and, within a few months, men who had served the national cause for many years while he was still in South Africa were loyally accepting his leadership and serving as his lieutenants. Some, however, were completely alienated, and before long a new party of Liberals grew up, with very little popular backing, but including men of high personal distinction who on principle rejected all forms of direct action and law-breaking, however non-violent.

By the end of 1920, when the Congress met again at Nagpur, Gandhi had formulated a new constitution for it. There were now to be village committees wherever possible; next above that came the union committees, then district committees, then provincial committees, and, finally, the All-India Congress Committee of 350 members. Each year a President was to be elected for the year. He had the authority to nominate a small Working Committee which was a standing executive capable of acting throughout the year. Anyone who paid an annual subscription of four annas (roughly four pence or five cents) could become a member of the Congress. It thus became a mass movement, at certain times with millions of paying members.

The government response to all this was cautious. In England, the Secretary of State, who constitutionally had the last word, was impressed by the fact that Gandhi was sincere in his desire to avoid violence and to calm excitement. But to most of the local officials in India, including the Viceroy, it appeared that he was stirring up sedition and that it might be wise to arrest him or even to expel him from India to some remote British colonial island before revolution broke out. For the time being, restraint won the day. Gandhi on his side seemed to believe that the government had no reason to object to mass civil disobedience.

He was not in fact advocating immediate and general civil disobedience. His programme was to be more or less phased. First, he urged young Indians to withdraw from all government schools and colleges; national schools were to be set up to replace them. Lawyers should refuse any longer to work in the law-courts; national arbitration boards must be set up to replace the government courts. The use of alcohol and drugs, from which, incidentally, the government derived a considerable revenue, must be abandoned. All foreign cloth must be discarded. Gandhi himself presided over bonfires of foreign cloth. Soldiers and police should withdraw from government service. Finally, there should be general refusal to pay taxes. Along with these actions, which were to be phased gradually under Gandhi's direction, the country must rid itself of communal antagonism (especially as between the Hindus and the Muslims); they must destroy the curse of untouchability. Forced labour must go. Such were to be the essential ingredients of the self-emancipation of India. Swaraj, said Gandhi, could not be given by the British. It could not be given by God. It must be earned and achieved by internal reform.

It is hardly surprising that neither his more politically minded colleagues nor the government believed that he could achieve such radical changes within a year or even within any measurable time. To a large extent, his admonitions fell on deaf ears so far as the educated classes were concerned. Few resigned from government schools and colleges; very few abandoned their legal practice. But the common people heard him gladly, especially the peasants and other villagers. India began to ring with the cry: "Mahatma Gandhi *ki jai*" (victory to Mahatma Gandhi). Too often, as he with characteristic candour insisted, this enthusiasm went no further than shouting. The people who came in crowds to listen went away to do none of the things he demanded of them. Hindus and Muslims still rioted against one another. Untouchables were still denied the right of access to village wells and other amenities. Only a very few took his message to heart, but, to those who did follow him, life took on a new colour. An elderly Muslim judge, Abbas Tyabji, who had thrown his lot with Gandhi, wrote: "God! What an experience! I have so much love and affection for the common folk to whom it is now an honour to belong. It is the fakir's dress that has broken down all barriers." Gandhi had by now abandoned the dress of middle-class townsman. To the end of his life he wore only handspun cotton clothes, a loincloth and, when necessary, a shawl flung round his shoulders.

As the new movement spread and as excitement grew, the government had to make up its mind how far it could let it grow without arresting the arch-culprit. The Ali brothers were arrested again. So were some of the Congress leaders, but Gandhi remained free. Partly, this was because, up to a point, it was realised that he was determined to avoid violence and his arrest might have led to violent outbreaks, which could not then be controlled.

At the time of a State visit from the Prince of Wales, when he landed in Bombay, the population as a whole observed *hartal*. That is to say, they all closed their shops and business and stayed at home. But a minority came out to do honour to the guest. Some of these loyalists were attacked by the mob and there were many casualties. Gandhi, who was himself in Bombay at the time, immediately began to fast, issued the strongest possible rebuke, and took the blame upon himself. He admitted that he had been playing with fire, and here was the result. However, he still hoped that the people of India as a whole were prepared for a truly non-violent campaign, and he soon resolved to start the general campaign of tax refusal in a single district, the Bardoli district of Gujerat, where the tax refusal of two years earlier had been well organised and where the people had shown a capacity for self-discipline. A few days before the date set for this, an incident occurred in quite another part of India, at a small town called Chauri Chaura, which altered the whole course of events. A demonstration was passing the police barracks; the police jeered at the crowd and a few shots were fired. Thereupon the crowd set fire to the police barracks and many policemen were killed. Instantly, Gandhi called off the whole movement of civil disobedience and declared that he had been blind to the real state of affairs. His politically minded colleagues were furious. Over months and years, the great revolution had been prepared. Here, just because of an isolated act of violence, the whole thing was thrown away and India was left in dismay.

From the purely political angle, no doubt the indignation of the politicians was justified. It is conceivable that if Gandhi had gone ahead, even though he himself and the other leaders would certainly have been arrested almost at once, the British Government

might have been brought down. Undoubtedly, widespread enthusiasm had been aroused. But this would certainly have been
accompanied by much bloodshed and hatred and bitterness. It
would not have been a non-violent revolution. To most of Gandhi's
colleagues, this did not matter much. Political freedom was worth
quite a lot of bloodshed. To Gandhi it mattered supremely. He
was not at bottom a politician, but a moralist. To him it was
better that the British system, much as he now hated it, should
continue for years rather than that it should be overthrown by
violence. The only free India he cared to see was an India that
had learnt at least in a large measure the way of non-violence.

The British Government, of course, was no more interested in
these high moral purposes than were Gandhi's colleagues. Seeing
their enemy in disarray, they realised that now was the moment to
arrest Gandhi. He was himself aware that this was bound to happen
soon, and so he issued the strictest injunctions that there must be no
demonstrations of any kind. This was published in *Young India,*
his weekly journal, on 9 March 1922. The following day he was
arrested. As the Viceroy wrote to his son, "not a dog barked."
But whether this was due to Gandhi's own influence, or to India's
disappointment and disillusionment with him, may remain an open
question. The government thought, as it often thought in later
years, that he had shot his bolt and that his influence would wane.
If he had been simply a political leader, their calculations might
have been justified. But what they forgot, just as many of his close
colleagues forgot, or never understood, was that he was really
something quite else: a moral leader, if you will, who was wrestling
with the immoral world of politics. His political opponents and his
political colleagues again and again overlooked this fact. But
the people of India as a whole never forgot it. In prison or out of
prison, in political favour or out of it, he remained for them the
Mahatma.

3

In the Villages
(1924-1927)

GANDHI was arrested on 10 March 1922. He was sentenced to six years of imprisonment and he was sent to the Yeravda Jail at Poona, not to the jail at Sabarmati, within a mile of the ashram. Owing to a sudden attack of appendicitis, he was released again, after the operation, on 5 February 1924. So the six years were reduced to less than two. Up to a point, there can be no doubt that Gandhi enjoyed prison life. At a later date, Rabindranath Tagore playfully described his prison terms as "arrest cures," and so no doubt they were. But it would also seem that, after a time, prison life irked him as it must irk any active man. The psychologists may be left to debate the problem of the connection (if any) between his desire to be free again and the sudden attack of appendicitis. In his very strenuous ordinary life outside jail, he did not fall ill, though we shall soon note that he had attacks of high blood pressure.

But it was characteristic of him that, although he was declared a free man on 5 February 1924, he did not return to the active politics of open rebellion against British rule till after the original sentence had expired. The government might say that he was free, but he did not consider himself fully free. These intervening years were spent in the work that was in fact always far more congenial to him than political life. He toured the villages of India, striving to release the masses of the people from age-old superstitions and from poverty and ignorance, and he undertook the first and perhaps the most impressive of his long fasts in an endeavour to induce Hindus and Muslims to cease from communal strife. Fortunately, his devoted and noble secretary, Mahadev

Desai, published full reports of his village tours; he himself wrote on some of these for his weekly journal, *Young India.*

Mahadev Desai's reports cover a series of journeys in early 1925 in Kathiawar (the extreme western seaboard of India, near to the place of his birth), in central India, in some remote districts of Bengal (north-eastern India), and elsewhere. This was followed by tours in Bihar (north-central) and Travancore (extreme south-west), described by Gandhi himself.

A few pages of quotations from these reports will give a much closer insight into the real life of Gandhi, into his heart, than chapters about his political actions.

This was the time when, first and foremost, he was trying to persuade every man, woman, and child in India to give some time to handspinning of cloth as the simplest means, the first step, in an attack on Indian rural poverty. So the first quotations may show him propagating this faith in East Bengal. Mahadev Desai says:

> There were on an average three or four meetings a day, and a plethora of addresses everywhere, but the meetings were, without a single exception, so orderly and those who presented the addresses so considerate that there was not much strain on Gandhiji.... Of all the meetings, those with the ladies stand out most prominently in the memory. There is not a place which I can recall where one sister or more has not come to Gandhiji with presents of khaddar pieces—dhoties, towels or table-cloths—some woven by themselves, and all woven out of yarn spun by themselves. At Chittagong, just as Gandhiji was leaving, a young girl came with a beautiful towel of her own spinning and weaving. At Noakhali two dhoties were presented to Gandhiji woven of yarn spun by 60 ladies of a village who fasted and prayed and devoted the whole of the fourth "Gandhi day" to spinning. At Chandpur most of the ladies made it a point to come with yarn of their own spinning, and at Mymensingh hundreds of ladies attended the meeting in spite of heavy showers of rain and spontaneously offered gold bangles and other ornaments along with the yarn. The meetings, far from being pandemonium, as in other parts of India, were, with one possible exception, models of silent and attentive gatherings. Along with every one of these meetings, there was a spinning demonstration which one could not leave

without added faith and hope. Hundreds of sisters have I
seen "slaving away at their wheels," as Gandhiji said.

Mahadev goes on to tell of Gandhi's talks with students:

The Comilla students had a definition of national education
from him. That education is national, he said, which educates
in you a sense of fellow-feeling for all your countrymen, which
teaches you to melt at the woes of your countrymen wherever
they may be. That education is national, which makes you
think in terms of the nation, which makes you calculate not how
a particular thing will benefit you individually, but what it
means for the nation as a whole. And nothing is so universally
useful as the spinning-wheel. At Dacca the students' meeting
was cancelled, but Gandhiji asked the students to come and
have a chat after all the public functions were over, and they
had more than they could even in their wildest dreams have
expected. Gandhiji, always at his best when provoked, unbosom-
ed himself when a friend objected that spinning was a waste
of energy and time, and another, that his advice took no account
of the division of labour. "Do I ask you to do spinning for
the whole of the day? Do I ask you to take it up as a substantive
occupation? Where, then, is the breach of the principle of
division of labour? Do you have a division of labour in eating
and drinking?" he passionately asked. "Just as everyone of
us must eat and drink and clothe himself, even so every one of
us must spin." "And it is a waste, you say? Fellow-feeling
for your countrymen, you say, you have in abundant measure?
And what is that fellow-feeling, without the milk of human
kindness? Do you feel anything like the love that a cow feels
for her calf or a mother for her baby? The cow's udders and
the mother's breast overflow with milk at the sight of their
young ones. Do your hearts overflow with love at the sight of
your famished countrymen? By spinning, my friends, you
demonstrate your love for them. You spin and you make
them shake off their idleness.... Spinning...has purpose and it
means added production. The purpose is that it serves as a bond
with the masses."

Here too in East Bengal, where the majority of the population is Muslim, with a large Hindu minority—today it is the Province of East Pakistan—he also pressed for better Hindu-Muslim understanding: "The Hindu and the Mussulman must each add a common article to his creed, namely, that he cannot live without the other." He believed that "God, who has placed together 70 million Mussulmans with 220 million Hindus, will have some mercy on us; he will make us live as brothers in spite of ourselves."

Ahimsa, which we may translate as harmlessness or as non-violence, was another of his constant themes. Thus, at Bogra, still in East Bengal, he said: "I shall tell you something about Ahimsa in order to strengthen your faith in it.... The spinning-wheel is an emblem of peace and ahimsa, and I have pinned my faith to it because ahimsa is not a policy with me, but a creed, a religion. Why do I regard it as such? Because I know that it is not *himsa* or destructive energy that sustains the world, it is *ahimsa*, the creative energy. I do admit that the destructive energy is there, but it is evanescent, always futile before the creative, which is permanent. If the destructive one had the upper hand all sacred ties—love between parents and child, brother and sister, master and disciple, rulers and ruled—would be snapped. Ahimsa is like the sun whose worship as the symbol of God our Rishis immortalised in the Gayatri. As the sun keeps watch over man's mortality, going his eternal rounds and dispelling darkness and sin and gloom, even so does ahimsa. Ahimsa inspires you with love than which you cannot think of a better excitement. And that is why faith in the spinning-wheel, which is a symbol of peace and love, is increasing as I grow older. And that is why I do not think I am committing an impropriety in spinning whilst I am talking to you. As I am turning the wheel, I am saying to myself: Why does God give me my daily bread, whilst He starves multitudes of men? Let Him starve me too, or enable me to do something to remove their starvation. And as I turn it I am practising ahimsa and truth which are the obverse and reverse of the same coin. Ahimsa is my God. When I look for ahimsa, Truth says, find it through me. When I look for truth, Ahimsa says, find it through me."

In Bengal, Gandhi was first and foremost concerned with promoting hand-spinning, but, in some other parts of the country, notably Travancore in the south and Cutch in the west, he found himself engaged in a battle against orthodox Hindus on behalf of the Untouchables or outcastes. Here is a report of some of the happenings in Cutch:

On the very first day of our arrival in Cutch . . . there was a public address, of course, attended by all that the lavish hospitality of the Cutchies could conceive. They could have been discreetly silent about things where they were on unsure and delicate ground. But that would be poor courtesy. So they eulogised Gandhiji's services in the cause of the "untouchables," stated that their relations with them were quite all right and requested Gandhiji to give them the benefit of his advice as to what more they could do in this direction. But in flat contradiction to all these sentiments, the "untouchables" were confined to a remote, safe corner of the meeting....."I should not mince matters," he said. "I have been calling myself an untouchable and a sweeper, not out of arrogance, or ignorance, or because I am westernised, but because I may serve them the better on that account. The western influence had nothing to do with my views about untouchability. They are the deliberate conviction of a man born and bred up in a purely orthodox Hindu atmosphere and tradition, of a man who had practised Hindu religious teaching by actually imitating his orthodox parents, of a man who had tried to study the human body as much as the Dweller of that tabernacle, of a man who had given years of study to the Shastras in perfect faith and devotion, of a man who had wandered throughout the length and breadth of India, discussing the matter with shastris and pandits, and who was more confirmed in his view as a result. You should have counted with them when you invited me. But even if you feel today that you have made a mistake in inviting a man of such views, you can still retrace your steps, and courteously send me back. I assure you I shall appreciate it and not misunderstand it. You must know that whilst I should feel honoured if you excluded me, I should feel deeply hurt if you excluded these friends. I can no more bear to be present in a place where they are slighted and insulted than a devoted student of

Ramayana can bear to stay in a place where the name of Rama
is dragged in the mire. Pray, therefore, either permit them to
come and sit with you, or me to go and sit amongst them. The
cordon that you have drawn goes right against the grain of my
being. Either remove that cordon or put me with these brothers.
But mind you, I want you to do what you do with the courage
of your conviction, and not to please me. If you exclude me I
assure you I shall congratulate you on your courage and your
instinct of self-preservation. But if you admit the 'untouchables,'
I adjure you to do so with the maturest deliberation, so that
you might not later have to be in the sorry plight of those people
at Mangrol [a village he had visited some months earlier in
Travancore] who after I left them recanted their views and
expiated for their sins. Let this be the first object lesson in
Satyagraha."

The warning went home and when the vote was taken, one
could not but be struck with the deliberation which was manifest
in the voting. There was a slight majority for the orthodox
view, and with perfect pride and pleasure Gandhiji asked for
permission to go and address them now from amongst the
"untouchables." There was not a flutter as the table was quietly
removed by the volunteers beyond the cordon, and in a few
minutes the meeting was listening to Gandhiji addressing them
from the new platform. It was a pure triumph of Satyagraha.

Next day a further meeting was held, so naturally, Gandhi and
his party looked forward to it with mingled feelings. There was
some doubt whether many people would turn up. It was known
that the orthodox had spent much of the night discussing the
matter. In the event, the meeting was very well attended, by
a much larger crowd than the day before, and a number of
caste Hindus, including some Brahmins (the highest caste),
sat with the "untouchables" and Gandhi and his friends. It
seems likely that the incident had some permanent effect on
caste rigidity in the whole of Cutch. At least, it was the first
effective challenge to the whole notion of untouchability in that
part of India.

Not that it had any effect on the towns and villages that he
visited immediately after. At a place called Mundra, there were

two separate enclosures, one for the untouchables and the reformers, the other for the rest. The president of the meeting, all the Hindu volunteers who kept order, even the Mussalmans of the town and the teacher of the school for untouchables, sat in the touchables' enclosure, and every effort was made to keep any caste Hindu from entering the untouchables' enclosure. In his speech that evening, Gandhi cried out: "If this is Hinduism, oh Lord, my fervent prayer is that the soonest it is destroyed the best." He tried to cancel the meeting arranged at the next place, Anjar, and wrestled with the president of the reception committee there to let him have two meetings, the first with the untouchables alone, the second with the rest of the community. But they would not agree. So, when it came to the time for the meeting, instead of speaking to the people about the spinning-wheel, about abolishing untouchability ("why speak to people who are unwilling to listen to my message?" he said) or appealing for subscriptions to the memorial fund for the late C.R. Das—the three topics that he was specially concerned with at the time—he led those who were willing to join him in a prayer chant, later familiar among all who attended his daily prayer meetings: "Raghupati Raghava Raja Ram, Patita Pavana Sita Ram." This prayer, repeated as a chant for minutes at a time, is to the Hindu worshipper who uses the name of Ram equivalent to the Lord's prayer for the Christian. That was all that the people of Anjar heard from him. Or rather, that was all that the high-caste people heard. A meeting with the untouchables alone was arranged after all.

Mahadev Desai adds to this that the position of the Untouchables in Cutch, even in those days, was not nearly as bad as it was in parts of south India and, in the course of his tour, Gandhi met some devoted workers who, in defiance of powerful opposition, were working to break down these barriers between man and man. He concludes his chapter with a paragraph in praise of two remarkable men; one, a man who had worked for over forty years in the State Education Department, and in his retirement was giving all his remaining energies to educational reforms and to the encouragement of hand-spinning. Nor had he, though a Brahmin, any attitude of superiority towards the outcastes. Of the other man: "Jaykrishnabhai, the botanist, is a unique figure. His passion for reclaiming the salty and sandy coast-soil of Cutch, and of covering the land with trees, is phenomenal. Trees to him are something more than living companions." And he too was free from the canker of superiority. It was such men as these whose efforts were assisted by Gandhi's visits as he moved all round India, and who continued the work of reform with renewed hope after he left.

Gandhi himself wrote the published reports of his tours through Bihar and the United Provinces. There is something new to be found at almost every place he visited, but here it must suffice to record one or two of his experiences. Thus, at a place in Bihar, called Giridih, he was challenged again on the efficacy and wisdom of his insistence on hand-spinning. His reply helps to elucidate his real purpose in this:

> I have said repeatedly that those only are expected and should be induced to spin who have no other paying employment and that too only during the hours of unemployment. The whole theory of handspinning is based upon the assumption that there are millions of men and women in this land who are idle for at least four months in the year.

These, in his view, were the many who could earn some slight addition to their meagre incomes by spinning their own cloth. Moreover, he urged that "the thinking part of India should spin for sacrifice by way of example and in order to cheapen khaddar" (handspun cloth). He added that, though not all should spin, all should wear handspun cloth, in order to assist their poor neighbours.

At another place, Forbesgunj, on the borders of Nepal, we get a vivid account of what was liable to happen at these village meetings when for one reason or another order broke down:

> The crowd was immense. The meeting had to take place under the fierce sun. The people had been waiting since morning without any shade overhead. The noise and the din were terrible. It was impossible for me to get any quiet; and volunteers were unable to restrain the vast crowd from coming to touch

me. The fact is that not much work had been done there before. The volunteers were new to their task. The poor fellows tried their best. Nobody was to blame. It was a new situation and a new experience for them. And the people were not to be deprived of what they must have considered to be the only opportunity of coming near me and touching me. It is an affectionate superstition; but it is also most embarrassing for me. I spoke to them about khaddar, about the spinning-wheel, about temperance, gambling and the like; but I am afraid it was all like foreign speech to them. Mysterious are the ways of God. Tens of thousands of people irresistibly drawn to someone or to something of whom or which they had but the vaguest idea. I do not know whether they profited by coming to see me, a perfectly strange being to them. I do not know whether it was worth while my going to Forbesgunj. Perhaps it is as well that we do not know the results of all we do, if only we do things for the service of God and humanity and do nothing which we know to be wrong.

Already, before this experience, Gandhi noted that the shouts of the crowds were almost unbearable to him and he had to stuff his ears to prevent himself from swooning. Many years later, when I was with him in the villages of East Bengal, he commented that the shouts with which he was received were intolerable to him and he put his fingers in his ears to shut out the din. Moreover, at that time, there was a further reason for his protest. The people were receiving him with the acclaim that was intended as a sign of victory and rejoicing. Yet it was soon after hideous communal killings, and he thought it would have been more fitting to receive him in silent grief.

These few pages may give some impression of the themes that were uppermost in Gandhi's mind as he travelled from village to village across India. But it cannot be said too often that, whatever he was doing, and wherever he was, the constant preoccupation of his mind was with the "dumb, semi-starved millions" of Indian villages, whose poverty and misery and superstition were a constant burden on his soul.

During the years following his release from jail, which means in effect the years 1924-28, though he was withdrawn from the political struggle as such, he was doing the utmost in his power to lay solid foundations on which a free and happy India could be built. And one essential for this was communal harmony. In India there lived at this time some two hundred and thirty million Hindus and some seventy million Muslims, besides other smaller religious groups: Christians, Sikhs, Parsis, Jews, Buddhists. (Jains and the Untouchable castes are sometimes reckoned as Hindus, sometimes separated from them.) The British Government had introduced into the early electoral system of India a communal franchise. That is to say, in each province of India certain seats were reserved for Muslims; others were reserved for all other religious communities. Muslim voters voted only in the Muslim constituencies, all other voters in the "general" constituencies. The proportions were based on the statistics of population. Moreover, it was the practice of the government to reserve some proportion of official appointments to members of the minority communities. Thus, there was a constant contest for jobs and for higher representation in government service and in political representation, especially between Hindus and Muslims, particularly in towns. This contest led in the mid-twenties to serious outbreaks of violence, chiefly in the large towns. Gandhi felt that his work of arousing political consciousness had contributed to this conflict and that he must try to stop it.

Following a riot in a town called Kohat in September 1924, where no less than 155 Hindus were killed, he announced that he would undertake a three-week fast, hoping thereby to induce the leaders of the two communities to be reconciled. The fast was undertaken in the house of his old colleague, Muhammad Ali, a leading Muslim, in the city of Delhi. Leaders of all religious communities gathered together in Delhi from all over India; they held a unity conference while the fast was in progress and agreed on a resolution affirming freedom of conscience and religious conviction and practice, but condemning all resort to violence in religious matters.

Gandhi hoped by fasting to purify himself, thereby to be a more fitting instrument for healing the wounds of the country. He broke his fast on 8 October 1924, in the presence of leaders of all religious communities, including the Anglican Metropolitan of India, Bishop Foss Westcott, and his beloved Christian friend

C.F. Andrews. For a time there was a hush; peace prevailed; but very soon the riots began again. The breach had not been healed. Indeed, though from time to time the two major communities seemed to draw nearer to one another, in the end the cleavage led to the establishment of the separate Muslim State of Pakistan. To what extent the British Government, or at least some of its local agents, fostered this conflict, it is not easy to say. The reason commonly given in England for refusing the demand for Indian self-government was that it would only lead to violent conflict and civil war all over India, and it seemed to be assumed that the Muslims would be able to dominate the Hindus by force. So the British must remain to keep the peace as far as possible. When I first visited India in 1927, I was startled to find British officials who quite openly said: "So long as we keep the Hindus and Muslims in conflict, our Government will not be in danger." Although Gandhi took upon himself the free burden of striving throughout his life, to bring harmony within and between the major and indeed all communities in India, there is no doubt that he considered the British Government to blame for the Hindu-Muslim conflict. Thus, in 1940, he wrote:

Why did Britain create the Princes and arm them with unheard-of powers? Surely for making her foothold secure.... Who created minorities? There is no majority save political majority. These things were, and still are, bulwarks of imperialism. No jugglery of words can hide this naked truth.

To the end of his life Gandhi was happiest when he was among the simple village people of India. In spite of his legal training in London, in spite of his many years of legal practice in South Africa, working from a city office, it was in the villages that he felt at home, and nowhere else. And, from the time when he settled again in India in 1915 to the day of his death in January 1948, his concern remained very much the same. He was concerned to persuade the people of rural India that their basic human interests were all one, and that the deep cleavages which had developed through the centuries between Hindu and Muslim, between caste Hindu and outcaste, so that many villages have, to all intents and purposes, lived in three distinct sections, were basically mischievous and involved a denial of the truth of universal brotherhood. Every part of his being rose up in denial of the notion that Hindus and Muslims were two nations. To him, this was just a simple false-hood which could never be tolerated. That men should adhere to their respective ancestral faiths he fully accepted; but this they could do with mutual respect and tolerance. Such divisions of religious faith could never break the bonds that unite the whole human family. If he were a reader of the writings of the great Italian patriot, Mazzini, he might well have echoed the words in which that great humanist appealed to the men of Italy to rise up and overthrow foreign rule:

> Free men and slaves, you are all brothers. Origin, law and goal are one for all of you.... Do not say, the language which we speak is different; tears, actions, martyrdom form a common language for all men, and one which you all understand. Do not say, Humanity is too vast, and we are too weak. God does not measure powers, but intentions. Love Humanity.

To Gandhi, the first need of the dumb masses was to overcome their vast poverty. He has often been quoted as saying that God comes to the starving man in the form of bread, and that many men were too poor to have any religion. It was this poverty that he was trying to fight all his life. He did not necessarily disagree with his socialist colleagues, Jawaharlal Nehru and others, but while they were working at their long-term plans, he was deter-mined to find an immediate first step to relieve the poverty of the half-starved millions. He saw this in the reintroduction of the spinning-wheel. India produces her own cotton. Yet the very men who produced their own cotton were often condemned to spend several months of each year in idleness. Why not spend this time in spinning and weaving their own clothes out of their own cotton? This at least would be a first step out of the pit of destitution. His emphasis on prohibition is also linked with this. He wanted to get rid of alcohol, not primarily for puritanical rea-sons, but because spending money on alcohol contributed to the misery of the village families. If, instead of spending their idle hours at the toddy shop, the village people could spend them in spinning and weaving cloth, their women and children would be doubly blessed. Visitors to India are apt to hear the story of prohibition from the angle of the middle-class citizen of Bombay: from men who can quite well afford to spend part of their income on alcoholic drinks and who see the disastrous social effects of the smuggling trade in a big city. Those who know the villages are apt to tell another story. Many villagers admit that they cannot easily resist the temptation of the liquor shop, but they wish they could, and, if the liquor shop is closed, they are unlikely to try and buy illicit liquor. This, at least, was the view that Gandhi had of the problem. He had the economic needs of the half-starved Indian villagers constantly in mind; he cared far more about them than about any political issue, even the issue of independence. Indeed, I have heard him say that, if he believed that the British would really be single-minded in treating the problem of poverty as the first problem to be tackled in India, he would be happy to see them continue to rule India indefinitely, even though he might be the only Indian to ask them to stay. Though he hastened to add that he was convinced that this could never be, as every alien government was bound to make its own security its first concern. Every day that he was in London at the time of the Round Table Conference on the future government of India, at almost every possible opportunity, he insisted that he represented the dumb, semi-starved millions of Indian villagers. He was ready to let the other Indians present there be the representatives of the towns and the vocal educated minority.

This emphasis needs to be made; for, in a world that has an obsession with politics, it is a man's political career that receives all the attention. In the later chapters of this book, we shall be obliged to give much attention to Gandhi's political activity. But it must not be forgotten that, throughout it all, he daily remembered the dumb millions he believed he represented. Their welfare was his constant concern. And he was never happier than when he was able to break away from the chains his political colleagues fastened upon him, holding him to the cities where the daily politics are made; back to the villages where he was at home among the people who understood, if anyone understood, the basic faith he had in God and in the way of non-violence.

4

Gandhi and Irwin
(1927-1931)

IN 1927 there was a change of Viceroys. Lord Reading's term ended and the British Government appointed E.F.L. Wood, thenceforth known as Lord Irwin, to succeed him. Lord Reading was a leading member of the old Liberal Party, a very able lawyer, a Jew by religion, a politician through and through. He had seemingly outwitted the Mahatma; he had arrested him at a time when political India was disillusioned with his leadership and, thereafter, no one had talked about the resumption of civil disobedience; the leading Congress politicians were favouring what was called Council entry—that is to say, getting themselves elected to the State legislatures in order to attack the government from the inside rather than the outside.

Lord Irwin was a different kind of man. He was a Conservative and an aristocrat, heir to a peerage. He was a devout Anglican. Arriving in India just at Easter time, he cancelled some of the festivities arranged in his honour so that he might attend an Easter service in Bombay. Such an act of religious devotion immediately caught the imagination of India. A few years later, I was solemnly assured that Lord Irwin always went to church in New Delhi on foot. Apparently this was not true, but it fitted the idea that India formed of this "tall, thin Christian," as Muhammad Ali described him in the first session of the London Round Table Conference. In any case, it certainly was true that when he toured the country he found opportunities to mix with missionaries and other non-officials, both Indian and British, who could see India from different angles. He was never hypnotised by the official viewpoint. C.F. Andrews was one of the men he met and occasionally conferred with; they had a good deal in common in their approach to religion.

It seemed reasonable to hope that he and Gandhi would be congenial. But, when they first met, each man was disappointed with the other. Lord Irwin summoned Gandhi, together with several other political leaders, to visit him. Gandhi crossed the country for this meeting. When they reached Delhi, the leaders were handed a document announcing that His Majesty's Government had decided to appoint an all-party committee of British Members of Parliament to examine the working of the Indian Constitution and to advise on any further steps towards self-government that they deemed appropriate. Indian political leaders were invited to co-operate with this committee—Simon Commission as it was called—presided over by Sir John Simon.

Gandhi was disgusted. Why travel across India to be given a document which in any case he and his colleagues considered to be an insult? The reply was a general agreement to boycott the Commission when it reached India; Gandhi endorsed this attitude. Instead of helping the all-British Commission, the party leaders decided to prepare an Indian-made constitution for India. An all-party conference was formed, which appointed a committee led by the distinguished liberal, Sir Tej Bahadur Sapru, and by Motilal Nehru, father of Jawaharlal Nehru; it included leading Muslims and others. They produced a notable document providing for an Indian Dominion; but it was then repudiated by several of the Indian parties, especially the orthodox Hindus and the Muslim League. Under these circumstances, the way was open for the younger leaders of the Congress Party, led by Jawaharlal Nehru and Subhas Chandra Bose, to demand that the Congress should abandon any idea of a compromise along the lines of Dominion status, which seemed to them to involve a continued subjection to Britain, and demand instead total and immediate independence.

Gandhi was not actively participating in the Congress leadership at the time, and he was not happy about this kind of demand, unless it were to be backed by some effective direct action. During the early months of 1928, he was under strong pressure to return to more active political leadership. The actual term of his prison sentence was now past; but, as the result of his constant touring in the villages, he had had something akin to a slight stroke. When I

first met him in March 1928, at his Sabarmati ashram, I noted
that one of his daily tasks was to assist some of the women of the
household in cutting up the vegetables for the daily common meals
of the whole community. He explained to me that the doctors
had warned him that he must stop all active work, for the rest of
his life, so he was finding daily occupations that would not over-
strain him. The remaining twenty years of his life indicate vividly
what importance he attached to the doctors' warnings. For the
time being, he was not ready to ignore them entirely.

During those days, he was visited by Motilal Nehru. I did not
know what they discussed together; but it is fair to assume that
Motilal was begging him to return to more active political leadership, especially as the younger generation was becoming increasing-
ly impatient of the failure to advance towards political freedom.
In Bengal, especially, there was a growing conviction that the
British would only be shaken out of their complacency by violence. Jawaharlal Nehru and other important young men were
averse to violent terrorism and knew that armed rebellion was
out of the question. So the only alternative to idle petitioning
was some open non-violent mass action or civil disobedience which
only Gandhi could lead.

By the end of the year, he had recovered his normal health
sufficiently to return to political life. At the annual session of
the Congress he persuaded the impatient young Congressmen to
accept a compromise resolution. This declared full independence
to be the goal of India's desire, but it offered the British Government a year in which to prepare a Dominion Constitution for
India, failing which steps must be taken to win full independence.

The "year of grace," 1929, was used by both nationalists and
the government. During the demonstrations against the Simon
Commission, one of the veteran leaders of the Congress, Lala Lajpat Rai of the Punjab, was struck by a young British police officer,
and died a few days later. On the Indian side, the cult of violence
was growing and a bomb was thrown one day in the central legislature, wounding one or two of the leading government officials.
Militant trade unionism was appearing, and the government responded by arresting a number of trade union leaders, some of
them communists, for conspiracy against the government. Their
trial took place at Meerut, and it dragged on for four years. Gandhi's

comment was: "It seems to me that the motive behind these prosecutions is not to kill communism but to strike terror."

Perhaps the most remarkable event of 1928, especially from the point of view of Gandhi and of those who wanted to demonstrate the strength of non-violent action, occurred in that very district of Bardoli in Gandhi's own province of Gujerat, which he had chosen in 1922 for the beginning of the abortive civil resistance of that year.

A local official had decided that the revenue assessment of Bardoli should be increased by thirty per cent. The peasants lodged a protest, but could get no redress. Members of the Bombay Legislative Council also pressed their case, but they got little redress from the government. Finally, the peasants invited Vallabhbhai Patel, formerly a successful lawyer but now a devoted follower of Gandhi and destined to be the strong man of the Congress leadership, to help them. He examined the documents, advised Gandhi that the peasants had a strong case, and Gandhi finally advised the peasants to refuse payment. The government took the sternest possible measures to break the resistance. Patel had warned them that they must be prepared for utter ruin. The children learned to sing a song: "If we are cut to pieces, we shall keep our pledge. Wake up brave fighters, the battle-drums have sounded. Wake up the brave, run away the coward." In spite of all the government could do in carrying away their crops and in bringing the rich to pay up, most of the peasants stood firm. They boycotted the local officials and their own neighbours who gave way. Independent observers came to report what was happening. Finally, the government yielded and appointed a committee to review the assessment. This committee reported that, instead of a thirty per cent increase, only five per cent was justified.

Vallabhbhai Patel thus earned the title of Sardar, the Leader, which he was always given to the end of his life.

Gandhi was greatly heartened by this event. The Viceroy was learning much. He had no wish for a head-on clash with the forces of nationalism, if it could be avoided. After a conference in London, where he was meeting members of the new Labour Government, he was able to announce that a Round Table Conference would meet in London, to which Indian leaders were to be invited, to try and work out an agreed constitution for India. When he made this announcement, the response in India was good.

A statement was issued over the names of Gandhi, the two Nehrus, and others, welcoming the declaration, but demanding the fulfilment of certain conditions if the success of the Conference was to be assured. These included the release of political prisoners, a general policy of conciliation in India, and majority representation of the Indian National Congress in the Indian deputation to the Conference. More especially, they insisted that the purpose of the Conference must be the preparation of a Dominion constitution for India, in other words a constitution that gave India the full substance of political freedom, without reservation of any powers. India must be as free as Canada or Australia.

On 23 December 1929, Lord Irwin met Gandhi, Jinnah, Sapru, and the elder Nehru, together with Vithalbhai Patel (Vallabhbhai's elder brother who was President of the Central Assembly and who had arranged the interview) to discuss the Round Table Conference. That morning a bomb had exploded under the Viceroy's train, so Gandhi congratulated him on his miraculous escape. But the rest of the interview was a failure. Both Gandhi and the Viceroy were disappointed. British opinion had expressed itself critically, and the Secretary of State in London had played down the importance of the Conference. So Irwin could give no such pledges as Gandhi and Nehru hoped for, and they went away to attend the annual Congress session a few days later where, under the Presidency of Jawaharlal Nehru, the Congress solemnly resolved to work for immediate independence and Gandhi was appointed to lead whatever action in civil disobedience he thought likely to be effective.

Neither Gandhi nor the Viceroy was eager to precipitate a new conflict. On the government side there were officials who urged the immediate arrest of those who were preaching rebellion against the government, but Lord Irwin was unwilling to act until open breaches of the peace should occur. On his side, Gandhi was ready to discuss ways of avoiding the conflict. At the end of January 1930, he suggested that there need be no conflict if the British Government would accept eleven points (perhaps he would have been satisfied with less than all the eleven); these included reduction of land revenue, abolition of the salt tax, scaling down of military and civil expenditure, release of political prisoners, a levy on the importation of foreign cloth. What in the world, said some of his own colleagues, have such measures as these to do with the political independence of India? Gandhi believed that such measures went right to the heart of the matter. These were the things that really mattered to the millions in the villages. They were not primarily interested in constitutions that might substitute brown exploitation for white. But there was no response from Delhi. Gandhi had perhaps rightly judged that the government would not respond to this kind of gesture; but at least he had given them a chance.

At the same time, 26 January was celebrated throughout the land as "Independence Day." It is celebrated now as "Republic Day." This first celebration was, of course, no more than an aspiration and a dedication. In many towns and villages, people met together to resolve: "It is a crime against God and man to submit to British rule."

To the general surprise, when Gandhi did in the end propose action in violation of the law, he chose the violation of the salt tax. To most observers this seemed a very small thing to concentrate upon. Not to Gandhi. His argument was that the salt tax hit the poorest of the poor. Even the poorest must eat salt. Therefore, in a country well supplied with natural salt, for the government to make salt a monopoly from which it took revenue was a crime against the poor. To Gandhi, the real crime of the British was that they did not respond to the needs of the poorest Indians.

At the beginning of March, he wrote a letter to the Viceroy, inviting him to help find a way to avert the coming conflict. He repeated his regret that the proposed Round Table Conference was not intended to prepare a free constitution for India. India could no longer wait:

> If India is to survive as a nation, if the slow death by starvation is to stop, some remedy must be found for immediate relief. The proposed conference is certainly not the remedy.... I know that in embarking on non-violence, I shall be] running what might be fairly termed a mad risk, but the victories of truth have never been won without risks, often of the gravest character. Conversion of a nation that has consciously preyed upon another far more numerous, far more ancient and no less cul-

tured than itself, is worth any amount of risk.

I have deliberately used the word conversion. For my ambition is no less than to convert the British people through non-violence and thus make them see the wrong they have done to India. I do not seek to harm your people. I want to serve them even as I want to serve my own.

He concluded his letter by declaring his conviction that, in an open conflict, if his followers remained truly non-violent, their sufferings "will be enough to melt the stoniest hearts."

Lord Irwin simply replied that he regretted that Gandhi was contemplating a course of action that was bound to involve violation of the law and danger to public peace.

In the early morning of 11 March Gandhi and seventy-eight companions set out on foot from Sabarmati Ashram to walk 241 miles to the sea coast, where they would then make salt from the sea in contravention of the law. Many sophisticated Indians, and most Westerners, thought the Mahatma had really taken leave of his senses this time; but he knew the mind of rural India better than any of them. This march was the beginning of a revolution.

For the time being the government held its hand. Perhaps the impression in official circles was that this curious revolution would perish in ridicule. However, Gandhi's march was reported widely in the press of the West as well as in India. At each village that they passed through, the villagers came in crowds to greet the pilgrims, and every morning and evening Gandhi held public prayers, when he spoke on his usual themes. On 6 April, after a night of prayer and fasting, and a bathe in the sea, Gandhi took a handful of salt from the seashore at Dandi, thereby breaking the law. He was not arrested.

Immediately, all over India, along the sea coast, peasants and fishermen followed his example. At the same time, meetings were held all over India to inaugurate mass civil disobedience. Jawaharlal Nehru, the President of the Congress that year, was one of the first leaders to be arrested. Many other leaders and law-breakers were in jail within a few weeks. But, so far, not Gandhi. He now gave notice that two government salt pans near Bombay would be raided. This led to his arrest on 4 May. The police came for him at the dead of night. His arrest led to a complete stoppage of work in many parts of the country. In a few places there were outbreaks of violence, but the Congress volunteers were generally successful in preventing this.

When the raid on the salt depots took place, there was plenty of police violence. As the first column of volunteers arrived, the police showered them with blows over the head, though they did not even raise a hand to ward off the blows. A second column advanced. They too were struck down. Other volunteers advanced, sat down and waited. The police in these cases beat them over the head or kicked them in their private parts. Some three hundred were taken to hospital. Accounts varied as to the amount of bodily damage done to these and other volunteers. But at least a few were seriously injured.

The Congress Working Committee met in May. (Or, rather, those who had been nominated by each man arrested to take his place; by the end of the summer, most of the members were four or five removed from the first members.) It decided to broaden the scope of civil disobedience. Boycott of foreign cloth and of liquor shops came high on the list. And now the observer began to perceive a very important difference between civil disobedience of 1930 and civil disobedience of ten years earlier. Then, the Muslim community had been actively engaged because of the Khilafat issue. This time, fewer Muslims participated.[1] But now, thousands of women took part. This was something new, something portentous, and it was due above all to Gandhi's influence. His fifteen years of residence in India, his intensive journeys through the villages, had made their mark both on him and on the movement. Now, removal of untouchability, an issue affecting every Hindu, but not affecting Muslims, was in the forefront of his mind. The principle of non-violence, involving capacity for suffering without retaliation, had been learnt from him

[1]This was true for the greater part of India but in the predominantly Muslim North-West Frontier Province, under the leadership of the remarkable Abdul Ghaffar Khan, civil disobedience was more intense and widespread than in any other part of the country except perhaps Bombay. The main point to note is that this movement, unlike the earlier one, called out support especially from those sections of the population who had responded to Gandhi's insistence on non-violence.

by tens of thousands. Such a campaign, and one which emphasised social and economic reform quite as much as political self-
government, appealed to millions of women. The politically
minded men were inclined to become more and more sceptical
about Gandhi's leadership. The peasants and the women of
India followed him gladly.

Thus it came about that, through that summer of 1930, day by
day, the streets of Bombay would be livened in the early morning
with songs of freedom sung by troupes of patriots rousing the people
to action. Later in the day, women could be found all over the
city, sitting outside the liquor shops and the foreign cloth shops,
plying their little "spinning-wheels" (called *taklis*), silently warning
every Indian that he must not buy from that shop. Sometimes
the stools on which these women sat through the heat of the day
were provided by the shopkeepers whose trade they were destroying. Many of the women had never taken any part in public life
before. Some came straight out of *purdah;* at the end of the day,
they would have no idea how to go home, and must patiently wait
till a husband or a son came to take them away.

H.N. Brailsford so perfectly describes the qualities in Gandhi
that led to this sudden emergence of thousands of women into the
public life of India that it seems appropriate to quote his words:

> For the interpretation of Gandhi's outlook on life one must
> never forget his mother's formative influence. From her he
> derived his habit of taking vows and she set the example of
> fasting. His originality lay largely in the fact that female ten-
> dencies were at least as strong in his mental make-up as male.
> They were evident, for example, in his love of children, in the
> pleasure he took in playing with them, and in the devotion he
> showed as a sick-nurse. His beloved spinning-wheel has always
> been a woman's tool. And is not satyagraha, the method of con-
> quering by self-suffering, a woman's tactic? The polar opposi-
> tion between violence and self-suffering is really a contrast bet-
> ween male and female patterns of behaviour. In Gandhi, the
> conservative and pacifist, his mother lived on; the male fighting
> instinct in him made him a rebel and a reformer.[2]

²Polak, Brailsford, and Pethick-Lawrence, *Mahatma Gandhi*, p. 168.

Later, one of his granddaughters, who lived with him after her mother's death, was to testify that he was to her just like a mother, and other women testified that they could open their hearts to him in a way that would have seemed quite impossible with other men.

During this civil disobedience campaign, there was certainly a wide awakening of women, in response to a call for sacrifice to causes that seemed to many of them far more real than political freedom as such. At one of the Indian homes where I stayed during that year while Gandhi was in jail, I noticed that it was the wife who was wholeheartedly enthusiastic for Gandhi; the husband, though an ardent nationalist, was a good deal more sceptical about the Mahatma's political methods.

Gandhi and all his colleagues were now in jail, but the plan for the Round Table Conference went forward, and it was still the hope of Lord Irwin and the government in England that ways could be found of bringing the Congress leaders to co-operate. For Irwin never fell into the error of much of British officialdom in India. He never believed that Gandhi and his colleagues were a small band of dangerous agitators with no serious backing in the country as a whole; a set of noisy men who could be safely shut away in jail while the sensible men, Indian and British, got on with the job of governing the country. This delusion never really deserted the ruling caste; perhaps it was fostered by their Indian colleagues who had good government jobs. But, however long the Congress leaders were held in jail, and however confidently the British officials and the press correspondents proclaimed that "Gandhi's influence is now waning," the event always proved that he was more popular than ever when he was ultimately released. And Irwin, to his credit, knew that the mass of Indian opinion backed him. Later that summer, I had been travelling about India and, on my return to Simla, Lord Irwin asked me my impressions. At that time a number of Indian propertied men, "loyalists" so-called, had allowed themselves to be enrolled in committees whose avowed purpose was to support the government in its campaign against the Congress civil disobedience. I happened to have met one such man, the chairman of an important pro-government committee in the decisive area of the United Provinces. He, no doubt, was aware that I was in India on a private mission of conciliation and that I was sympathetic to the

Indian claim for political freedom. None the less, I was quite astonished to find him openly saying to me: "You know, Mr Alexander, we are really all in favour of the Congress aim of self-government, though some of us question their methods." When I repeated this to Lord Irwin, he simply said, reflectively: "Oh yes, I think that is quite typical." The then Governor of the United Provinces had sent a private note to his officials warning them to have nothing to do with me. One of his "loyal" Indian officials showed me this document, and was evidently amused. This same official had a portrait of Jawaharlal Nehru, the "arch-rebel," hanging on the wall of his bedroom, and he made it clear that he continued in government service because he believed that free India would need experienced civil servants. Later he held a high position under his hero, Nehru.

In his autobiography,[3] Lord Irwin (later Earl of Halifax) uses the expressions common to the officials with whom he inevitably worked all the time, calling the Congress leaders extremists, and so on. But the pact that he made with Gandhi a year later, and all his interventions in the House of Lords in the later years of his life when Indian affairs were under discussion, make it clear that he was far removed from the usual limitations of British Indian officialdom.

His efforts to get the Congress leaders to the Round Table Conference in the autumn of 1930, however, failed. The Conference met, but the Congress leaders, Gandhi included, were still in jail. Probably, their absence was more effective than their presence would have been. The moderate leaders, men of the calibre of Sir Tej Bahadur Sapru, Srinivasa Sastri, and others, were able all the time to insist that for them the Conference would be a failure if it did not lead to some result which they could "sell" to the Congress leaders. They knew well enough that they by themselves could never persuade the Indian people to accept some half-way house which left the substance of power with the British. The new constitution must give the substance of freedom to India and must be seen to be doing this; otherwise a further period of frustration would result. The Labour Government, through its representatives in the Conference, was perfectly willing to agree to

[3]Earl of Halifax, *Fullness of Days*, Collins, London, 1957.

some such plan. So were some, at least, of the Liberal Party representatives. With the Conservatives it was not so easy. The government representatives in effect took the line: You, loyal and moderate Indians, should tell us what you want; then we can draft it into a constitutional framework. And so this procedure was followed. At one stage, one of the British secretaries told me that the Conservative representatives were becoming very restless. But the argument was used: What is the alternative? These men with whom we are dealing, who have suffered in India for their refusal to toe the line of the Congress extremists, are our best friends; let us not betray them. And the Conservatives were reluctantly carried along. For some of them, no doubt, the fact that a Conservative Viceroy was known to be in agreement with what was happening must have carried weight.

In situations of this kind, often the greatest contributions are made by men who work largely behind the scenes, and whose names never get into the headlines. One such man who attended the Round Table Conference in 1930 needs to have his name recorded. This was K.T. Paul, an outstanding South Indian Christian, the one non-Catholic Christian who was invited to London for this Conference. I was able to watch him at work week by week. As a Christian who knew the West well, he was able to interpret the mind of India to the Prime Minister, the Archbishop of Canterbury, and other people of influence, and to talk frankly. But the strenuous work of that autumn and the November fogs undermined his health. On his arrival in India he wrote me a letter full of hope for the future of Indo-British relations, but confessing that he was still suffering from the English fogs. A few weeks later he was dead. In so far as the first Round Table Conference opened the way to Indian freedom, K.T. Paul was no less surely one of its faithful architects than Motilal Nehru who died of his jail experiences in February 1931, or Lajpat Rai or others in the accepted role of the great pioneers. Gandhi himself never overlooked the contribution of those who were outside the main Congress front.

As a result of the efforts of such men as K.T. Paul, and others better known in the story of Indian nationalism, as a result, too, of the active sympathy of the leaders of the Labour Government with the aspirations of India for freedom, such good progress was made

in working out the framework of a free constitution for India
that, on their return to India, Sir Tej Bahadur Sapru and Srinivasa
Sastri, two very able and distinguished Indian liberals, felt able
to interpret the work of the Conference in a way calculated to
create greater confidence in the intentions of the British Government. Lord Irwin showed himself ready to co-operate and proceeded to release Gandhi and the other Congress prisoners.
Gandhi was as ready as ever to talk with his British opponents.
Although he had been disappointed in his first meeting with Lord
Irwin, he was willing to try again with him now, and there followed
two weeks of talks between the two men, leading to the famous
Irwin-Gandhi Agreement which ended non-cooperation for the time
being and brought the government and the Congress nearer to
mutual understanding than at any time before, perhaps nearer
than they were ever to be until the very dawn of independence in
1947.

Gandhi and Irwin had each been disappointed in the other when
they first met. Now they discovered each other and confidence
between them grew rapidly. What happened? It is not easy
to say. No doubt the process was a gradual one, growing from
day to day as they met and talked. Lord Irwin, in his memoirs,
written many years later, wrote thus of Gandhi:

As with all great men, different aspects stand out for different
people. That which gave him his exceptional position in India
was something different from that which won him the admiration of friends in Western countries, which is another way of
saying that the man himself was larger than any of the attempts
made to paint his portrait. There was a directness about him
which was singularly winning, but this could be accompanied
by a subtlety of intellectual process which could sometimes be
disconcerting. To appreciate what was passing in his mind
it was necessary, if not to start from the same point, at least to
understand very clearly what was the starting point for him;
and this was nearly always very human and very simple.

I remember when I first went to India talking about him with
C.F. Andrews who, I imagine, was closer to him than any other
European. He said, as indeed was clear when it came to the
Round Table Conference, that Mr. Gandhi cared little for cons-

titutions and constitutional forms. What he was concerned with was the human problem of how the Indian poor lived. Constitutional reform was important and necessary for the development of India's personality and self-respect; but what really mattered were the things that affected the daily lives of the millions of his fellow-countrymen—salt, opium, cottage industries and the like. I have no doubt this was true, and although it was easy to smile at the devotion of Gandhi to the spinning-wheel, while Congress was largely dependent for its funds upon the generosity of wealthy Indian millowners, the wheel none-the-less stood for something fundamental in his philosophy of life. He was the natural knight-errant, fighting always the battle of the weak against suffering and what he judged injustice. The claims of Indians in South Africa, the treatment of Indian labourers in the indigo fields in India, the thousands rendered homeless by the floods of Orissa, and above everything the suffering arising from communal hatreds—all these were in turn a battlefield on which he fought with all his strength for what to him was the cause of humanity and right.

One of the most significant points in this estimate of Gandhi is to be found in the reference to C.F. Andrews. To many European residents in India, official and unofficial alike, Andrews was a hated man who was to them a traitor to his race and nation. He was the known friend of Gandhi; he lived as an Indian; he openly condemned much in the British system of administration. Yet Irwin was so different from the conventional Viceroy that early in his term of office he had taken the trouble to meet Andrews and to get an authentic, close-up picture of Gandhi, which he accepted as true. Perhaps, too, we may see here why the two men had been disappointed in each other at their first meeting. Irwin had perhaps expected the Gandhi he learnt of from Andrews to be more understanding of a Viceroy's position and more easily assured by general statements of good intentions than he found him. Gandhi had expected the Viceroy of whom his friend Andrews had such a good opinion to be more openly in favour of full Indian political freedom than he appeared to be. They needed a longer time together before each was able to discern the essential integrity and reasonableness of the other man. This they fully achieved in the early months of 1930 in a series of eight meetings lasting in all about twenty-four hours. When the Delhi Pact was signed, some Indians hailed Irwin as a second Mahatma. But the Pact was bitterly opposed by British officialdom and by many Congress leaders, including Jawaharlal Nehru. Only Gandhi's great prestige induced the Congress Working Committee to call off civil disobedience. Many on each side felt that their leader had signed terms of surrender.

Unhappily, the confidence that two men are able to find in each other cannot be handed on to other men who have not been through the process of conviction. Within a few months Irwin was due to retire. His successor, Lord Willingdon, was much more conventionally minded, less ready to defy the advice of the long-term British officials. And, by the time Gandhi came to London for the second Round Table Conference, the Labour Government in London had fallen and the Conservative Party, very few of whom agreed with Irwin's point of view, was to all intents and purposes again in power in England.

5

The Round Table Conference
and After (1931-1932)

IT WAS already clear to Gandhi and his colleagues in the Congress leadership that the Willingdon administration was not intend-
ing to carry out the Irwin-Gandhi Pact in the spirit of its two
authors; so the question of Gandhi's attendance at the Second
Round Table Conference, which was summoned to meet in London
at the end of September 1931, was not easy to answer. What
was the point of his going to London if the British Government had
no intention of acceding to the demand of the Congress? And,
if there was to be a renewal of conflict in India, he would naturally
wish to face it with his colleagues.

On the other hand, some of his friends in England who had been
much encouraged by the spirit and tone of the first conference felt
that much might be achieved if that spirit still prevailed. Even
after the British Election, which almost destroyed the Labour
Party for the time being, it remained true that there were in the
government not only Ramsay MacDonald, as Prime Minister, who
in his earlier life at any rate had openly supported the demand for
Indian freedom, but also the Lord Chancellor, Lord Sankey, who
had been, and remained, the chairman of the Conference and who
let it be known that he was staying in the government in order to
see the Indian Round Table Conference through to a successful
conclusion. Accordingly, several telegrams went to Gandhi from
some of his friends in England, begging him to come. How far
he was influenced by these telegrams, it is impossible to say. But
he came.

This was the first time that I was close to Gandhi for any length
of time; I was able to spend a day or two in his household in

London each week helping C.F. Andrews and his other friends
to cope with all manner of visitors and various incidents. It may
not, therefore, be inappropriate to give some space to the daily
life, as I saw it then, of the Mahatma. First, however, it is necessary to record briefly what happened in the Conference itself.

The Congress Working Committee had decided to appoint
Gandhi as their sole representative to the Round Table Conference. He was accompanied by Pandit Madan Mohan Malaviya, of the Hindu Mahasabha, and by Mrs Sarojini Naidu, both
of them members of the Conference, and both of whom normally
shared his point of view. But their presence did not appreciably
lighten his burden. On almost every topic he was obliged to
speak, and he never had a free moment for preparing his speeches.
When I asked his secretary, Mahadev Desai, why the Congress
had not nominated any other member, he replied that they were
not sure that all would speak with one voice. The only thing
they were sure of was that all would approve whatever line Gandhi
thought it right to take.

His personal staff consisted of two secretaries, Mahadev Desai
and Pyarelal Nayar, his youngest son, Devadas—"nice fat
Devadas," as one of the India Office officials called him—and
Miraben (Miss Slade) who took charge of the domestic side and
found a wonderful little dairy quite near the Knightsbridge office,
which supplied most of the essential foods. But I must return to
the domestic scene when we have seen what happened in the Conference.

The change of government in fact meant a complete change of
tactics whatever Lord Sankey may have hoped to the contrary.
It is important to realise how the Conference was composed. Not
one of the fifty or sixty Indians who attended had been elected by
any body of electors. Everyone was chosen by the Viceroy.
They were chosen to represent every aspect of the public life of
India. There were not only members of the Muslim League (and
some other Muslims too), but also a number of Indian Princes or
their Ministers. There were two Indian Christians, a Catholic
and a Protestant. There were Sikhs and Parsis; there was Dr
Ambedkar who was assumed to represent the sixty million Untouchables—although it cannot be doubted that, outside a limited
area in or near the city of Bombay, if any group of Untouchables

had been invited to nominate a representative to the Conference, they would probably have nominated Gandhi who had been fighting for them against the caste Hindus ever since his return from South Africa and who was known to them by name as the Mahatma throughout the land, whereas those who knew of Dr Ambedkar would hardly be hundreds of thousands. This is, of course, no reflection on Dr. Ambedkar, a remarkable man, wo had succeeded in rising from his childhood of oppression and degradation to a position of importance in the public life of the country. Then there were special representatives of Anglo-Indians (people of mixed blood), of the European business community, of Indian commerce, and so on.

The early days of the Conference were occupied in an attempt to find means of bringing the minority groups into some agreement with the majority, which means the Hindus. But the composition of the Conference made this impossible. If they had known that the issue of the Conference was to be genuine self-government, then they would have had some incentive to agree; but in spite of the ingenious but ambiguous formula of the Irwin-Gandhi Agreement, reserving some essential matters "in the interest of India," it became clear that no substantial power was to be transferred at all. The British, not the Indians, were to decide what was "in the interest of India."

So long as Gandhi was in jail, together with all his colleagues, there was some desire on the part of the minority members to find a way out that might open new vistas for the active participation of the Congress. But with Gandhi in London, all alone, they could and did proceed to isolate him and make it appear that he was a solitary figure representing "extremism," while all the rest were good fellows who knew how to behave and who could now demand all sorts of special favours for the groups they were supposed to represent. In the end, the so-called minorities got together; they claimed to represent among them well over half of the population of India, and they made a common demand. One man only refused to participate in this absurdity, namely, Dr. S.K. Datta, the Protestant Christian.

Gandhi, on his side, claimed that he represented 85 per cent of the people of India. Even H.N. Brailsford thought that this was rather an extravagant claim. But, in fact, whether justi-

fied or not, it was based on a simple calculation. At that time
(and the position is not so different today) 85 per cent of the
people of India lived in villages, the other 15 per cent in towns
and cities. Gandhi was not thinking of voting strength, still less
in terms of various religious communities. He was ready to
concede that the other members of the Conference could speak
for the townsmen, including the Hindus of the towns: religious
communities mattered nothing to him. What he claimed was that
he could speak and was constantly speaking for the "dumb, semi-
starved millions" of villagers. At a meeting that he addressed
at Chatham House (home of the Royal Institute of International
Affairs) someone asked him at question-time how he substantiated
this claim. He replied in a single phrase: "By right of service."
If we recall his years of work both at his ashram and "in the
villages," the justification for this claim will be clear.

Although the Government in England and every one else knew
in their hearts that Gandhi represented as much as all the rest
put together, yet from the point of view of British opinion and
even perhaps from that of the successful outcome of the Conference, it would have helped if he had brought with him one or two
non-Hindu colleagues. There was, for instance, Dr M.A. Ansari,
a most distinguished Muslim leader, loyal member of the Congress,
but at the same time widely respected among Muslims who were
quite outside the Congress Party. I asked Gandhi one day why
he did not urge the inclusion of Dr Ansari. "I should like the
other Muslims who are here in London to invite him," was his
reply. Which other political leader of our time would suppress
his trump card out of consideration for the feelings of unscrupulous
opponents? Similarly, the Congress could have sent an Untouchable who would have worked with Gandhi instead of opposing
him.

There was a moment when it looked as if the government
was seriously trying to come to terms with Gandhi. He had been
out of London for various week-ends: he went to Lancashire,
where he quickly made friends with the mill-hands, some of whom
were out of work, partly because of the boycott of foreign cloth
organised by Gandhi in India. He spent a week-end in Cambridge and another in Oxford, and one in the Quaker College,
Woodbrooke, at Birmingham. Then a second week-end was

arranged at Oxford in the Lodge of the Master of Balliol, A.D. Lindsay, later Lord Lindsay. I was invited to this meeting, but I never learnt exactly who planned it, though I suspect that Dr S.K. Datta, Henry Polak (Gandhi's old friend from South African days), and C.F. Andrews were all in the plot. Two or three leading Oxford scholars were present, such as Dr Lindsay, Professor Gilbert Murray, and Professor Coupland. Malcolm MacDonald represented his father, the Prime Minister, and the civil servant who was secretary to the Conference also attended, representing the government officially. After a difficult session or two, which served to show how far apart were the minds of men who thought principally in terms of constitutional provisions from the man whose mind was for ever in the midst of the starving villagers, the later sessions were much more fruitful. Minds seemed to be meeting to good purpose. Malcolm MacDonald appeared to be the only Britisher present (apart from Gandhi's special friends) who had no difficulty in appreciating the outlook of the Mahatma. He, after all, had grown up in the Labour Movement and understood the kind of politician who has a passion for social justice and looks at proposed legislation from one point of view only: will it help in the struggle against poverty and social injustice?

As we left Oxford, Dr Datta, not usually an optimist, said to me: "I believe we have done some real business this weekend." But he was mistaken. Whatever the explanation, the government was not interested in following up the work done at Balliol. They had, no doubt, their own Conservative members of Parliament to consider, most of whom, in the words of the Secretary of State, Sir Samuel Hoare, "hate Gandhi like the devil." Nor were they willing at that stage to turn their backs on the forty-nine whom they had invited to London, in favour of the one who represented the heart of India.

The Conference continued along its appointed course to a conclusion that gave Gandhi nothing of what he and his colleagues demanded. He returned home empty-handed, to face a new and much longer conflict with the government. But before we go on to that bitter chapter, let us have a further look at Gandhi the man as he appeared during those weeks in London.

As is well known, he accepted the invitation of Muriel Lester to stay at Kingsley Hall, Bow, in east London. He had wished to be among the poor of London, but I think he concluded that most of the people of Bow were as well off as the lower middle class of such a city as Bombay. Poverty by Indian standards was hardly visible. However, he was certainly among the working class people, and they took to him at once. Was it his directness that they liked, or the plain fact that for him simplicity of living was no affectation? He was perfectly content in his cell on the roof, with the minimum of furniture. Even in the coldest November days his only concession to the climate was to add one more wrap round his shoulders; his lower legs were still bare as he took his brisk early walk in the dark round by the smelly gas-works and along the dirty canal. One of those days, in the dawn light, a man working on his sooty allotment stopped for a moment to stand and gaze, and then shouted after him: "Go it Mr Gandhi; I'm with you and you'll win."

But Kingsley Hall was a long way from St. James' Palace, where the Conference met each day; so a house was taken at 88 Knightsbridge, to be his office and to house his staff, Mahadev, Pyarelal, and Devadas. There they lived and had their food. On an upper storey of this house lived Dr S.K. Datta and his British wife. Mrs Datta made herself responsible for the domestic arrangements. She engaged a cook and a girl to look after the front door. Bernard Aluwihari, a Ceylonese student of Oxford recommended by Jawaharlal Nehru, spent his days looking after the telephone and adding gaiety to the scene.

The week after, all these arrangements had been made, Dr Datta came to me and said: "We are going to lose the cook. Mahadev and the others are terribly unpunctual and erratic about meals. They seem to expect them at all sorts of times. The cook has her food spoilt, and she never knows when she can go out. Do you think you can speak to Mahadev about it?" I did so. He, with the utmost goodwill, similingly said: "You know how it is with us. We must always be available when Bapu [Gandhi] needs us. It is no use for us to promise to be punctual. We could not keep the promise." And I left for Birmingham. Next week, when I arrived, I asked Dr Datta: "What has happened to the cook?" "She is still here," he said, "but I don't think she will stay long." She never left. The girl at the door also stayed to the end, though the door bell was apt to ring at any hour from six in the morning to ten at night, and she certainly got no regular time off. Why did they stay?

Chiefly, the reason was that they discovered within a few days that they were not just domestic servants, but they were Gandhi's personal friends, an essential part of his family, for whom he cared just as much as he cared for Mahadev or Devadas or any of us. He never asked for time off. He certainly worked longer hours than any of them. And yet he was never too busy to be interested in their family doings or other personal affairs.

During that period of Indo-British history, it was not only members of Parliament who "hated Gandhi like the devil," but also the picture some of the popular press had painted of him, as a dangerous rebel and political extremist, meant that there was a strong and widespread prejudice against him. Accordingly, on his arrival in England, the government decided to afford him full protection from molestation and they assigned two experienced Scotland Yard detectives to look after him. These two men quickly became his personal friends. They too became, in effect, part of his ever-growing family. He gave them his list of engagements each day and they became his timekeepers. Punctuality was a virtue he confessed that he had learnt from the West, and he hated being late.

One day while I was in London, a lady appeared at the Knightsbridge house, half an hour before the time Gandhi was due to leave for some engagement. She explained that she was the wife of one of the detectives. Her husband had talked so much about this remarkable man from India that she had decided to come and see him at close quarters for herself. But she knew that he was always terribly busy, so she did not want him to know of her visit. She just wanted to see him at close quarters as he left the house. Word was in fact taken to him of her presence and as he left the house he stopped and had a few words with her, enough to bring the almost inevitable laugh. Did he ever fail to have some light or playful comment which made those who met him feel at ease with him?

That was not the end for her. A few weeks later, Gandhi found time to go and have afternoon tea at the house of this detective, though this meant a long drive out to South London. Next day the detective commented: "Of all the men I have had to look

after, Mr Gandhi is the busiest, except perhaps Lloyd George
when he was Prime Minister during the war. But Mr Gandhi
is the only one who has ever found time to visit me in my own
home."

However, it was not every man or woman who got such a positive impression of Gandhi during his sojourn in England. The
eastenders understood and liked his directness, even his sharpness,
but the sophisticated middle class or upper class reacted differently.
Nor was this confined to the right-wing imperialists who hated
him for his "disloyalty" to the Empire. Many liberals who
in principle were favourable to Indian self-government (usually,
perhaps, with the reservation that it must come when they, the
liberals, saw that India was ready for it) were disappointed and
even disgusted with Gandhi. Why? An adequate answer to
this question would go far to explain why the British rulers of
India and the nationalists could never understand one another.
The answer is, however, not altogether simple. It can only be
unravelled by looking first at the man, Gandhi, and then at the
national movement that he represented.

Gandhi had never visited the West since he had become "the
Mahatma." The ordinary Englishman assumed that he was no
doubt a saint in his personal life, but that he somehow combined
this with the shrewdness of a political leader and the hair-splitting
of a clever lawyer. But all this is wrong. In the first place,
the expression "Mahatma" should not be translated as "saint."
A man can be a great soul without having all the qualities that
are normally thought by modern Anglo-Saxons to be the marks
of sainthood. Selfless and thoughtful for others Gandhi certainly
was, to a pre-eminent degree. His serenity in difficult circumstances was remarkable even for an Indian. During the most tiring
and mortifying days of the Round Table Conference, it was always
he who kept his temper unruffled and could laugh away the irrita-
tions that sometimes vexed even his close intimates. So far, one
might say he was a saint indeed. But he was not always gentle
in his dealings with others. He sometimes did not appear to be
very sensitive to their feelings. He believed in outspokenness;
he liked others to be frank with him; and he practised frankness
with others. He was particularly severe on any kind of self-
importance. More than once I heard people who had met him

express their resentment that he had not chosen to treat them and their ideas with the seriousness that they thought would have been appropriate. He could treat with severity even those he loved very dearly. There was an occasion when Charlie Andrews, of all men, was accused of some misbehaviour. Gandhi did not say to the accuser, "You must be wrong. Andrews could never have done such a thing," though one may fairly assume that he did in fact think just that. On the contrary, he summoned Andrews, cross-questioned him searchingly, and thereby demonstrated to the accuser that his accusation was false. Andrews, who was much more of the saint (Western type) than Gandhi, did not complain of being thus treated. He did not say, as many another might have said, angrily: "You surely know me too well to suspect me of such base behaviour."

The political aspect of the matter is also far from simple. To most liberal-minded Britishers, the ideal men to deal with were the Indian liberals, men of the temperament and outlook of Sir Tej Bahadur Sapru and Srinivasa Sastri, men who, however ardent their patriotism, were of the view that in political action all forms of direct action must be ruled out, however non-violent. To them, rational persuasion was the only way. No other way was permitted. Gandhi rejected this view, not because of impatience, but because he interpreted human nature differently. While I watched him in London, I was again and again impressed with his patient desire to meet his political opponents and to sit down with them and reason with them. And he always showed the genuine courtesy of a man who would seriously listen to his opponent with the hope of understanding him better and perhaps learning something new. Indeed, this very generosity towards his opponents was often alarming to his political colleagues. They never knew when he might come away from some talk with a British statesman—or, indeed, with some much less important person—saying: "I must change my line of action. I have learnt something that I have overlooked."

So impressed was I by this endless patience in the use of the art of persuasion that I asked him one day why from time to time he abandoned the use of persuasion and adopted a policy of direct action. His reply was to this effect: "Because human beings are not always ready for persuasion. Their preconceptions

may be so deeply rooted that arguments do not touch them at all.
Then, you must touch their feelings. Nothing else will change
their minds." But, at this point, he parted company with those
who argued that, sooner or later, as between nations, there must
be a resort to the arbitrament of force. That, he said, still did not
prove who was in the right; it only proved who was the stronger.
Even though sometimes an armed rebellion might shock the ruling
authority into a change of policy, even if the revolt was suppressed,
yet it caused widespread suffering and bitterness which should
be avoided. The best way to avert this was for the aggrieved party,
in this case the Indian people, to demonstrate the strength of
their conviction by self-suffering — by inviting suffering rather
than inflicting it. If they showed great determination in thus inviting their rulers to hurt them, while refusing to hit back, sooner
or later, the rulers would begin to ask themselves whether, after all,
their rule (of India) was as good and beneficent as they had assumed.
For, if it were, how would so many good people, including simple
peasants and other unsophisticated men and women, be ready
and eager again and again to invite imprisonment and other
suffering?

All this was so new a doctrine that most English liberals
failed to understand it. Well-intentioned people would listen
to Gandhi addressing some meeting in London and came away
saying: "He is not in favour of non-violence at all. I heard
him say there would have to be bloodshed before the British leave
India." What he had said was, of course, that he was expecting
more violence committed by the British soldiers or police on the
civil resistance movement that might need once again, or more
than once, to be attempted. The blood would be shed by his
followers, but it would be their own blood, not the blood of the
British.

One other incident of Gandhi's stay in London needs to be
discussed here. This is the visit he paid to Buckingham Palace.
Some weeks before he left India, when his coming was still doubtful, an Indian student in London discussed the problem of his
attendance at the Round Table Conference with a friend of mine.
He said he hoped the Mahatma would not come, because if he
did he would be obliged to go about London in a frock-coat
and that would not be right. In fact, he did nothing of the

sort and, as part of his determination to live as his own natural self, he was only too happy to refuse all invitations to social functions. But then he was confronted with the invitation from King George V to a function at Buckingham Palace. What was he to do? To those who think of him as a political revolutionary, it might seem that the obvious thing was simply to refuse to go. But that was to overlook essential elements in his make-up. He was the very soul of courtesy, and he was determined not to offend if he could help it. So messages went to and fro. He would be happy to break his rule, provided it would not be inappropriate for him to attend in the clothes he always wore. The reply came from Sir Clive Wigram, the King's Private Secretary, that his dhoti and shawl would be in order. I think he would have preferred to be told that unfortunately the King could not make an exception for anyone. However, the answer was reassuring, and he and Mahadev Desai set out for the Palace, hoping for a pleasant social occasion which might at least bring a little sweetness into a painful situation, for certainly the conference itself was giving him no cause for comfort. They returned deeply distressed. What had happened?

The King, it appeared, had taken the opportunity to give Gandhi a severe political lecture. The occasion which was to have been entirely non-political, an occasion for pleasant social intercourse, which indeed he would gladly have missed altogether but for his sense of propriety, had been for him totally spoilt by what he and Mahadev could only regard as the King's complete disregard for the proprieties.

It is curious to see how this incident was regarded on the other side. Sir Clive Wigram wrote to the Viceroy in India as follows:

His Majesty was, as is his custom, very nice to [Gandhi]...but ended up by impressing on him that this country would not stand a campaign of terrorism and having their friends shot down in India. His Majesty warned Gandhi that he was to put a stop to this....Gandhi spluttered some excuse, but H.M. said he was responsible.[1]

---

[1]Harold Nicolson, *King George the Fifth*, p. 509.

In his own diary, King George gives a similar account, and was evidently very pleased with his performance. Alas, kings share the frailties of other mortals. To make Gandhi responsible for the terrorist crimes, which he had battled against all his life, was about as misguided a comment as could possibly have been made. So, even if it had been proper to talk politics on an occasion when it was understood that there would be no politics, the political comment made by King George was totally, even brutally, wide of the mark. His unfortunate intervention that day can have had no effect but to convince Indian nationalism that the grandson of Queen Victoria could not be given the respect that all India had had for the great Queen. Contrary to their hopes, the monarchy was just as fully involved in the political struggle as the Ministers of the Government.[2]

Before Gandhi's visit to London the Indian National Con-

---

[2]Since I wrote this chapter, my attention has been drawn to a full account of this incident at Buckingham Palace. (Viscount Templewood, *Nine Troubled Years*, p. 590.) Lord Templewood was at that time Secretary of State for India and was closely involved in the whole affair. It will be seen that his report substantiates what I have written. He is kinder to the King than I have been, but it is clear that it was Gandhi who saved the day, and Sir Clive Wigram's remark, "Gandhi spluttered some excuse," is false. It seems likely that the King did not even listen to his guest's courteous response. Here is what Lord Templewood has to say on this incident: "It was arranged that at the party I was to fetch up Gandhi at a suitable moment for presentation to the King. When the time came, Gandhi's khaddar made it easy for me to find him amongst the black coats and ceremonial clothes of the delegates. When I presented him, there was a difficult movement. The King was obviously thinking of Gandhi's responsibility for civil disobedience. However, when they were once started, the King's simple sincerity and Gandhi's beautiful manners combined to smooth the course of the conversation, though more than once I became nervous when the King looked resentfully at Gandhi's knees. When the conversation was drawing to an end, the King, the most conscientious of monarchs, evidently thought that it was his duty to warn Gandhi of the consequences of rebellion. Just, therefore, as Gandhi was taking his leave, His Majesty could not refrain from uttering a grave warning. 'Remember, Mr. Gandhi, I won't have any attacks on my Empire.' I held my breath in fear of an argument between the two. Gandhi's *savoir faire* saved the situation with a grave and deferential reply. 'I must not be drawn into a political argument in Your Majesty's Palace after receiving your Majesty's hospitality.' They then took leave of each other as friendly guest and host. A very honest King, and a great diplomat, I thought to myself and what exquisite worldly manners the unworldly possess."

gress had for years taken the view that the struggle for Indian freedom must be won in India and that there was no need to have any special representation in London. The British Government would ultimately yield, not to representations made by some emissary in London, but by the growing strength of the movement in India itself. But when Gandhi came to London he found that a dynamic young Indian, V.K. Krishna Menon, had started a vigorous agitation and had formed an organisation called the India League. More recently, another group of Indians had formed a body called the Friends of India. This was less openly revolutionary, but was none the less supporting the demand of the Congress for full self-government. The two groups did not show any affection for each other. In these circumstances, some of the Britishers who accepted Gandhi's demand, and who wanted to see his and the Congress' point of view more openly interpreted in England, conferred with him during the last days of his stay about ways and means of doing this. He accepted the need, and he realised that we were a very small number with no funds available for setting someone free to give full time to such work. But, if we saw no objection to support coming from India, he believed he could find the funds, provided we could find the right person for the work. He very generously asked me if I would undertake it. I was clear that I could not do this, but I promised to give all the help I could to a full-time worker. He then suggested that we might ask Agatha Harrison. Miss Harrison, who a few years earlier had made a remarkable effort to rescue the exploited child workers in the factories of Shanghai, had been spending the autumn of 1931 helping C.F. Andrews with his writings, and she had become an important part of the Knightsbridge household. I asked her to come up to Gandhi's room, and he explained to her what we had been discussing. Would she do it? She naturally put some searching questions about what he would expect of her, with whom should she work ("with Horace, and anyone else that you agree to ask to work with you"), and about finance. Within a couple of days she had accepted, and the finance had been guaranteed by G.D. Birla. Thus began the activity of the India Conciliation Group and Agatha Harrison's unceasing, single-minded, and utterly selfless work which never ended till freedom came to India in 1947 and which, in a slightly

different form, still went on until her untimely death in 1954—
due to her determination, at the age of 69, to work as if she were
only 39.

Our first job came speedily. Gandhi had hardly left Europe
when the press announced that he had given an interview in Rome,
on the eve of his departure by ship, announcing that he would
start another civil disobedience movement as soon as he reached
India. Before he left London, Gandhi had assured some of us
that he would try not to embark on any fresh direct action against
the Government. He had been much disturbed by the news
coming from India of fresh ordinances introduced by the government and by the imprisonment of some of his close colleagues,
especially Jawaharlal Nehru and Abdul Ghaffar Khan of
North-West Frontier Province. One of the first things that
Agatha Harrison had undertaken for him was the typing of some
copies of the new ordinance for strengthening the hands of
the executive in Bengal. As she worked through it, she commented
that even to read it made her nearly sick. These things were
happening; it was clear enough to Gandhi that the new Government in England was quite out of sympathy with the Irwin
approach. So he had already warned Nehru before his arrest
that he could get no help from London in withstanding the new
repression.[3]

In spite of all this, he had made it clear that he would take no
precipitate action. He would try to see the Viceroy, hoping still
to find ways to avoid a new conflict. What were we to make of
this Rome interview? As we read it, we were quite incredulous.
Not only were we sure that he would not have said what was
reported. To those who knew him, it looked like a clever travesty.
And that is exactly what it was.

When it was possible to get word from him, he denied that he

---

[3] I happened to be in the Knightsbridge office when the cable to Nehru was
being sent by telephone; this was done by Bernard Aluwihari. The woman at
the other end of the telephone did not seem very intelligent. At last the message
was correctly taken, but the name at the end was too much for her. She had
apparently never heard the name "Gandhi." So, slowly and patiently, Bernard
said: "G for God; A for Ass; N for Noodle; D for Devil; H for Hell; I for
Idiot." As he finally put the phone down he turned to Agatha and myself with
a magnificent gleam of triumph.

had given any interview. So far, so good. But then, what had in fact happened? It was difficult to believe that the interview, published over the name of Signor Gayda, Mussolini's top press man, was a pure fabrication. Within a few days of his arrival in Bombay, Gandhi was in jail and those who had been with him in Rome were in jail with him. So the full story was not available till years later, when the damage Mussolini had intended had been well and truly done, and most people had forgotten all about it or rather had registered, in spite of denials, that Gandhi had obviously been more outspoken than any of his friends had expected.

Miraben told the story in detail; and this is it. There was a reception in Rome for Gandhi. Many people had attended it. At one stage, the questioning became very intense, and one man (evidently Signor Gayda) had put a number of questions. But there was to be no publicity. None of the Indian party paid any special attention. Miraben, however, was listening all the time (she certainly would be) and Gandhi had said nothing different from the things he had said again and again in England. In other words, there had been just that clever distortion that would suit Mussolini's hope of sowing discord between India and Britain. No doubt, the conflict between the government and the Congress in India would at best have been slightly delayed if there had been no "Rome interview." It is evident that both the Viceroy in India and the India Office in London were determined to reverse the Irwin policy. Nothing that Gandhi could have done would have saved the situation. So, in spite of King George (who, paradoxically, had expressed his approval of the Irwin-Gandhi conversations a few months before), the blame for the long conflict that ensued must be placed squarely on the British authorities, especially in India, where the Irwin-Gandhi pact had been bitterly resented and where officialdom was still determined to crush Gandhi and the Congress. Some months after, the new effort to crush the Congress had begun, I had an opportunity of visiting Lord Irwin in his Yorkshire home. His comment was to this effect: "It is much easier to start a repression of this kind than to bring it to an end. I wish I could see what this leads to." Such considerations probably did not enter into the thinking of the officials in India. They assumed that they could crush the Congress so that it would never rise again. They persuaded themselves that it did not really represent any deep sentiment in the minds of the masses. The event proved them wrong. The more the leaders went to jail, the more they became national heroes. Even after nearly twenty years of independence, those who want to become political leaders in India are well advised to be able to declare their *bona fides* by producing a good jail record.

It has been necessary to deal at some length with the episode of the Rome interview, because at the time it damaged Gandhi's reputation among many people in England who were prepared to think well of him; and the denials, even when they came, were not wholly convincing, because they did not provide any adequate explanation. Gandhi denied that there had been any interview. Signor Gayda retorted that it was all based on the notes he made as Gandhi answered his questions. In fact, both were speaking the truth—except that, in Signor Gayda's case, he should have added that he carefully doctored his notes so as to produce the desired effect.

In a sane world, Gandhi's visit to Rome could be ignored and the visit he paid to Romain Rolland in Switzerland and the conversations that those two remarkable men had together would figure as the truly historic part of his journey across Europe. But such talks cannot be trapped by the pedestrian pen of the biographer. At such points (and they are innumerable in the life of Gandhi) the biographer can only salute and pass by, reminding the reader that what can be recorded in print is far less than half the essence of his life lived among all sorts of men.

A few days after his return to India, Gandhi was back in prison, and there he might well have remained for many years but for the fact that the British Government took a step in regard to the new Indian Constitution which Gandhi had already declared he could never tolerate. Having already given separate representation in the Indian Parliament to the Muslims, they now proceeded to propose separate electorates for the Untouchables, thus perpetuating their status of social inferiority to the caste Hindus. Gandhi had, of course, fought against this stigma all his life. As we have seen, for years he had made the destruction of the stigma of untouchability a central point in all his Indian public campaigns. Dr Ambedkar, the Untouchable who had been invited to the Round Table Conference, welcomed the government's plan. In the immediate future, it would be likely to put him at the head of a powerful party in Indian political life. Gandhi had no wish to deny him such personal satisfactions. But he saw that such a separation would have the effect of making permanent the inferior social status that he was determined to destroy. Unlike a party of workers in the West, such a party would, in every section of India, inevitably remain a permanent minority. The cleavage between the Untouchables and the caste Hindus would be deepened. The caste Hindus would tend to rally in opposition to reform. The Untouchable minority would be defeated again and again, for ever.

Gandhi was arrested on 3 January 1932. In March, the government announced that they would themselves propose a "communal award," as the various groups represented in the Conference had been unable to agree. Gandhi then wrote from prison to warn the Secretary of State, Sir Samuel Hoare, that he would resist with his life the separation of the Untouchables into a separate electorate. The award was issued in August. The Untouchables were separated. Gandhi thereupon announced that he would begin a fast unto death in September. This appeared to be a way of putting pressure on the British Government. But Gandhi insisted that it was nothing of the sort. His fast was directed, he said, not at his enemies but at his friends. "Fasting," he said, "stirs up sluggish consciences and fires loving hearts to action ... Nonviolent pressure exerted through self-suffering by fasting ... touches and strengthens the moral fibre of those against whom it is directed."

Pandit Malaviya, orthodox leader of the Hindu Mahasabha, summoned leaders of the Hindu community to meet in conference. In Delhi and Calcutta, temples were opened to Untouchables, from which they had been excluded. A leader of the Untouchables from southern India, M.C. Rajah, joined in the effort to find a settlement. Finally, Dr Ambedkar was induced to come to the conference, though he had in the first place dismissed the fast as a stunt.

Gandhi began his fast on 20 September and the day was observed as a day of fasting throughout the country. By the 26th a compromise plan had been worked out which Gandhi felt able to accept. Separate electorates disappeared, but the Untouchables were given a percentage of seats in the legislatures that would give them representation according to their numbers. In the event, they were if anything over-represented, at the expense of the high-caste Hindus. This, no doubt, seemed still to give legal recognition to their special status. But the conference adopted a resolution which said: "Henceforth among Hindus no one shall be regarded as an Untouchable by reason of his birth."

This all happened in 1932. Even in 1967 there is plenty of evidence of the continued observance of untouchability in many parts of India. Does this mean that Gandhi's fast and the solemn declaration of the caste Hindus after its termination were meaning-less? It does not mean that. It does mean that ancient social abuses, especially perhaps in a country of such size and diversity and poor communications as India, cannot be wiped out by the life-work of a Mahatma or by constitutional decree (under the constitution of free India, the status of untouchability is abolished). With the best of goodwill from the government and social reformers, these deep social cleavages in the pattern of life of the multitudi-nous villages of India can only be transformed by a long process of pressure and by the slow changing of men's minds. But this does not mean that Gandhi's fast of 1932 was futile. Henry Polak commented at the time: "Gandhi has given untouchability a smashing blow, from which it can never recover." That is as fair a comment as any. When the whole story of the destruction of untouchability comes to be written (which may not be possible for another fifty years), while the influence of world concepts of human equality and democracy and the influence of Christian missions will no doubt be conceded, together with other forces, I think the decisive date for the beginning of the final process of emancipation will be Gandhi's fast of September 1932.

Typically, he realised that a symbol of the new status was of the first importance. So he resolved to destroy the pejorative term "untouchable." Instead, he began to call them "Harijans," which means, "children of God." He argued that every religion insists that God is the friend of the helpless and the oppressed. The Untouchables, therefore, deserve the name of children of God; but, according to this argument, it was doubtful whether the caste Hindus could claim to be His children. He looked forward to the time when they too would deserve to be called Harijans. But that would only be when the stigma of untouchability was totally wiped out of India. The word "Harijan" has caught on, and is now very generally used, though it still has to compete with the official expression, "Scheduled Castes," an invention, no doubt, of British officialdom.

6

Constructive Work
(1932-1939)

GANDHI was constantly falling out with his colleagues of the Indian National Congress. For most of them, pure politics, which meant the displacement of the British by a national government, was at all times the most important consideration. It is true, no doubt, that Gandhi was just as impatient for the disappearance of the British as any of his colleagues. But his fundamental philosophy was different from theirs. To them, the question of Indian fitness for self-government did not arise. For Gandhi it did. Not, indeed, in the same sense as for the British who thought that a people must fit itself for self-government by trying doses of gradually increasing strength: let them first run municipal and local government well; then provincial government, with "safeguards," meaning no control for the time being over such essential services as defence and finance; finally, full responsibility for the central government would follow. Gandhi's political philosophy was different. To him, the essential evidence of fitness for self-government was shown by the capacity of the Indian people for self-discipline. And this could be shown in two main ways. Mass civil disobedience could show their ability to suffer without retaliation in resistance to the authority of the British Government. Beyond this, their ability could be tested, not by running local government under British tutelage, but rather by undertaking large-scale economic and social reforms under their own leadership. To Gandhi this latter activity, which he called "the constructive programme," was quite as vital an aspect of true ahimsa, or non-violent social life, as the non-violent resistance to the government. To many of his colleagues, it appeared to be nothing but a retreat from the political struggle.

In 1932, nearly 78,000 volunteers had offered civil disobedience and had gone to jail. But month by month the numbers offering resistance to government edicts had steadily decreased. In January the official records showed nearly 15,000 convictions; in September, less than 3,000. The Willingdon government was determined to crush the Congress. There was to be no Irwin-like parleying with the leaders of rebellion. British officialdom believed that, if they continued to treat the Congress with sufficient severity, Indian opinion would forget Gandhi, or treat him as a failure, as one who had misled them, and opinion would rally in support of the moderates. Provincial self-government would proceed under British leadership and gradually the country would be prepared for full self-government. In spite of Gandhi's fast in September 1932, during 1933 the government was inclined to believe that it was achieving its purpose. The dangerous men were all in jail. Congress funds had been forfeited. The nationalist press was gagged. Civil disobedience was to all intents and purposes dead. And, what was more, Gandhi, the arch-rebel, was concerning himself entirely with the harmless issue of untouchability. In fact, many of the Congress leaders were inclined to agree with the government's estimate of the situation. They were angry with Gandhi for deflecting the attention of the country to the social problem of untouchability. How could this help the struggle for freedom? But, as usual, the event seems to show that Gandhi had a deeper insight into the realities of the whole Indian situation than either the British Government or the political leaders of the country. He saw, not for the first time, that the longest way round is the shortest way to the goal.

His weekly paper, *Young India*, had been suppressed when he was arrested. He never attempted to revive it. Instead, he now started a new weekly, *Harijan*, which was in the first place devoted entirely to the welfare of the Harijans and other social issues. During the early months, he edited the paper and wrote a good deal of it himself, from jail. Then, after a series of minor clashes with the government and a vain attempt to persuade Lord Willingdon to meet him, with a view to the formal cancellation of civil disobedience, he undertook a three weeks' fast for self-purification, so that he would be better fitted for carrying on his great task of converting Hindu India and of providing better economic and educational opportunities for the Harijans.

In August 1933, he was finally released from jail by the Government, but his jail sentence had not expired, so he confined himself, for the time being, to Harijan work and neither wrote nor published anything about politics. On 7 November 1933, he set out on a tour which occupied him for nine months, during which he covered altogether 12,500 miles, much of it on foot, calling on caste Hindus to purge themselves of their prejudice and sense of superiority towards the Harijans, and the Harijans to abandon some of their habits, such as the eating of carrion, which caused them to seem unclean to their high-caste neighbours. As he toured, he collected money for his Harijan fund. Gandhi was always a prince of beggars. It would be impossible to guess how much money he collected during his life-time to aid in rehabilitating the poor of India. He readily accepted alike the thousands of rupees he could get from wealthy merchants and the jewellery that poor women took off their own arms and ankles. The small gifts from the poor, no doubt, gave him more satisfaction than the large donations from the rich. It is recorded that when, in southern India, in an area where the worst tyranny of untouchability prevailed, a girl took off her gold ornaments and gave those to him, he declared: "Your renunciation is a truer ornament than the jewellery you have discarded." When women asked for his autograph, he only gave it in exchange for a bangle from their wrists. During this tour, he collected eight lakhs of rupees (800,000 rupees; 1 rupee equals 1s. 6d. British money, or 15 cents American). All this was collected personally in cash or in kind—as he travelled from place to place—all or nearly all from villagers. Many of the villages he visited were quite "off the map."

He had some severe opposition to meet from the orthodox. In one place a bomb was thrown at his party, injuring seven persons, though not Gandhi himself. In March 1934, there was a severe earthquake in Bihar, and Gandhi interrupted his Harijan tour to visit the earthquake zone. Agatha Harrison, who was travelling with him for part of the time, was impressed by the fact that, even as he travelled among villages that had been totally destroyed, his main concern seemed to be to prevent the people from sitting down under their disaster, waiting for the government or other outside agencies of goodwill to come to their rescue. The people still had their physical strength and their tools. Let them get to work rebuilding what had been destroyed.

Gandhi declared that the earthquake was an act of God in retribution for the Indian sin of untouchability. Such an "unscientific explanation of physical phenomena" brought a vigorous rejoinder from Rabindranath Tagore (though Tagore was, of course, heart and soul with Gandhi's efforts to destroy untouchability). Tagore suggested that the orthodox Hindus might just as well claim that this was a warning from God that Gandhi's reform efforts must be stopped. And, in any case, why should a rural area of Bihar, a province where untouchability was much less rigidly enforced than in southern India, be singled out by God for this horrible act of vengeance? Gandhi's reply, though it may not seem to be a logical one to Tagore and other critics, at least helps to show his philosophy of life, and especially his refusal to accept a dualistic philosophy:

We do not know the laws of God nor their working. Knowledge of tallest scientist or the spiritualist (should this perhaps be "the most learned theologian"?) is like a particle of dust. If God is not a personal being for me, like my earthly father, he is infinitely more. He rules me in the tiniest detail of my daily life. I believe literally that not a leaf moves but by his will. Every breath I take depends upon his sufferance.

Gandhi was so essentially a man of action that it is not easy to watch the growth of his mind across the years. As we leave him striding through the villages of India during the middle thirties of the century, we may perhaps stand back for a moment and try to understand what were the foundations on which he had built his life, and how his religion or his philosophy grew and developed in response to the innumerable currents of life that he encountered. Let it be noted that he himself, when he came to write his autobiography, in the late 1920s, called it *The Story of My Experiments with Truth*. That indicates quite a lot. It shows a truly scientific approach to life. He believed in experiment; his goal was truth, but not some absolute truth that he expected to reach in the course of years. Rather, truth was to him infinite. Man could discern partial truth; he could see glimpses, enough to live by; but, at each turn in the upward path, fresh vistas would appear, sometimes leading to a modification of the truth seen from a lower, more limited range of country. Consequently, he was not satisfied to accept the authority of any religious system as final. Nothing in human understanding could ever be final. So, neither the "tallest scientist" nor the most learned theologian could give final answers to the questions about the significance of life and the universe. Every authority must be tested by human intelligence in the light of experience. Thus, in these years of activity for the Harijans, texts from the Hindu Vedic writings might be produced by his critics showing that there was some degree of sanction for the observance of untouchability in the ancient religious customs of India. But, in that case, it was time to recognise the imperfections of the Vedas. A new age could revise the wisdom of the ancients and reject what appeared to be false or at least no longer applicable.

Gandhi had been brought up as an orthodox Hindu, of the *baniya* or trading caste, though in fact his father was not a trader or shopkeeper; he was the Minister of a small Indian State. Like a great many other young men, Gandhi did not think much about religion or fundamental questions when he was young. He accepted the Hindu system in which he grew up without much question. His first experience of Christians was unfavourable. They ate meat, they drank wine, but, more serious than this, they were intolerant and said rude things about Hinduism. As a young man he had been induced by a friend to eat meat for a time, believing that this might give Indians the physical strength to stand up to the all-powerful Englishmen. But, as he hated doing things that he could not talk about to his parents, he soon gave up meat-eating. It was only when he found himself in an entirely different surrounding in "Christian" England, as a student of law, that he began to think seriously about fundamental values and about the truth and falsehood in various religious systems. Both in England and in South Africa, he became intimate with Christians who commanded his respect. One of them persuaded him to read right through the Bible. He found much of it very tedious and uninspiring. But, when he gave a promise, he kept it. So he went right through and, when he suddenly arrived at the New

Testament and read the Sermon on the Mount, his heart and head
responded with enthusiasm. These were authentic truths to him;
these were the things his heart had been seeking for.

But he rejected the schemes of salvation that his evangelistic
Christian friends presented to him as essential Christianity. It
was the person of Jesus that caught his imagination, not any eccle-
siastical dogma. So he saw no reason to stop calling himself
a Hindu or to begin calling himself a Christian. Indeed, he found
the Hindu religious philosophy more logical and profound than
the Christian faith as it had been expounded to him. Once he
had discovered the Christian gospels, he found himself driven
back to his own great scriptures. In the end, it was the Bhagavad
Gita especially, which he had first learnt from his mother, that
gave him the greatest help and confidence as he faced the problems
and frustrations of life. Towards the end of his life, he came to
claim that he was not only a Hindu but also a Christian, a Muslim,
a Buddhist, a Sikh, a Parsi, a Jew; in other words, he had learnt
so much from all the great scriptures of the world that he honoured
all the great religious leaders and found it wrong that their followers should spend their time and energy fighting one another as
if any single religious system were perfect or had a monopoly of
truth.

But we may still fairly ask: what did he mean by "God" ? The
term "God" is used constantly by men and women all over the
world and there are a thousand different senses in which it is used.
What did it mean to Gandhi? And was he consistent in his use of
the term?

He often declared that he did not accept the idea of a personal
God. But it is not quite obvious what he meant by "personal."
Apparently, he was rejecting the idea of an anthropomorphic God.
He was aware that men love to project their own image and create
a God who is simply a glorified human being. The writer of the
Book of Genesis pictures God, the Creator, as saying: "Let us
make man in our own image." Which is equivalent to saying
that man is creating God in his own image. Such a human God
was rejected by Gandhi. As the years went by, he came to identify
God with truth. First, he saw God as truth; then he turned the
words around and insisted that Truth is God. So that every man
who seeks for truth, whether the scientist or the philosopher or

the man of action who is striving after some worthy goal of human endeavour, is in Gandhi's view worshipping God, even though he calls himself an agnostic or an atheist. But although this was what Gandhi said he believed in, many of his habits of mind stuck to him throughout his life and seemed to deny his declared philosophy about God. He called God "he" all the time, rather than "it"; although in such a passage as we have quoted, where he justified his contention about the Bihar earthquake, he was deliberately rejecting the idea of the fatherhood of God, yet he still spoke of his "maker"; in at least one passage from his voluminous writings he looked forward to the time when he will, like a tired child, at the end of the day, "lay his head in the lap of his maker." Pictorial language, no doubt; he was always inclined to write in simple terms that make some sense to the ordinary unphilosophical reader. Yet such a conception suggests a very "personal" attitude to God. He certainly believed that his God was a potent life-force. He believed, evidently, that there was purpose behind the universe: the force he called "God" was not a blind force. Truth, after all, is not a purely abstract expression. It may not seem very easy to imagine oneself "laying one's head in the lap of truth"; but Gandhi might have said:

Why not? Is not the whole of our human personality, with its deep emotional centre, its passion for investigating truth, its devotion to beauty, all a part of the creative force that may be called the "truth" of the universe? Whatever the power behind the universe, it obviously includes every aspect of human nature and human aspiration. Call it the life-force, call it truth, call it love, call it what you will. This is the ultimate reality which I, Gandhi, like to call God, and I am content to put myself into its hands [pictorial language again].

Gandhi also believed that God made His "will" known to him as an inner guide. Again and again in his life, when he was wrestling with some tremendous issue, whether political or moral—and for Gandhi all issues were fundamentally moral—he would announce after making his decision that it had come to him as an urgent inner summons, sometimes almost as an audible voice. Thus, at the beginning of his Harijan campaign, while he was still

in prison, he was acutely conscious that many of the caste Hindus
who had accepted the Poona Pact were not ready to implement
it. They had presumably accepted it in order to save his life, that
is to say under pressure of his fast. For weeks he wrestled with
this problem of their seeming insincerity or at the least their lack
of enthusiasm; at last he announced that he was about to fast
for twenty-one days. Here was no coercion, except the pure
coercion of love. He would not desist if anyone did anything
different. The intention of the fast was self-purification, and
perhaps an appeal to the conscience of his fellow-Hindus. What
led him to this fast? Here are his own words. One night, as he
wrestled with his problem, something had happened:

> I saw no form. But what I did hear was like a voice from afar
> and yet quite near. It was as unmistakable as some human
> voice definitely speaking to me, and irresistible. I was not
> dreaming at the time I heard the voice. The hearing of the
> voice was preceded by a terrific struggle within me. Suddenly
> the voice came upon me. I listened, made certain that it was
> the voice, and the struggle ceased. I was calm. The determi-
> nation was made accordingly; the date and the hour of the fast
> were fixed. Joy came over me.

We may note that he declares: "I made certain that it was the
voice," not just *a* voice, but *the* voice. Although he does not say,
"the voice of God," the inference is that that is what he means:
at least, the voice of eternal truth, not just some passing fancy
rising from his own subconscious mind. Clearly, if the voice of
some absolute truth is calling for some specific action, the authority behind his action is far greater than if it were just "a voice."
And I think Gandhi very firmly believed that it had this quality,
and wished others to believe it. Yet, if someone who claims not
to believe in God at all were to argue with him on such lines as
this. "Oh, yes, I too, in my scientific work am often impelled by
an urgent sense of duty, by my inner sense of integrity, to pursue
some difficult enquiry," Gandhi might have said: "That is the
same thing; that is just what I mean." But the difficulty remains
that, so long as terms like "God" and "the inner voice" are used,
it appears to most people that a claim is being made for direct

access to an authority beyond and outside that of the most sensitive
conscience.

There is still an apparent contradiction between his frequent
insistence that the voice of God or of ultimate truth was demanding
certain actions from him, in other words his conviction that he
knew what God demanded of him at a special time and place, with
his emphatic statement: "We do not know the laws of God or
their working." Perhaps, he would have said: "But sometimes
He does reveal His will clearly for each man, showing him his duty,
if only he will reduce himself to a cypher and listen to the inner
prompting." In other words, not every man rightly interprets
the truth that is being given to him. His ability to disentangle
the real truth of his own being from the whims of his own wilful-
ness will depend on his self-discipline. Any man may deceive
himself. Many do deceive themselves. Those who, usually as
the result of long years of self-discipline, come to have the fullest
apprehension of truth, are the men and women whom the world
calls its saints and seers. Moreover, though Gandhi was willing
to stake his life on his sense of divine direction, once he had heard
the voice, he was always humble enough to say even at the moment
of his great decisions: "I may be wrong. If so, it is better
for the world that I should be allowed to die."

Gandhi had grown up in an atmosphere of religion. Then,
when he went to England for his legal training, he found himself
in the midst of late Victorian Protestant Christians. In South
Africa, also, evangelical Christians were among his intimate
friends. So it was natural he should express himself in terms that
involve, for instance, the assumption that there is a power for
righteousness, usually called God, and that man can and should
seek to be aware of the source of his true well-being, God in fact.
Gandhi kept abreast of the change towards a world of human
thought that tended to dispense with the old-fashioned ideas of
God. There were young Indians who tried to convince him that
he ought to be an atheist. There were some among his close colleagues who were agnostics. But he continued to have a strong sense
of communion with a spiritual power whom he called God, even,
though he insisted that to him God was truth and not a personal
being. It is not easy to put the fundamentals of Gandhi's religion
into a few sentences, or even into any words at all. But two things

can be safely said, one negative, the other positive. On the negative side, he had discarded the anthropomorphic being with strong human passions who can be figured as a man in the manner of classical art, whether eastern or western. On the other hand, his faith was no mere intellectual notion about the nature of life. It was the essence of his being, the breath of his daily life. Without his daily prayers and other religious exercises, he could not have lived, or, if he had lived, his life would have been very different.

Gandhi's life was so full of action and fresh development that it is not easy to find an appropriate moment for standing back and trying to understand what were its main driving forces. It is often assumed that, once he had forged his weapon of satyagraha in South Africa and launched on his life of non-violent political action, he had nothing more to learn, or at least he did not add much more. He had arrived. But this is hardly the whole truth. No doubt, his later life was built on the foundations so well laid in South Africa; but he grew in maturity and in the sureness of his convictions as the years went by. It was only in his later life that he began to speak not only of God being truth, but also that Truth is God; it is in his later years that we find him constantly repeating that truth and non-violence are his two anchors, his fundamental values.

In the period we have now reached, the mid-thirties, he was travelling across the length and breadth of India, proclaiming these eternal values, and finding their application in various fields of social improvement. His activity in these years was in many ways a repetition of his activity between the first and second great civil disobedience movement. The emphasis was different at some points, especially, of course, in making the battle against untouchability the centre of his whole campaign. It was different also in that he was now concerned to build a number of permanent organisations for carrying on the constructive programme.

First of all, there was the Harijan Sevak Sangh, the society for the service of the Harijans, which he brought into being. Originally, this was an organisation composed entirely of caste Hindus, for Gandhi felt it was their job to serve those whom they had hitherto oppressed. Ultimately, some of the Harijans themselves joined the board of this society, so that they might advise the caste Hindus how best to serve the Untouchables. Week by week, the pages of the paper *Harijan* recorded the lists of temples, wells, and schools thrown open to the Harijans. Some wealthy caste Hindus adopted Harijan children into their families or paid for their education. Such adoption was a flagrant violation of the rigid caste rules that had bound Hinduism in most parts of India for many centuries. It is impossible to know how widespread such adoptions were, even under Gandhi's powerful influence. I confess that, even as late as 1960, when I visited a village near Delhi and met the chief family of the village belonging to a high caste, I was amazed to find that, as only daughters had been born to the family, they had adopted a Harijan boy from another section of the village to be the heir to the family lands. One had assumed that it would be chiefly in the towns, among the sophisticated, that ancient caste taboos would be put aside. Villages are always liable to be more conservative in social affairs than towns. But it must never be forgotten that Gandhi made a stronger appeal to the villagers of India than to the townsmen. They understood his language and his thought forms, whereas sophisticated townsmen were always apt to think of Gandhi as a medievalist who wanted to put back the clock of human progress. It is, probably, fair to assume that Gandhi's effort to break down untouchability by bringing Harijan children into high-caste Hindu homes has been quietly penetrating into many Indian villages.

During the thirties, Gandhi's zeal for handspinning and weaving in no way abated. He gave much attention to the All-India Spinners Association, and nothing pleased him more than to see some new and more successful model of a portable spinning-wheel. He continued his own daily handspinning; yet he never became an expert spinner. In his hands the thread continued to break; but he was never discouraged. There was also the All-India Village Industries Association which fostered such industries as paper-making, the weaving of mats, the pressing of oil, bee-keeping, the husking and grinding of rice, and the making of gur (which is the full sugar content of the sugarcane).

Gandhi did not reject all machinery. As he pointed out, the human frame is the most perfect machine of all. As for modern machinery, he had long ago recognised that the sewing-machine was a true labour-saving device, in that it saved women from some of the perpetual labour about the household which is the lot of almost every housemother in every corner of the globe. And, if there were sewing-machines, there must be factories for their production. Gandhi had several objections to modern industrialism. First, the concentration of industry in large cities tended to promote overcrowding of people, away from the earth and nature, and thereby promoted immorality. Moreover, in such a country as India, especially where labour is plentiful, the important thing is to find useful work for all, not to concentrate work in the hands of a few. Then, too, he was concerned at the inhuman monotony of repetitive manufacturing processes and the loss of any sense of creative joy in work. Industrial workers tend to think of work as a curse, to be reduced to as few hours in the week as possible. But creative work is a joy and the man who enjoys his craft is happy to continue working all day long. So, as far as possible, Gandhi tried to reconstruct village life, by bringing back to the villages of India as many of the processes as possible that are naturally connected with the primary producer.

This was also the period when Gandhi brought to fruition his ideas about education. The educational system brought to India by the British seemed to him to put too much emphasis on literacy, as if man's basic needs are reading and writing. It should be recognised that Western education has developed largely from medieval times, when schooling was provided for quite a limited section of the population, namely, those whose life was to be spent in clerical occupations. The great majority of the people learnt their life's work from their parents or by apprenticeship to some skilled craftsman. Literacy was not supposed to be universally desirable. Even some of the rulers of States in those centuries could not read or write, nor did they wish to do so. In the eighteenth and nineteenth centuries, as the demand for literacy increased, schooling in the arts of reading, writing, and arithmetic gradually spread to the mass of the people. And so the British in India, as also other European colonial powers in other parts of Asia and Africa, responded to the demand for widespread education by providing imitation of the schools in vogue in Europe. This system seemed to Gandhi, as indeed to a good many other people, to be a misfit in rural India. Therefore, in the 1930s, he was largely instrumental in the establishment of a committee, under the leadership of Dr Zakir Husain, a distinguished pioneer

in education (now President of India) to propose a plan of education
which would connect the schooling of the children with the daily
life of the village.   Thus, what is today known as "Basic education"
was born.

The essence of basic education is that in each school some craft,
whether spinning or weaving, or gardening or carpentry, should be
the centre of the life of the school, and that other activities of
the children, whether reading, writing, arithmetic, geography, or
history, should be closely related to the basic craft.

The plan for basic education, as first proposed, gave rise to
much controversy.   It was said that the new schools should to a
large extent be self-supporting.   In other words, the produce of
the craftwork should be sold, to help pay for the wages of the
teachers.   Partly, this was intended to meet one of Gandhi's
strongest objections to the British educational pattern.   Under
the existing system, education was a provincial subject, and the
main source of revenue available to the provinces for supporting
schools was obtained from the sale of alcoholic drinks and drugs,
and other kinds of excise duty.   To Gandhi this was an abomina-
tion.   He declared that he would rather have no schools at all
than have them supported by an immoral tax, as he called it.   So
some other source had to be looked for.   In ancient India the
"forest schools" were supported by the local community.   A
village or a group of villages would see to it that the teacher, the
"guru," was provided for.   To revive this ancient system might
no longer be wholly practicable.   But at least some part of the
support of the teacher might be met by the sale of the produce of
the school, if much of the time of the children were to be given to
useful craftwork.   Critics immediately suggested that Gandhi was
prepared to turn all the children of India into pitiful little wage
slaves.   The schools, instead of being centres of light and hope,
would become little factories, where the chief driving force would
be the determination of the teacher to get the maximum productive yield out of the children.   Gandhi did not accept this criticism.
But the basic schools that were set up in due course did not, as
far as I know, ever seriously try to become self-supporting by the
sale of their produce.   The problem of adequate revenue for the
payment of teachers remained unsolved, and still remains so.   On
the other hand, those who have watched a class of children all

busily plying their little *taklis* or spinning-wheels must recognise
that they appear to get plenty of pleasure from this rhythmical
activity. Most children are dexterous with their hands. They
soon learn not to break the cotton thread. The sight of such a
class at work is like the sight of a beautiful dance—only that the
children are dancing with their hands, not their feet. As the
classical dances of India give almost more attention to the rhyth-
mic motion of arms and hands than to the movements of legs and
feet, this kind of school exercise may fairly be likened to a simple
dance.

There was plenty of political excitement in India during the
nineteen-thirties, and Gandhi, even though there was no civil
disobedience, was actively involved.

As we have seen he grew up in one of the many Indian States,
in territory that was not directly administered by the British.
These States included some vast territories, with millions of inhabitants; others were no more than large estates, covering a few square
miles; others came between these two extremes. All were bound
to the British "Paramount Power" by treaties, and the British
appointed residents to each State or group of States to advise the
ruler. When advice was offered, the ruler was expected to attend
to it; but as a rule the Indian Princes were left to run their States
very much as they chose; most of the States were autocracies, so
that they were not unaptly described as "bad," "worse," or "hell."
There was no rule of law, no check on the way the ruler spent the
taxation he raised, no suggestion of a democratic government.
The State of Rajkot, in which Gandhi grew up, where both his
grandfather and his father had acted as ministers to the ruler, had
a better record than some; but everything depended on the whim of
the ruler. A good father, who might rule with real concern for
the welfare of the people, might be succeeded by an irresponsible
son.

By the nineteen-thirties, the wind of democratic sentiment was
blowing across the wholly invisible boundaries from British India
into the Indian States. Nothing could stop it. However, Gandhi
himself, unlike his young colleague, Jawaharlal Nehru, was not prepared to encourage this movement. He did not feel that the time
had come to antagonise the rulers of the States. In 1938, following
action by Nehru in the State of Mysore, which Gandhi thought

rather ill-advised, he persuaded the Congress Working Committee to pass a resolution which declared that the Congress as such would not interfere in the affairs of the States, though at the same time the States' subjects were assured of general moral support in their own independent efforts to achieve a measure of reform, and individual Congressmen, such as Nehru himself, were permitted to help them.

Within a very short time, Gandhi found himself involved directly in the affairs of Rajkot. His close associate, Vallabhbhai Patel, had helped the local reformers to win a notable victory through civil disobedience, and the ruler, or Thakore as he was called in this case, agreed to appoint a committee of ten, seven of them to represent the popular movement, to carry out reforms. However, the Thakore, partly under pressure from other rulers, partly under the advice of his own minister named Virawala, backed out again. Civil disobedience was resumed, and severe measures of repression were taken by the government. Mrs Gandhi insisted on joining the movement and she was sentenced to imprisonment.

Gandhi himself was ill at the time; but he decided to go to Rajkot; he made enquiries which satisfied him that the Thakore had gone back on his word. He would not listen to Gandhi's remonstrances, though Gandhi felt that he was almost a father to the young man. So Gandhi began a fast without limit of time, and he became extremely ill. With the consent of Gandhi himself, appeals were made to the Viceroy to intervene. He invited the British Chief Justice to carry out an inquiry. This was accepted by the Thakore, and Gandhi broke his fast. The Chief Justice found that the Thakore had broken his promise; so the committee of ten was to be appointed as first agreed. However, excitement grew. The Thakore's friends demonstrated against Gandhi. He then retreated, declaring that his appeal to the Viceroy was wrong, that he ought to have preferred death, and that he had harboured feelings of distrust towards Virawala, which were quite improper for a satyagrahi. So he apologised to the Viceroy and the Chief Justice for the trouble he had given them, and claimed that the Thakore and his minister must be free to act as they thought right, without regard to the new award. So they did. Political prisoners were all released, their confiscated lands were restored, and full civil liberty was promised. But there was no political reform. If anything, in Gandhi's own opinion, the new scheme of government was worse than it was before. No wonder his critics asked what right he had, in order to satisfy his conscience, to throw away the hard-won gains of the 75,000 people of Rajkot.

During these years, in the political sphere, things had been happening that showed at least that the British Government meant what it said. Even while they were wholeheartedly supporting the Viceroy in India in his attempt to destroy the Congress Party and to discredit Gandhi's political leadership, the Conservative Government in England went laboriously ahead with their new plan for extending self-government. In India, the picture was one of a continued struggle between the British authority and the Congress Party, in which for the time being the British were successful. To the English observer, what was more apparent was a long-drawn-out parliamentary battle between the Conservative Government of Stanley Baldwin, with Sir Samuel Hoare as his chief lieutenant at the India Office, piloting a long and complex measure for reforming Indian Government through the House of Commons in the teeth of bitter opposition from Winston Churchill and a small group of Tories, but with the support of the two opposition parties, Labour and Liberal. Almost the only voice among the political leaders of England to suggest that the Hoare Bill did not go far enough, rather than going too far, came from Stafford Cripps, who at this time was on friendly terms with Nehru, and who accepted the demand of the Indian National Congress for immediate self-government. The India Bill gave self-government to the Indian provinces; but in the Central Government, the British still kept full control of such vital matters as defence, foreign policy, and the financing of the main Central services.

When this new Act came into force in 1935, the Congress Party had to decide whether they should contest the provincial elections, with a view to controlling as many of the provincial governments as possible. Although Gandhi did not like the new Act, he encouraged the Congress to fight the elections, and the result, even with the very restricted franchise of that time, showed how far the government was still from crushing the Congress Party. In seven of the eleven provinces they were able immediately to form a ministry that had the backing of an effective majority. Within a few months, they had captured the ministries in two other provinces. But they made one questionable decision which had unfortunate results. In the United Provinces, the largest and most populous of the provinces of north India, there lived perhaps the most highly cultured Muslim community of India. The majority of the population of this province, however, was Hindu. At the time of the elections, Congress and Muslim League—already perhaps the most important Muslim party in India as a whole, though not yet the power, it was soon to become—had fought the elections side by side, so that the Muslim League expected to be included in any ministry that might be formed. The election results gave the Congress a majority over all other parties, so they decided, on the principle of "majority democracy," to form their own ministry alone. They did invite some leaders of the Muslim League to join the ministry, but this offer was refused. Accordingly, as the Congress included Muslim members, the ministry was formed from the Congress alone, including some Muslims.

The effects of this action on communal relations in the country as a whole were not immediately apparent and the ministries in the main acquitted themselves well, and began to get busy with social and economic reforms, including some that were dear to Gandhi. Madras was outstanding. This was the only province where a leading Congressman, C. Rajagopalachari, decided to head the new ministry. In all the other provinces, the ministries were formed by men of the second rank, as the Congress leaders considered that, until the full battle of freedom was won, their first job was to reserve themselves for the battle with the British, which they believed would still have to be fought. They were not at all convinced that the grant of provincial self-government held with it any intention of the British to part with power over the Central government. When war came to Europe in September 1939, and the Viceroy without waiting to consult any Indian representative declared that India was at war with Germany, they felt that their suspicions were justified, and all the provincial ministries resigned.

7

"Quit India"
(1939-1945)

WHEN WAR came to Europe again in 1939, the Congress High Command was divided in its attitude. Jawaharlal Nehru, perhaps the only Indian leader who followed world affairs closely, and for their own sake, not merely for their repercussions on the Indian national struggle, had been watching the growth of the power of the Fascist States in Europe, Germany, and Italy, with alarm no less than was felt by most people of democratic sympathies in the West. The British Government under Neville Chamberlain, and successive weak French governments, seemed to him to be following a policy of disastrous appeasement, with no will to stand up against the dangerous aggressiveness of the two Fascist dictators. The civil war in Spain had seemed to him to be the prelude to what was coming upon Europe. The British Government's efforts to treat the Franco "rebels" as of equal authority with the legitimate Republican Government of Spain seemed to indicate that the British Government was at heart sympathetic to the dictators rather than to the struggle for democracy.

When, therefore, the British Government, following the invasion of Poland in September 1939, finally, declared war on Hitler's Germany, Nehru and those who saw things as he did began to hope that the tide had turned, and that at last the British Government had woken up to the true menace of Fascist expansionism. In that case they were ready and eager to stand beside the British and all other people who were now prepared to withstand Hitler. But the test of British sincerity would be shown by their action in India. If they were really converted, let them show their change of heart by inviting full Indian participation in the struggle; in fact by inviting the leaders of the national movement in India to take over effective control of the Central Government in Delhi. In September 1939, there can be little doubt that the leaders of the Congress would have settled for something a good deal less than a total British withdrawal. Participation in the Central Government by a few of the Congress leaders, together with one or two Muslim League leaders, might possibly have brought a united India into the war against Hitler. But, for whatever reason, the British Government did not attempt to bring this about. Following the letter of the law, they called on the Viceroy to declare India at war, and no effort was made to extend the basis of the Delhi Government.

Gandhi's own position was slightly different, here as often before. His political thinking was not in full harmony with the Congress leaders. Several years before, he had resigned his membership of the Congress, leaving his old colleagues free to follow lines that he knew he could not wholly approve. Yet the personal bond remained close. Nehru, Patel, Rajagopalachari, Rajendra Prasad, and his other colleagues would constantly visit him to confer about the policies they were planning.

Gandhi did not disagree with Nehru in his analysis of the condition of Europe. Perhaps, he did not use such expressions as "fascism" so freely. But early in 1939, he wrote a letter to Hitler, warning him that, if war came to Europe, it would be Hitler's responsibility; he would have to bear the main guilt. This letter received no reply. Whatever Mussolini may have thought some ten years earlier, Hitler evidently had no interest in trying to court the favour of the leaders of "rebel" India. But Gandhi, though he agreed that the war was mainly due to the policies of Hitler and Mussolini, remained fundamentally a pacifist. He would have preferred to support the British and French in 1939 with benevolent neutrality, rather than with active military force.

The Viceroy at this time was Lord Linlithgow. He and Gandhi apparently liked each other, and Lord Linlithgow made it easy for Gandhi to meet him from time to time. The very day after he had announced that India was at war, he invited Gandhi to meet him (4 September 1939), and they met again at the end of the same month. But these talks were quite abortive. Gandhi had made it clear that his personal sympathies in the war were with Britain;

knowing as he did that any great war would be largely an air war, he was appalled at the prospect of the destruction of such buildings as Westminster Abbey and the Houses of Parliament. Moreover, Gandhi was not interested in bargaining. If India was prepared to support Britain it should be unconditionally. But his colleagues in the Congress leadership could not agree to this. Their statement of 14 September made it plain that they could support Britain not from any sentimental attachment to that country, but only if there were such a clear statement of war aims that all the world could see that this was a genuine war of those who believed in democracy—meaning democracy in all parts of the world—against the dictators. To this demand there was little response. In so far as there was a response, all the emphasis was the old one on the need to give full guarantee to the minorities. There was no suggestion of giving the leaders of the Congress any positions of real authority. So, in October all the Congress ministries resigned; in several provinces the British Governor took over responsibility for the government. In others, and as time went on, the number of these increased, new ministries were formed in which the Muslim League had a predominant influence. Moreover, in March 1940, the Muslim League, under Jinnah's leadership, had announced that, in the parts of India where the Muslims were in a majority, namely, the north-west and the north-east, independent States should be formed, with full powers of defence, external affairs, communications, customs, and all the rest.

But Gandhi, as usual, was not thinking in terms of political bargaining. The whole world was faced with destruction, and he wanted to find some way to avert this evil. Perhaps, there were ways in which India could help to rescue the world. At the end of 1940 he wrote: "It is my certain belief that only non-violence can save India and the world from self-extinction." But by then much more had happened. During 1940, and especially after the beginning of the "blitzkrieg," the British Government made proposals that might have interested the Congress leaders very much a year before. Now there were serious suggestions for bringing the leaders into the Viceroy's executive council. But it was too late. The gulf between the Congress and the government had grown deeper. Already, there was talk of civil disobedience. On the government side, even while proposals for expanding the executive council were being made, the Viceroy was sending private messages to the Governors of the provinces, warning them to be ready for thorough and drastic action against the Congress if civil disobedience began. The simple fact was that both sides distrusted each other. Even after several years of Congress government in the provinces, British officialdom still regarded the Congress as their "enemy," not to be conciliated but to be crushed. Many Congressmen were equally convinced that to try to come to an understanding with the British was a waste of time and effort. As usual, Gandhi took a line of his own. For a time, when it looked as if those Congressmen who were eager to join in the war against the dictators, and who hoped for an agreement with the government, were in the ascendant, he had withdrawn from all participation, wishing to be free to preach against all participation in every kind of war. But when it became clear that there could be no co-operation between the government and Congress, he was invited to lead the Congress in expression of open disapproval of the government's policies. Many Congress leaders now wanted a full-blooded civil disobedience movement; and this was what the government was anticipating. But Gandhi was determined not to embarrass the government. So the movement he led was a movement of individual disobedience. In the first place he himself chose the men who were to court arrest, and gave them exact instructions about how to act. They were to make public statements opposing the war, and if possible all wars. Therefore, he first of all named a man who until then had not been in the public eye, Vinoba Bhave, who shared his conviction that all war was to be resisted, and that aggressive force should always be met by non-violent action. Another of those chosen by him for individual disobedience was Freda Bedi, English wife of an Indian, and not in the active political leadership. Thereafter, Jawaharlal Nehru and other Congress political leaders, many of whom were not pacifists, but were now determined to resist the government's war policies, followed and were arrested. So the movement grew until, by May 1941, over 2,500 individuals had been arrested. All these had taken some individual action. There had been no mass demonstrations. Meanwhile, the government had plenty of recruits for the fighting forces, men who joined the forces for the usual reasons. And although the jails must have been full, the normal machinery of the government was not interfered with. So everyone was satisfied, except those Congressmen to whom the war against the dictators in Europe meant little or nothing, and who wanted to take advantage of the desperate position in which Britain found herself after Hitler had overrun Europe, in order to press the demand for Indian freedom. After Japan came into the war, some of these went to Japan, in order to enlist in armies that were fighting the British. For such action, Gandhi, of course, had no sympathy at all. But before that happened, already the government, responding with courtesy to their courteous opponent, had released the prisoners.

Such was the position at the end of 1941. The early months of 1942 saw the victorious drive of Japanese forces across southeast Asia. At any time, India herself might be threatened with invasion from the east. At the same time, in Britain, one effect of the closing of ranks was the strengthening of the War Cabinet by the inclusion of Sir Stafford Cripps, who became leader of the House of Commons. Cripps was generally regarded as a left-wing socialist, and he had shown a personal interest in Indian freedom and had made friends with Nehru. Although in ideology they were remote, Churchill and Cripps became personally attached; and it was presumably Cripps who persuaded the arch-imperialist, Churchill, to permit him to make a fresh effort to break the deadlock in India. A special sub-committee of the British Cabinet was set up to help Cripps to prepare new proposals which he might take to India. These proposals were in two parts. For the future, they recognised the right of India to full self-determination after the war, although with the dangerous qualification that any province or Princely State might vote itself out of the Union. For the moment, there were no proposals for constitutional change; but the plan involved the expansion or reformation of the Viceroy's council, in such a way that Indian nationalism would have a full say in the direction of policy, including defence. The obvious difficulty of such a plan was, once again, that it was expecting men of two nations, who profoundly distrusted each other, to work together as a united team. If a man of Cripps' outlook had suddenly become Viceroy perhaps such a plan might have worked. But it would have been almost impossible for men of the outlook of Nehru to work as happy colleagues with the top British civil servants, under the chairmanship of Lord Linlithgow.

Moreover, the fundamental assumption of the Cripps proposals was the belief that everyone in India was united in the desire to resist the Japanese threat by armed defence. Many Congress leaders did wish to do just that; but Gandhi, though he had no wish to substitute a Japanese occupation of India for the British, was still determined to have no part in armed defence. The furthest he would go was to say that, if India were satisfied that the British had undergone a change of heart in the matter of Indian self-government, they would do nothing to impede the military defence of India on the part of British and American troops.

The Cripps proposals were, of course, secret; no hint of their content reached the press until they were presented by him to the Indian leaders. So it is worth recording, as an illustration of the genuineness of the change (for the moment) in the British approach, that a day or two before he set off for India, when the plan was being finalised, he invited the India Conciliation group to meet him in London and to confer on his proposals. I was asked to chair this meeting. I recall, in my welcome to Sir Stafford, I failed to say that, of course, it was a strictly confidential occasion. Nor did he immediately insist on this. Apparently, he trusted us all. Later I interrupted him to say this, and he then underlined the need to keep it to ourselves until he made his announcement in India. As far as I recall, we did not offer any special comment or suggestions; but Agatha Harrison, our indefatigable secretary, who even in war time managed to keep a close watch on the course of Indian opinion, with special emphasis on Gandhi, expressed grave doubts about the adequacy of the proposals. A year earlier they might have been acceptable; but she feared that, once again, they would prove to be too late. She was right.

Gandhi himself took little part in the discussions with Cripps. Reluctantly, he went to Delhi for a day or two; then he withdrew to Sevagram, and, as Mahadev Desai told me a few months later when I was at Sevagram, he knew nothing of the final talks with Cripps, or their breakdown, until he saw it in the newspapers. A rumour had spread about that the Congress leaders were nearly ready to accept the proposals, when one of them put through a long distance telephone call to Gandhi, who urged them to reject, which they accordingly did. This story is a complete fabrication. Nevertheless, he had made it quite clear that he did not like the Cripps proposals, which he described as a post-dated cheque (which, of course, it was). Moreover, he found time to write a long personal letter to me—the first letter I had from him in years—complaining that a good man like Cripps should not have identified himself with such bad proposals. Why did they seem to him to be so bad? It is not easy to know, even after all the things he himself said.

Proposals for bringing India into partnership in order to prosecute a war more successfully would hardly appeal to the man of non-violence. But he knew that India was not non-violent. So, if there was a danger of invasion by the Japanese, was it not proper that India should undertake the best possible armed defence? Moreover, it was Gandhi who, in 1939, in accordance with his usual practice, had insisted that there ought not to be any bargaining with the British. Help should be offered to them in their emergency without conditions, if it were to be offered at all. In 1942, some of his old colleagues, such as Rajagopalachari, who had worked happily enough with the British during his term as Chief Minister in Madras, believed that the best way to "convert" the British was to help them unconditionally. Rajaji and some others were favourably impressed by the Cripps proposals. Why not accept proposals which, from a government headed by Churchill, were surely more far-reaching than anyone could have imagined a few months earlier? Looked at from the British end, it was indeed amazing that Churchill and such colleagues as James Grigg and John Anderson, two men with records of government service in India, should have been prepared to go so far. But Gandhi was never interested in political compromise as such. He was a Victorian evangelical who believed in "heart conversion," nothing less. When he met a man like Irwin, who seemed to him to be utterly sincere, a man of complete integrity, he was prepared to meet him more than half way. Cripps, perhaps, seemed to him to be too much the able lawyer, who was determined to sell his goods, and to make them out to be rather better quality than they really were. Gandhi was not conscious of any heart conversion of the British Government.

Whatever the reasons, he did not like the Cripps plan; and it may well be that his known opposition was one reason for their final rejection; though the reasons given in the letters sent by Maulana Abul Kalam Azad, as President of the Congress, to Cripps, were fair enough in themselves. So the Cripps mission failed, and all was set for another open conflict between the government and the Congress in the late summer of 1942. It was clear enough to one who was in India later that year that the Delhi establishment of officialdom had disliked Cripps and his mission, and were eager to have another go at the old enemy, the Congress, with Gandhi as enemy number one. This time they would demonstrate finally that Gandhi and Nehru really counted for nothing in India.

The articles Gandhi was writing in his weekly paper, *Harijan*, during the months after the failure of the Cripps mission, showed that he had now made up his mind that a more drastic effort must be made to induce the British Government to part with power at once. Why was this? Quite simply, it would seem that the answer must be: the Japanese threat. By March 1942 the Japanese had overrun Burma. Japanese bombs were dropped in Ceylon and south India. It was widely anticipated, by both Indians and British, that the Japanese would soon attempt an invasion of India, probably starting by descents on various parts of the coast of Bengal or Orissa. In that event, what would be the response of the Indian people as a whole?

The British Government, though it no doubt regretted the failure of the Cripps mission, believed that they could cope with such an invasion. Many thousands of additional troops were arriving in India from the West, first from Britain and later from America, during the summer of 1942. Many thousand additional Indian troops had been recruited. The Delhi authorities never believed that the population as a whole was hostile to the British, so they were not unduly disturbed that the Congress leaders were still unwilling to co-operate. Gandhi had a wholly different picture. He believed that the mass of the people was, in fact, completely alienated from the British Raj; if the Japanese came, he believed that a great many would be either indifferent or would actively help the Japanese. He wanted the whole country to be united in resisting such an invasion. He sent his English follower, Miraben, to the coastal districts of Orissa to find out what the feelings of the people really were in regard to a possible invasion by the Japanese. She reported that the people in the villages were estranged from the government by stories of racial discrimination brought by refugees from Malaya and Burma, and by the "scorched earth" policy already adopted by the Government in Bengal, where most of country boats, on which the fishermen depended for their livelihood, had been destroyed for fear they might be used by the invaders. The people, reported Miraben, were confused, but their dominant feeling was of distrust and fear of the government.

Gandhi believed that the only way to overcome this confusion, and to present a united front to the invader, was for the British to "quit India," leaving the country to the leadership of its own trusted sons. Such an act, he believed, would immediately change the attitude of the people to the British. It would also bring the communities of India into harmony, as they would learn to work together against a common danger. As first expounded, his "quit India" policy involved the withdrawal of British troops. Nehru and others of his colleagues insisted that this was quite unrealistic, as it was out of the question that India, without any training, could offer effective non-violent resistance to the Japanese. The withdrawal of Western troops would be an invitation to the Japanese to come. Gandhi, therefore, in spite of his conviction that a truly non-violent opposition to the Japanese could be undertaken and would be much the most effective, gave way on this, and agreed that an Indian national government would invite the armies already in the country to remain for the period of the war.

One thing can be stated without qualification. Throughout this period, Gandhi was never pro-Japanese, nor was he ever anti-British. He genuinely believed that, if the British would hand over authority and create an Indian national government without delay, it would be the greatest triumph for the British: "The transmutation of ill-will into goodwill towards Britain was worth all the battleships and airships." The recognition of India's independence would be a great victory for the British people.

In the midst of the world's greatest orgy of destruction, Gandhi was more than ever determined to seek for non-violent alternatives for armed conflict. It was a notable concession on his part to accept the continuance of armed forces for defending India against the anticipated Japanese invasion. Gandhi on his side worked out in some detail a plan of action for non-violent non-cooperation with the invaders if and when they arrived. As far as action against the British was concerned, he did not get the opportunity to put any plan into action; but it is clear from notes he had prepared that, if he could not get any response from the Viceroy, the sort of action he planned would still avoid all mass demonstrations; it would have included the illicit manufacture of salt, as in 1931, and a general refusal of land tax. Members of legislatures were to resign. There was to be no interference with the activities of the military, and those who were engaged in essential government work were to continue in their work. "Our object is to make it clear that we will never tolerate Japanese, Nazi or Fascist invasion, nor British rule." His final words in this memorandum are typical: 'If anybody has the spirit of communalism (i.e. any who have bitter feelings against Muslims or the Muslim League) or harbours hatred or ill-will in his heart against any Indian or Englishman, he will best help the struggle by keeping aloof."

It has seemed important to emphasize this; for, when the conflict came, in August 1942, there was far more violence than at the time of any previous civil disobedience; and the government insisted that this was a deliberate policy on the part of the Congress, and especially of Gandhi himself. He was in prison, and unable to defend himself, though ultimately, in the next spring, he undertook a three-week fast on this very issue—of self-purification, no doubt, but also of vigorous protest against the government's accusations.

Let it be confessed that his action in the summer of 1942 was difficult for any Britisher to understand. The writer had lately reached India from beleaguered England, in order to assist civil defence in Bengal. Under the circumstances of the time, the issue of the war was paramount in the thinking of every Britisher who, therefore, assumed that any action taken in India that challenged government authority at that moment could only help the Japanese and Hitler. When my colleague, Richard Symonds, and I visited Sevagram in late June, we had long talks with Gandhi, and felt convinced that he was in no hurry to embark on a civil disobedience campaign; so that it was with something of a shock that we read the Congress Working Committee's resolution of 14 July, forecasting a civil disobedience movement to be led by Gandhi, and insisting that "British rule in India must end immediately." The purpose, indeed, was to make India "a willing partner in a joint enterprise"; but at a time when British and American arms seemed to be defeated almost everywhere, it hardly seemed to make sense to suggest the immediate total change of the Indian government.

After a further visit to Sevagram, I wrote a letter to Gandhi, in which I pointed out that a civil disobedience movement just at this time would seem to every Englishman, including those most friendly to India, like a stab in the back. He prepared a carefully reasoned reply to this, which was to have appeared in the first August number of *Harijan;* but by then he was arrested. Of course, there were weightier voices among his colleagues, especially Rajagopalachari's, persistently saying the same thing, and pleading with Gandhi not to take any action against the British Government at that moment; but they were unable to convince him. On 7 August the All-India Congress Committee, a much larger body than the Working Committee, met in Bombay and endorsed the "Quit India" resolution, leaving it to Gandhi to decide how and when to act. He addressed the Committee thus: "The actual struggle does not commence this very moment. You have placed certain powers in my hands. My first act will be to wait upon His Excellency the Viceroy and plead with him for the acceptance of the Congress demand. This may take two or three weeks. What are you going to do in the meanwhile?" In effect his answer was: "Get on with the constructive programme, spinning and the rest. Act as if you were free men." "After my last night's speech," said Gandhi to his Secretary, Mahadev Desai, "they will not arrest me." But how wrong he was! The arrests of the Congress leaders, including Gandhi, took place a few hours after he said this. There was to be no more parleying, no more attempts to bridge the wide and deep gulf that separated the two sides. Gandhi was not to be given the opportunity to get the movement under way this time.

It is charitable, and perhaps not unreasonable, to suppose that the government genuinely believed that, if they acted like this, and arrested leaders all over the country, there would be no trouble; for their constant thesis was that the Congress, far from representing the mass emotion of the people, was only a crowd of noisy patriots who knew less of the mass mind than the British officials scattered up and down India. Many thousands had been joining the forces. Did not this indicate that the ordinary Indian villager was loyal to the British? Apart from the charismatic personality of the Mahatma who could rouse the villagers to action, the rest of the Congress leadership, including Nehru, appeared to British officialdom to be noisy agitators, with little following.

No doubt, by this time some British officials had become aware that the support given to Congress Party candidates at every election indicated a widespread support for the full demand of the Congress for immediate independence; but even as late as 1944 I met an experienced, intelligent, and liberal-minded official who commented: "Do you notice that the Indian press never even refers to Nehru nowadays? They have forgotten all about him." I could not help wondering what he expected daily newspapers—however ardent their devotion to Nehru—to say about him when he was languishing in jail and any news about his life in jail was guarded in official secrecy. Yet any Englishman who was not in an official position knew how false this was. Especially if you were known to have some sympathy with Gandhi and the Congress, Indians who were notoriously "loyal," and who wore Western clothes and co-operated with the government, Christian and Muslim, no less than Hindu, would come to you privately and express strong support for Gandhi. Did the government really not know, for instance, that men in the armed forces would find opportunities to talk privately to Nehru before his imprisonment and ask him what they should do? "None so blind as those who will not see"; and so the Delhi authorities remained blind to the extent of discontent throughout the country.

They had plenty of opportunity to learn as soon as the arrests became known. In many places something akin to revolution broke out on such a scale as to cause much disturbance to the smooth running of official machinery, especially in the north-east, where the menace of Japanese invasion still hung over the land. The newspapers were not allowed to print the reports of the worst events; so, much of what happened never became known. Rumours may have made it seem worse than it really was. But in due course, when the government was well on top again, and the country outwardly peaceful, the government itself published reports of many incidents of violence, just to show how wicked the Congress leaders had been, especially Gandhi. For he was made out to be the chief culprit, the architect of all the violent sabotage. The government insisted that secret orders had been sent out and that the whole thing had been planned.

What was the truth? As has been shown already, as far as Gandhi was concerned, he had prepared draft plans for action, which would have restricted the "open rebellion" (as he himself called it) to action that would not have seriously embarrassed the government, though he hoped it would demonstrate the strength of conviction in India that the continuance of British rule was intolerable. But Gandhi did not represent ordinary political opinion at this time any more than at earlier times. The younger generation had found his scrupulous policies almost intolerable in the early 1930s. By 1942 the number who were determined to teach the British a sharp lesson had grown. There was by this time a widespread pro-German as well as pro-Japanese sentiment in India. Not that they liked Hitler as they knew little or nothing of Nazi concentration camps. All that they knew was that the Germans were fighting the British. A German missionary friend of mine told me that, in the early months of the war, a number of Indians had said to him: "You know we want you [the Germans] to win." They were incredulous when he assured them that he wanted the British to win.

This younger generation welcomed Gandhi's declaration that the time had now come for an open rebellion, to oblige the British to "quit India." Gandhi had been arrested without the opportunity to issue instructions; so without delay they made up their own minds about what needed to be done. They knew they were not expected to murder Britishers; but that did not rule out sabotage of many kinds, including the burning of police stations, tearing up railway lines, and generally attempting to destroy government property. Especially in Bihar, Bengal, and Assam there was plenty of activity of this kind. It was embarrassing to a hard-pressed government in war time; but also it was the kind of thing that a government can respond to with vigour and confidence. If the rebels had taken their gloves off, so would the government. This kind of thing was much easier to cope with than Gandhian non-violence.

As news of these events came through to Gandhi, he was deeply disturbed. The first thing that happened after his arrest was the sudden death of his devoted and remarkable secretary, Mahadev Desai, a man only fifty years old, who had spent his entire manhood in complete devotion to Gandhi. He was arrested with his master and friend. A week later he fell dead at his side. It is thought that he was deeply distressed at the prospect that Gandhi might undertake another prolonged fast. The sudden action of the government had indeed come as a profound shock to Gandhi. The world in which he lived was so far removed from the thought-world of British officialdom that he had never dreamed that they would act so quickly and so sharply. But the fast was delayed for some months, while correspondence went to and fro between the Viceroy and Gandhi on the matter of the violent activities that had followed the arrests. The correspondence began in friendly terms. The two men had, in fact, liked each other. But as it continued, it became more and more harsh. So, in the end, on 10 February 1943, Gandhi began a twenty-one day fast—a "soothing balm," as he himself described it, to comfort him in the light of the accusation from his friend, Lord Linlithgow, that he, Gandhi, could possibly have encouraged or countenanced the violence that had occurred. This time the government did not release him, but they gave permission for him to be visited by friends, with his own consent. I was one of those he generously let in for a visit. "Strictly for ten minutes only," I was warned as I went in. However, neither Gandhi himself nor the doctor who was in the room watched the passage of time. When I was able to leave his room, about twenty minutes later, the initiative was entirely on my side, and it was not easy to tear myself away from his conversation, though he could only talk in whispers.

As I sat down beside his bed, a typical smile of greeting spread over his face. "Well, so you have come to see me during my fast," he said. "But I must tell you that it is a fraudulent fast. You will understand that this is a capacity fast. I have no intention of dying. During my fasts now I must always take some lime in the water I drink. After a week, the doctors warned me that, unless I was willing to add a little more lime, I might not pull through. So I had to give way. That is why I say it is a fraudulent fast." It did not seem to me that surviving for three weeks on a slightly increased diet of occasional lime-juicy water was a bogus fast; but it did seem entirely typical of Gandhi to judge himself with such severity. So I later told this tale to my friends in letters to England. Months or years later I was shocked to find that in British Government circles the story was being told that Gandhi's three-week fast in Poona in 1943 was a bogus one, and that he had allowed himself to take normal food rather than die. I think Churchill was one of those who told this story. But, unfortunately, Churchill always tried to convince himself that Gandhi was a fraud. Probably, Gandhi said just the same thing about his fast to others; so the story may have come from various sources. In any case, it still seems necessary to expose the truth of the matter.

There was naturally a strong movement among his friends in Poona to try to get Gandhi released, in the hope that he would then end his fast; but this attempt seems to have been ill-conceived. He had said he would fast for twenty-one days. He had said nothing about his release. It would presumably have made no difference. One day his son, Devadas, who was visiting his father each day, told me he was much more concerned about his mother than about his father. And he was right. His father made a good recovery from the fast. His mother died a year later, in February 1944, thus ending a remarkable married life of sixty-two years. Gandhi thought he had come to terms with death long before this. But the gap left by his devoted companion was very deep. Soon afterwards he became ill with malaria; and in May he was unconditionally released. By that time there was a new Viceroy, and some of the bitter feelings of 1942 had dimmed, at least on the British side; but hardly on the Indian, where all the leaders were still in jail, completely silenced. Gandhi felt no satisfaction at his release. The government would not let him see any of his Congress colleagues. However, in July 1944 he wrote to Jinnah, and in September they had a series of meetings. But they could not agree. Jinnah was determined to have the Muslim League accepted as the only representative voice for all the Muslims of India. As the Congress had always been non-communal, and was at this moment under the presidency of a Muslim, Maulana Azad, Gandhi could not possibly agree to Jinnah's demand. He also demanded the partition of India on religious grounds in advance of independence. Gandhi took the view that if partition were to take place, it should come after independence. In other words, let the Muslims agree to independence for an undivided India. Then, if they found that the Hindus were trying to keep them in subjection, they could demand separation for the Muslim majority areas. Gandhi believed to the end that if the country could be united in freedom, the demand for Pakistan would soon disappear. Plainly, the difference between the two men was fundamental. Jinnah had no intention of compromising on his demand for Pakistan.

In 1945 Gandhi began to tour the country again, and in the latter part of the year he spent weeks or even months in Bengal. He was destined to spend a great part of his last years in Bengal, so it may be useful to see just what Bengal meant in the picture of India as a whole.

British rule in India grew out from Bengal, more than from either Bombay or Madras, the other two major early trading settlements. Calcutta was the city from which the East India Company ruled its Indian domain; and it continued as the imperial capital till the move to Delhi in 1911. This move was a blow to the pride of Bengal. Up to that time, Bengal had contributed a great part of the leadership to the national movement. After that, and especially after the death of C.R. Das, this leadership faded out— though it was restored in a new shape by Subhas Chandra Bose, a man twenty-eight years younger than Gandhi, who had challenged Gandhi's leadership more than once in the thirties. Bose was for a much more aggressive political hostility to Britain. When the war came, he escaped to Japan, and there he formed the Indian National Army, to fight alongside the Japanese against the British. He died in an air crash in Formosa.

Gandhi belonged to west India, not to the east; and it was often said that he had comparatively little following in Bengal. It is true that none of the Congress leaders who were close to Gandhi was from Bengal. It is also true that his way of non-violence did not seem to make a wide appeal to the intellectuals of Bengal; but then it did not appeal widely to intellectuals anywhere. Nevertheless, the bonds he had forged when he was at Santiniketan, on his return from South Africa, were never broken; and Rabindranath Tagore, although temperamentally so unlike Gandhi, held him in the highest regard to the end of his life.

At the time of the Congress arrests in 1942, one of the most rebellious areas in all India was the coastal district of Midnapore, in West Bengal, just the area where the Japanese, advised perhaps by Subhas Bose and his friends, might attempt an invasion. British troops, lately arrived from England, were stationed there; and they found that, instead of fighting the Japanese, their job in the autumn of 1942 was to follow up revolutionary suspects, who moved about from village to village. They did not enjoy beating up Indian villagers at all. A few months later quite a different job was given to them. In October, a severe cyclone hit Midnapore, and tidal waves spread ruin over the countryside. Already, Bengal was running short of food, which could no longer be imported from Burma, which was in Japanese hands, so the people of Midnapore were rendered destitute. Relief was organized from Calcutta, and the British Army officers, who by now knew the district well, gave useful assistance in its distribution. They no longer visited the villages to beat people up, but to feed them. However, things went from bad to worse. Food stocks had disappeared. People in Midnapore began to say: "Those who perished in the cyclone were the lucky ones." The villagers crowded into Calcutta, but the queues outside the rice shops were so long that many got nothing. They began to drop dead in the streets. By the end of 1943, it was reckoned that nearly two million people had died of famine in Bengal. No wonder all eyes, including Gandhi's, were turned to Bengal. The Central Government in Delhi was slow to recognise the gravity of the situation; but when Lord Wavell became Viceroy, he immediately turned the army on to help in relief measures, and before long the famine was under control. Adequate food was brought from other parts of India. Distribution was continued until the next harvest.

When Gandhi visited Bengal he was concerned to see for himself what had happened, and also to learn the full Midnapore story. When the local Congress workers told him with some show of pride about their acts of sabotage in 1942, he was bound to tell them that such acts did not accord with non-violence. Non-violence did not only mean non-killing. The destruction of bridges and roads could not change the hearts of men. If there was violence in their hearts, he would almost have preferred the clean violence of killing men—the men they hated. As he toured Bengal, as ever he called his hearers to accept the non-violent way of life, and urged them to self-help in overcoming their recent disasters. B.R. Nanda has summed up this episode of Gandhi's life in these words:

When we recall the emphasis which Gandhi had placed on the training of the people for non-violence since 1934, when we recall his anxiety at the growth in the pre-war years of indiscipline and the spirit of violence, and his studied restraint in conducting the individual civil disobedience movement of 1940-41, we wonder how he could have permitted what was certainly a dangerous plunge in the surcharged atmosphere of that period. He knew the risk inherent in a mass movement in the midst of a global war which had brought the Japanese to the gates of India. But he also saw the passivity of the people and the possibility that they might succumb to the Japanese invader. To rouse a final assertion of their national self-respect without hatred or violence required a miracle, but miracles had happened before....

The courage with which he stood up to the Government, the indomitable faith which he asserted in non-violence at a time when violence seemed to have triumphed all round him, the tenacity with which he attacked the cobwebs which official propagandists spun around the events of 1942—all this raised him further in the esteem and affection of millions of Indians.

8

The End of British Rule
(1945-1947)

IN THE SUMMER of 1945, even before the atom bombs were dropped on Hiroshima and Nagasaki, and before the surrender of the Japanese, Lord Wavell had released all the Congress leaders, and had brought the leaders of Congress and the Muslim League together in a fresh effort to bring these popular leaders into the Viceroy's Executive Council. There need be no doubt about his sincerity; characteristically, when his effort failed, he blamed himself and no one else. But his failure was due to the same old trouble that had led to the breakdown of the Gandhi-Jinnah talks. Jinnah claimed that only he could nominate Muslim members of the Council, and that the Congress nominees must either be Hindus or from some other religious community. But the Congress had always rejected the claim that a Muslim was in any sense different from the rest of his countrymen. In their view, Jinnah's "two-nation" theory was false. In order to get things moving, however, the Muslim President of Congress, Maulana Abul Kalam Azad, was willing to nominate non-Muslims only, for the time being. But Gandhi was not prepared to abandon the principle, even for a moment. He was perfectly willing to see a majority of the Council Muslim, if that would satisfy Jinnah; but it would not. He rightly saw that if he accepted this, he on his side would have abandoned his principle. Gandhi went so far as to suggest that all the members might be chosen by Jinnah; and he repeated this proposal from time to time during the next year of negotiations. But, whether or not he could ever have persuaded the Congress leaders to agree with this (and it would seem doubtful), neither Jinnah nor the government would agree to it. So, once again, the negotiations broke down. What would have happened next, if there had been no change of government in Britain, must be a matter of guess-work. Following their victory at the polls, the Labour Party took office in England; and for the first time, they had a clear and considerable majority over all other parties in the House of Commons. In England, this does not mean that the other parties can be wholly ignored, especially where foreign or imperial policies are involved. In important issues of this sort, it is customary for the government of the day, however large its majority in Parliament may be, to consult the opposition leaders before embarking on new policies. This happened in the development of the new Labour Indian policy; but it was now true that the new government could make up its own mind about that policy first, and then proceed to invite the co-operation of the opposition leaders, who were aware that the government was in a position to act, if necessary, even without the consent of the opposition.

Those of us who had been hammering on the doors of the India Office for years past had an impression of a great change of attitude. Up to 1945, one had felt that the attitude of official Britain was: "Of course, we are ready to bring the Congress leaders (or more likely they would say: 'The Hindu leaders, including the Congress and your friends Gandhi and Nehru') into full partnership any time; but you see what happens. They cannot agree with the Muslims. As long as that goes on, we are bound to continue our rule." And in unofficial conversation, what they seemed to be saying was: "There will never be agreement so long as we can foresee. Full self-government cannot be expected for another twenty years or more. The present Congress leaders are an impossible lot in any case. We don't believe they represent much except as trouble makers. It is far better for the millions of India that British rule should continue, for self-government could only bring conflict and inefficiency and mass starvation. So please stop your starry-eyed and foolish idealism about their capacity to govern themselves."

The change of government brought a startling change of emphasis. It may not have been obvious at once to the ordinary citizen of England, and it certainly took a long time to convince the Indian public that there was a real change. Even the officials at the India Office found Lord Pethick-Lawrence, the new Secretary of

State, very much like a good old-fashioned liberal. And had not Attlee, the new Prime Minister, been a member of the Simon Commission, whose proposals for the evolution of Indian self-government in 1928 had hardly been revolutionary? The one man the officials were afraid of was Sir Stafford Cripps, but he was not in a position, perhaps, to exercise much direct influence on Indian policy.

Those of us who had been active in the India Conciliation Group, however, soon began to find a new wind blowing. The writer, who had been in India with a section of the Friends Ambulance Unit in 1942 and 1943, and whose presence had once or twice been embarrassing to the government (and perhaps to the F.A.U.) had been trying to return to India in the summer of 1945. Amery at the India Office pointed out that passages to India were still so difficult that many wives of officials had not yet been able to join their husbands, from whom they had been separated for years. Would it be decent to give priority to someone who was known as a critic of government policy, and whose presence in India might only stiffen Gandhi in his intransigence? But a few weeks later, when I talked to Lord Pethick-Lawrence, he simply said: "You are just the people who can help us"; and within a few months, both Agatha Harrison and I were in India, and in daily contact with Gandhi and other recently released Congress leaders. It was, in fact, extremely difficult to convince them that the new British Government was determined to part with power. They had seen little or no difference between the two earlier Labour governments and the Conservative governments in their approach to Indian problems. Had not the conflict of the Irwin period taken place with a Labour government in office? And if the new government meant business, why did it not immediately release all the political prisoners, instead of doing it slowly and piecemeal? It was clear that nothing but strong acts would convince the men and women who had spent the last three years or more in jail. Why should a victorious Britain be more generous to Indian nationalism than the hard-pressed Britain which had only been willing to go as far as the Cripps proposals of 1942? And in any case, would Britain, just trying to recover from the devastating effects of the war and the air-raids, have time to make India anything but a secondary issue in the next few years? Gandhi was at least as sceptical as many of his colleagues.

At the beginning of 1946, a parliamentary delegation, consisting of members of the three major British parties—Labour, Conservative, and Liberal—from both Houses of Parliament, visited India, on the initiative of the government, not indeed to expound a new policy, but primarily to indicate the concern of Britain to have a close-up view of India after the war, and to judge what the strength and demands of the main Indian parties now were. It was noted that one of the Labour members was Reginald Sorensen, who had for years been almost the only member of the House of Commons who consistently pleaded the "Congress" view in Parliament. Even liberal-minded fellow-members had found his views "very extreme." All the members of the delegation appeared to be friendly towards Indian aspirations. But they were as cordial to Jinnah as to Gandhi; their tour of India no doubt helped to reassure some; but the scepticism of most Indian nationalists was much too deep to be so readily broken down.

In February, it was announced that three Cabinet members of the government would soon leave for India to negotiate a settlement. And on 15 March, Attlee in the House of Commons defined government policy in words which were at some points a good deal more explicit than anything a Prime Minister had ever said before:

> India must choose what will be her future constitution. I hope that the Indian people may elect to remain within the British Commonwealth.... But if she does so elect it must be by her own free will.... If, on the other hand, she elects for independence, in our view she has a right to do so.... We are very mindful of the rights of minorities, and minorities should be able to live free from fear. On the other hand, we cannot allow a minority to place a veto on the advance of the majority.

Some of the other phrases in this speech sounded very much like the old cautious language that had been used over and over again; so in spite of these new words, the speech did not yet convince sceptical Congress leaders that the wind had changed. Most people were inclined to wait till the Cabinet Ministers arrived, to see how far they were prepared to go. The Cabinet Mission reached India on 24 March 1946. It consisted of Lord Pethick-Lawrence (the Secretary of State for India), Sir Stafford Cripps, and A.V. Alexander.

The first two were already familiar with India from recent visits, and both were known to Gandhi. Alexander was new to all this. He was the least radical of the three; indeed, it was rather ingeniously suggested that, although all three were members of the Labour Cabinet, they might also be regarded as representing the three parties in England. Cripps was the convinced, even rather left-wing, socialist; Pethick-Lawrence had the temperament of a Liberal; Alexander was in some respects a Tory. Anyhow, they made a good team. It was expected that their work might occupy a month, perhaps a little more. But they did not leave Delhi for England till 29 June. That is to say, in order to complete their task, they stayed on through the torrid heat of May and June, when the thermometer is rarely below 80°F, and often above 100°F. To be sure, they were much of the time in air-conditioned rooms. But they were working hard all the time. Pethick-Lawrence was already in his seventies. Cripps had a breakdown which necessitated absolute quiet for a week. Probably, it was this persistence, more than any other factor, which finally convinced India that they meant business, and that they would not allow any hurdle placed by the Muslim League or any other party to stop the handing over of political authority.

Elections had been held all over India, which had resulted in a complete victory for the Congress Party in all the "general" seats throughout the country, whereas all the specially reserved Muslim seats in the Central Assembly were won by the Muslim League. In the Provincial Assemblies, the results were similar, except that in the predominantly Muslim North-West Frontier Province, the Muslims who supported the Congress and who opposed Jinnah on Pakistan won a majority of the seats. In the Punjab also, Jinnah had not yet consolidated his position; and the Unionists, who opposed partition, were still strong enough to form a new ministry with Congress support, leaving the Muslim League in opposition. But in the other crucial province, Bengal, where the two religious communities were nearly equal in numbers, the Muslim League had by this time been able to capture the ministry.

When the Cabinet Mission arrived in India, it was clear that the Congress and the Muslim League were the two really powerful all-India parties who, if possible, ought to be brought into an agreement before the final handover could take place peace-

fully. The Mission spent its first few days meeting every kind
of leader of various parties and minorities, also the British Governors
of provinces, and anyone else who had a fair claim to be heard;
but thereafter they settled down to discussion with the leaders of
the Congress and the Muslim League, the former including Gandhi,
who had come to Delhi at the request of both the British Mission
and the leaders of Congress. Gandhi gave his personal views to
the Mission a few days after its arrival. He urged the immediate
release of political prisoners who were still being detained. Also,
in order to convince the people that the needs of the poorest were
of paramount consideration, the salt tax should be abolished. As
for the Interim Government, let the British invite Jinnah to head
any government he might care to form. In this way Gandhi still
hoped to avoid the division of the country, and to convince the
Muslims that they had nothing to fear by entering freely into a
united India, free from British control. It was, in fact, Gandhi's
conviction all through that the British order of procedure was
wrong: first let them hand over effective authority to whomsoever
they would; then, and only after that, let the Muslim electorate
decide whether it really wished to secede out of India. So long
as the date and the method of the British withdrawal remained
uncertain, he was convinced that the Muslim League would find
every excuse for demanding more and more. Bargaining would
continue. Not only the Muslim League, but other pressure groups
—the Princes of the semi-independent States, the Untouchables
who followed Dr Ambedkar, the Anglo-Indian community and
others—would insist that their interests should be fully safeguarded.
But Gandhi felt that all their fears were in the main unjustified, and
that a strong Congress government, under the leadership of such a
man as Jawaharlal Nehru, who throughout his life had loathed
communalism, especially Hindu communalism, and who was
determined to make India a secular State; one who, moreover,
counted Muslims among his closest personal friends—such a government would soon reassure the minority religious communities.
But if even that prospect did not satisfy the British or the Muslims,
then Jinnah could form the new government. In any case, let the
British stop the game of holding out the carrot of freedom just in
front of the donkey's nose, promising to put it into its mouth as
soon as there was agreement on what could never be agreed upon.

But he could not persuade the British, not even Pethick-Lawrence and Cripps. They went on striving for an agreement as to how much of the carrot should go into which mouth.

Agreement between the Congress and the Muslim League was not achieved in the first round of talks in Delhi in April; so the government invited leaders of the two parties and Gandhi to a further session of the conference at Simla at the beginning of May. A house belonging to the family of Sir Maharaj Singh and his brother and sisters, a mile or more away from the Viceregal Lodge, was offered to Gandhi, and he was asked what staff he would need to accommodate. This question led him to a moral crisis which needs to be described, even though none of those closest to him seemed fully to understand what it was or why it came to a head at this moment.

When he began to prepare a list of those who at the moment were helping him with his work, he found it quickly mounted up. The exact number I do not now recall, but I believe it was over thirty. Quite a big entourage for a saint who tries to live at a minimum standard. Anyone might have commented thus; and so, apparently, he suddenly felt. He gathered his secretaries together, and his household, and told them that he had come to the conclusion that he must manage without them. None of them were to come with him to Simla. This meant, especially, that his secretary, Pyarelal Nayar, who had been with him constantly since the death of Mahadev Desai, and indeed for some years before that, was no longer to stay with him. The same was the case with several others who had been very near to him and usually working along-side him for months or even years. The company who shared the house with him at Simla for the next ten days included his close colleague, Vallabhbhai Patel, and his daughter Maniben, who acted as housekeeper, and summoned us peremptorily to meals. (If we delayed for five seconds at our writings when the bell had rung, the voice of Maniben would be heard: "So you do not want any food today.") Acharya Kripalani, another old colleague in the Congress leadership, was there, and Khan Abdul Gaffar Khan, sometimes called the "Frontier Gandhi," a tall Pathan frontiersman, who had been converted to the way of non-violence, and had organised the Khudai Khidmatgars, sometimes called "Red-shirts"—but they were in no way communist—in order to

bring peace and well-being to the impoverished and warlike tribes
living between India and Afghanistan. It was mainly due to the
work of Abdul Gaffar Khan and his brother, Dr Khan Sahib, that
the Muslims of the frontier had voted against the Muslim League
and for the Congress in recent elections. Gandhi also invited
Agatha Harrison, Sudhir Ghosh, and myself to be with him. Sudhir
was a young Bengali who, whilst a student in Cambridge, had been
in touch with the India Conciliation Group in London; he thereupon
started a group to promote Indo-British understanding in Cambridge, and on his return to Calcutta he induced the Anglican
Bishop of Calcutta, Dr Foss Westcott, to head a group for conciliation and understanding there. During the imprisonment
of the Congress leaders, he was in touch with Rajagopalachari,
who was exploring ways for building bridges between the British
and the Congress, and between Gandhi and Jinnah. When Gandhi
was released, Sudhir came into direct contact with him. Gandhi
was impressed with his ability to win the confidence of British
officialdom, and he made much use of him in the next few months.
Sudhir had quickly won the ear of the members of the Cabinet
Mission, and during the time at Simla he usually accompanied
Gandhi as he set off each morning to join the talks at the Viceregal
Lodge. Rajkumari Amrit Kaur, who was a sister of Sir Maharaj
Singh, and who shared with another brother the house nearest to
the one where Gandhi was living and who for several years had
undertaken secretarial work for him, shared with Agatha Harrison
the job of coping with the immense correspondence that poured in
on Gandhi, day by day. Of course, he always undertook a great
deal of letter-writing, in answer to his innumerable friends and
correspondents, with his own hand, or rather his own hands; long
before this he had trained himself to write with either hand; so
when one hand was tired he turned to the other. Now that he had
dismissed his secretarial staff, or most of it, he tried to cope with
an even larger proportion himself; but to do it all was a physical
impossibility; and although he worked his mind and body over
longer hours than most people, he knew that there was a limit;
and that, as he himself put it, "overworking the body is a form of
violence." So in fact there was plenty of work during those days
for both Amrit Kaur and Agatha Harrison who I believe was the
only one of us who could use a typewriter. Nevertheless, one of

Amrit's brothers expressed some indignation that the Mahatma's conscience should have thrown away the help of Pyarelal and thereby put a very heavy burden on his sister. I am not sure that she was really doing any more than she had often done before.

Agatha, Sudhir, and I—Gandhi once referred to us playfully as "the three persons of the trinity"—were also encouraged to help in the informal contacts with the staff of the Cabinet Mission. Cripps had brought with him for this mission two men, both of whom I had met earlier; Bill Short, army man with a long association with India, who had a special intimacy with the Sikh community, and Woodrow Wyatt, a young Labour member of Parliament, who had been giving some attention to Indian affairs. After breakfast each morning, armed with my binoculars, I would set off down the "wrong path," leading away from Simla; if any of the patiently waiting journalists accosted me they would say: "Are you going to look for birds?" "Yes" was my truthful reply. But, having reached the lower road, I turned along it towards Simla; and unless the birds delayed me, as they sometimes did, within thirty or forty minutes I found myself at the hotel where Bill and Woodrow were living, and would try to review the progress made the day before, as it had appeared to their chiefs and to mine. Sometimes they dropped some useful tip, which I could take back to share with Gandhi later in day. Of course, there was direct confrontation each day between the three groups of leaders; but as everyone knows, even with the best of good will, those who stand on different sides at such a time do not always carry away the same impression of what has been said and intended.

Often it seemed as if they were boggling over incredible trifles. I found myself saying again and again, *solvitur ambulando;* but no doubt that was due to my Western impatience, and partly to my confidence that the British Ministers meant business this time. On the Indian side, though part of the explanation may have been that there were too many lawyers, who could split too many hairs, the main reason for their insistence on dotting every "I" twice over and crossing every "T" was that their profound distrust, following long and recent imprisonments, was not yet put to rest. The old steel-frame of government in India was still working; and from Gandhi's point of view, the refusal even to abolish the salt tax as a gesture of accepting what he and his colleagues cared most about seemed to mean that there was still not that change of heart he was looking for. Even these Cabinet Ministers seemed to believe that they knew best what was in the interest of India.

One afternoon, as I was walking back towards Summer Hill, the car with Gandhi and Sudhir overtook me. They stopped and picked me up. As I got into the car, Gandhi said: "Horace, you must try to think of the best Indian judge or arbiter to settle one or two outstanding points. We seem to have reached agreement this afternoon, but there are one or two matters still to be decided, and someone from neither of the two major communities must be found to arbitrate. Probably a Christian would be the best." This seemed to be good news. Jinnah appeared to have capitulated. Gandhi's impression was supported by the Cabinet Mission. Alas, next morning Jinnah explained that he had not meant what they all thought he had meant. The agreement of yesterday fell apart again. In the end, the Simla talks had to be abandoned without any agreement. It was left to the Cabinet Mission to work out proposals which in due course they submitted to the Congress and Muslim League leaders.

The Cabinet Mission's plan rejected the Muslim League's demand for partition. It emphasised the need to keep India united. It attempted to meet the fears represented by the Muslim League by an ingenious plan. The Union of India, including all the Princely States as well as the provinces, would have authority over foreign affairs, defence, and communications, with power to collect revenue for these purposes. Next, the country would be divided into three groups; a north-west group of provinces, a north-east group, and the rest. In the north-west, the majority of the population would be Muslims, and in the north-east Muslims and Hindus would be about equal. Provincial autonomy would remain for many important subjects, and no province would be forced into a group against its will. Thus, although Assam, a province with a majority of Hindus, was provisionally assigned to the north-east group with Bengal, it could decide to opt out of it and remain with the main group of peninsular India. Provision was also made for the setting up of a constitution-making body. The procedure laid down was as follows. In the first place, the provincial representatives would meet in three sections. These sections would then proceed to settle Provinicial Constitutions and decide whether any group constitution should be set up for those provinces. This was coupled with a provision giving the freedom to Provinces to opt out of the group, some time after the election under the new constitution to be framed by majority of the representatives of the Provinces in the section under the new constitution. This was, roughly, the Cabinet Mission's plan for avoiding partition.

Gandhi's first reactions to this plan were favourable. He congratulated the Cabinet Mission for having evolved a plan which meant that at last the British would get off India's back. On two successive days, at his evening prayer meeting in Delhi, which was daily attended by hundreds of people, he spoke in warm praise of the Mission and its plan. So it was with some perplexity that even some of his close friends found in the next number of *Harijan*, his weekly paper, the following rather cryptic sentences:

> After four days of searching examination ... my conviction abides that it is the best document the British Government could have produced under the circumstances.... My compliment, however, does not mean that what is best from the British standpoint is also best or even good from the Indian. Their best may possibly be harmful.

His approval was however subject to the condition that no province should be forced to belong to a group against the wishes of its own representatives in the section, since the Cabinet Mission had claimed that the whole basis of their plan was voluntary.

As the days went by, it became more and more clear that he was unhappy about the whole plan, and wanted the Congress to have nothing to do with it. Why? It is difficult at this range of time to be confident, but his reason seemed to be that the freedom to a Province to belong to a group or not which had been given in an earlier part of the Cabinet Mission's statement was in effect taken away from the Province itself and made over to the majority in the section which would settle the provincial constitutions. He still wanted to see the British handover power to some responsible Indian interim government, either the Congress leaders or, as he himself kept urging, to Jinnah and his colleagues of the Muslim League; then let them decide whether India was to remain united, what powers were to be with the States, and what with the

Centre, and so on. In fact, his whole approach was different from that of the Cabinet Mission.

It seemed strangely ironical that his deepest cleavage was with the Secretary of State, Lord Pethick-Lawrence. Lord Pethick-Lawrence, as a young man, had identified himself with the suffragette activity in England; he had been sent to jail, where he refused food and submitted to the intolerable humiliation of forcible feeding. To the end of his life, he defended this action, and claimed that, when people are denied the full use of democratic rights (as the voteless women of England were), they are justified in resorting to civil disobedience, and have the right to make their rulers as uncomfortable as possible. He had sympathised, therefore, with the civil disobedience movement led by Gandhi in India, and had supported the Indian demand for self-government when very few British people did so. Now he and Gandhi seemed to be unable to understand each other. Lord Pethick-Lawrence took the view that, so long as he was Secretary of State, he must discharge his responsibilities, and he could not hand them over to any Indian statesman, whatever popular backing he might have in the country. He was determined to find the quickest possible way of transferring power, but it must be by constitutional methods, and it must be done in such a way that anarchy would not result. In other words, he must try to act in a way that would satisfy both the Congress and the Muslim League.

The atmosphere was so strained that a group of Quakers who were in close touch with both sides (Cabinet Mission and Congress leaders)—Agatha Harrison, Ranjit Chetsingh, and I—invited them all to an informal evening party at the New Delhi Y.W.C.A., where Agatha was staying. This was thought to have broken some of the ice; I recall that Mrs Sarojini Naidu, in particular, assured us towards the end of the evening that she believed it had done real good in making possible some frank informal conversation. Confidence, she thought, had been to some extent restored. Yet at the end of the evening, when Lord Pethick-Lawrence had left, Gandhi turned to us and said: "Did you notice that, as he stepped into his car, he said 'good-bye' to me? I think that means that he is not expecting to see me again." We were at pains to make sure, as we naturally believed, that his "good-bye" was no more than a polite salute "until we meet again in a day or two."

An amusing incident at the same time may be recorded. Although they were meeting in conference frequently, letters were exchanged in an effort to clear up misunderstandings. One day when Nehru came in to see Gandhi, the latter showed him a letter he was proposing to send to Lord Pethick-Lawrence. Nehru suddenly burst out laughing: "You can't address him like that," he said, "as if you were addressing God." Gandhi had begun his letter, "Dear Lord." (After all, why not? You address a letter to a commoner, "Dear Sir," so why not a Lord, "Dear Lord"?) From such trivial examples, one may see that even for a man who had used the English language, as much as Gandhi had done, over many years, there was still room for plenty of misunderstanding. It was, in fact, just for this sort of reason that he invited people like Agatha and myself to be with him. He often showed us his drafts of letters, to get them vetted from the angle of English mentality; and Agatha would say from time to time: "Gandhiji, I wish you could alter this phrase. It sounds harsh, and I don't believe you really want it to"; and as soon as he got the point, he would revise it accordingly. Perhaps it would have been useful to have an Indian national vetting letters from Viceroys and Secretaries of State.

On receipt of the Cabinet Mission's plan, Jinnah replied that no answer could be given by the Muslim League until the Working Committee had met; and this could not be for another ten days or so. Hence, there was a further adjournment, and Gandhi was invited to spend the time at one of the Birla mansions in the Himalayas at Mussoorie. Sardar Patel went there with him. He encouraged Agatha and Sudhir and myself to come for a few days. Agatha decided to remain in Delhi, but Sudhir and I went to Mussoorie. We returned to Delhi sooner than Gandhi, and he sent a message through me to the Cabinet Mission. I forget its exact purport; but it seemed on the whole to be reassuring; so when I reached Delhi, Agatha and I got in touch with the Mission, and asked if we might come round. "Yes" was the reply. They were all together, and would be glad to see us. The Muslim League Working Committee was by then in session, and its statement was expected at any time. I made my report to the three Cabinet Mission members, and we remained talking for a time. Suddenly a government messenger appeared, bringing a letter, which he handed to

Lord Pethick-Lawrence. He spent two or three minutes reading it, while the rest of us remained silent. Then he passed it on to Sir Stafford Cripps who began to read it. After a moment, he said to Lord Pethick-Lawrence: "May I read it out?" "By all means." So he read it out. It was the reply from the Muslim League. The opening phrases were full of indignation, because the Cabinet Mission had not agreed to the immediate establishment of Pakistan. However, when all the subsidiary clauses with their criticism and complaints were out of the way, the substance of the letter followed, accepting the Cabinet Mission's plan, as a step towards Pakistan. "I do not mind how much they abuse us, provided they accept," said Lord Pethick-Lawrence.

I was specially interested in this acceptance, for Gandhi had just assured me at Mussoorie that he had no doubt that Jinnah would reject the plan. He was not always right in his estimate of Jinnah.

The Congress in due course also accepted the Plan, again with certain reservations, so that each side was inclined to say that the others had not genuinely accepted it. But Gandhi had in the end thrown his weight against acceptance; and there was still plenty of misunderstanding and discord. The tangled negotiations of that summer have been adequately described in various books, and need not be repeated in detail here. In the end, the leaders of Congress were asked to form a provisional government, still presided over by the Viceroy, and Jinnah was very indignant. He began to prepare for revenge. But, if Gandhi's advice had been followed, the Congress leaders would not have been invited to form the new government, and the British might have been obliged to ask Jinnah to do this, which was exactly what Gandhi had begged them to do, whereas Lord Pethick-Lawrence and his colleagues thought such a course quite unrealistic.

Jinnah and the Muslim League considered that they had been betrayed and, accordingly, planned a Direct Action Day of protest, during the middle of August. In the great city of Calcutta, where the two religious communities were almost equally balanced, the effect of all this was a frightful orgy of killing. For several days, Muslim and Hindu toughs went about the city slaughtering every member of the opposite community they could find, using all kinds of murderous weapons they could lay hands on. The total number killed during those days has never been exactly ascertained, but it ran into thousands. Some weeks later, the killing and pillage spread to east Bengal, where many Hindus were driven from their village homes, and some were killed. Gandhi went to east Bengal, to try to stop the strife. He was always more at home among village people than in the towns. He soon decided that his task was to walk from village to village, meeting Muslims and Hindus, persuading the Muslims, who were in a majority there, to treat the Hindus as their brethren, and at the same time restoring courage to the terrified Hindus, persuading them to return to their villages and to rebuild their homes. In this undertaking he could count on nothing but opposition from the Muslim League, for Jinnah's thesis was that Muslims and Hindus constituted separate nations, and ought to live in separate States. When they began killing one another, therefore, Jinnah felt that his thesis was supported, and that the right solution was to give the Muslims their own State of Pakistan, and the Hindus, if they were in a minority, should leave the area and migrate to some predominantly Hindu area. The great and populous province of Bengal, which was predominantly Muslim in the east and Hindu in the west, had for some time been ruled by a Muslim League ministry (still with a British Governor, of course, who had special duties in respect to law and order); the Chief Minister was H.S. Suhrawardy. I had known Suhrawardy quite well a couple of years earlier, during the Bengal famine and its aftermath, when as Minister for Civil Supplies, he had actively encouraged the Friends Ambulance Unit, with which I was associated, in its efforts to relieve the suffering of the village people, especially the children.

One day in the summer of 1946, as I was walking alone with Gandhi after his prayer-meeting at Delhi, we began to talk about Bengal and about Suhrawardy in particular. I think I spoke of some of his good qualities, which I had noticed during those earlier years. "Do you realise that he is a bad man? " asked Gandhi. I replied: "Yes, I daresay; but I am not quite sure what you mean by that. We are mostly partly bad and also partly good, aren't we?" "Dr Jekyll and Mr Hyde," he commented. "I read that book by Robert Louis Stevenson in South Africa many years ago. There is much truth in it." When, a month or two later, he began his pilgrimage ' through the east Bengal villages, Gandhi asked for Suhrawardy's support in his work. He got a promise of

qualified support. Whenever he ran into difficulties, he appealed
to Suhrawardy for help, and to some extent he got it. One day
during that autumn, I happened to be in Writers' Buildings (the
name of the old Bengal secretariat), and I was talking to Suhra-
wardy's secretary. He told me of a letter that had come from
Gandhi in east Bengal. In this, Gandhi had recalled an occasion
some twenty-five years before, in the days when many of the present
Muslim League leaders were still active members of the Congress.
A committee meeting was being held in Calcutta, which the young
Suhrawardy was attending. After most other members had spoken,
Gandhi had said: "Let us hear what Suhrawardy Sahib has to say."
"You should not call me that," said young Suhrawardy. "What
should I call you then?" asked Gandhi. "Call me your son." In his
letter of October 1946, Gandhi recalled this incident of long ago,
and added: "May I call you my son today?" Suhrawardy showed
this letter to his secretary, and he was visibly touched by it.

Meanwhile, there had been widespread outbreaks of violence in
Bihar, the province next to Bengal to the west. Here, Hindus, the
majority community, attacked and slaughtered their Muslim neighbours who fled from their villages. "Now," said many people, "Mr
Gandhi must go to Bihar, for his job is to stop this barbarous action
of the Hindus—his own community." He did not see that to be
his duty. He still believed that his job was to stay in Bengal,
fighting the fear that had overtaken the Hindu minority there. He
called on Muslims of courage to go to Bihar and infect the Muslim
villagers with courage, so that they would return to their homes.
And in fact his close friend, Abdul Ghaffar Khan, from the
Frontier Province, did go there and tried to restore the courage
of the Muslim community.

Some time during the winter, I arranged to spend a few days
walking with Gandhi in east Bengal. Before leaving Calcutta, I
called on Suhrawardy. "Had he any message for Mr Gandhi?"
I asked. "Yes," he replied, "give him my love and tell him to go
to Bihar as soon as possible." I duly delivered this double message
of affection and criticism, and we agreed that the mixture was
typical Suhrawardy "Jekyll and Hyde." "Hyde" was still assuring
people that the old man was a fraud, and that it was only simple-
minded Britishers who were taken in by him. One day I took
Muriel Lester to call on Suhrawardy. She was spending a few

weeks passing through India. He treated her to this kind of talk, perhaps to see if he could get a rise out of her. "That is very interesting," she said quietly: "I have heard the same kind of thing before."

The chief things I recall from the days I spent with Gandhi in east Bengal are seemingly remote from his mission of peace and healing. One evening, when he asked me to come into the hut where the village people were giving him hospitality for the night, I noticed that they had draped the ceiling with a beautiful fabric, dark blue or nearly black, covered with golden stars. Gandhi was looking down at the ground, as he normally did. I could not help wondering if he had noticed his ceiling. "What a beautiful ceiling you have here," I said. "Yes," he replied, "I am very fond of the popular art of Bengal. It is simple and beautiful." But, as I have already noted in an earlier chapter, the triumphant shouts of welcome with which the villagers received him made quite another impression on him. Not only did he find this kind of reception wholly inappropriate; he also found the shrill cries unpleasant to the ear; he stopped his ears while it lasted.

Gandhi knew that his presence in many of these poor villages was embarrassing for the people, who were determined to give free hospitality to him and his companions. He cut down his personal attendants to the minimum; but he also made arrangements for one or two press correspondents, and for an occasional visitor, such as I was. From time to time one of his political colleagues from Delhi came for a day or two. With this in mind, he insisted on having the least possible space for himself. One of his granddaughters was with him, and she shared the same room, at times the same bed. There had been references to this in the press, which I had not seen, and one or two of his colleagues, including Sardar Patel, had written to him, imploring him not to embark on such "experiments" when he was engaged on such a vital political campaign. At one of our talks together, Gandhi explained all this to me. He made it clear that he had decided that it was right to act as he was doing on two grounds: first, because of the acute problem of accommodation in these poor villages, where a number of the families would be normally sleeping all in one room (though never, of course, both sexes in one bed, except for husband and wife); but beyond this, he felt obliged to test his granddaughter's assertion that she had absolutely no sexual feeling, but regarded him as her mother (her mother had died). And as he told me all this, he went on to say, with something like enthusiasm:' 'If I can show that sexual feeling can be totally conquered, it will be of real value to the human race.'' It is certain that Gandhi always had deep interest in matters connected with sex, and had strong and unusual convictions here, as in so many other fields of human behaviour.

After telling me all this, he asked me to think it over, and he hoped that the next day I would have some comment to make—he added that he wanted me to give my judgment "as a Christian." I felt as if he was thinking of me as a substitute for his beloved Charlie Andrews, who had died several years before, and whose opinion "as a Christian" would no doubt have been well worth attending to. However, I did my best next day, and began by saying that one of my mottoes had always been: "Moderation in all things." To illustrate this, I said that I could never feel any admiration for St. Simon Stylites, living on the top of his pillar. Gandhi replied that he liked my motto; and as for Simon Stylites, he agreed that he was not an admirable character. He even got angry when his food was not brought punctually. But Gandhi felt that, perhaps, I had not understood the pressing reasons for his action. However, he would see what others of his friends would say. A little later he wrote to tell me that he had reverted to separate beds for his granddaughter and himself, owing chiefly to the pleading of his old friend, Thakkar Bapa. He still was not convinced that what he had done was anything but good in itself, but his friends wanted him to desist, so out of deference to their wishes, he had done so.

Thakkar Bapa is a name that is presumably hardly known in the West, so ignorant are we of the truly great men who live in "remote" parts of the world, and so limited are our sources of information. But in a truly civilised world, his fame might well have outshone the fame of others, perhaps even of Gandhi himself. A.V. Thakkar, at this time a man of nearly eighty years, had given his whole mature life to the needy, as a member of the remarkable Servants of India Society, founded by G.K. Gokhale. He fought for the redemption of the Indian untouchables and for the many tribal people of India; he lived among them and helped them to help themselves. He was never in what is normally called "politics," so his desire to see Gandhi abandon this particular experiment had little connection with the political issues that were uppermost in the minds of his political colleagues. He was one, whose long life of selfless service had given him the best right to speak out on moral issues.

Here was Gandhi, embarked on one of the noblest public actions of his whole life, spending months in walking from village to village of east Bengal, bringing back goodwill and understanding after the communal riots that had rent the Noakhali district, yet at the same time so vividly aware of the personal moral problems that beset mankind in all ages and in every part of the world that he was determined to demonstrate if he could through his own actions that the mind of man could be master of sexual impulse. It was typical of him that he would not use the argument that this was not a convenient moment to undertake such an experiment. He was confronted with a situation, and he must meet it as it came to him.

During my few days with him I noted several things that had not been evident to me before. Certainly he was giving his full mind to the main job on hand. As he went round the stricken villages and watched the re-building of houses, he discussed the details of house-building as if he were a professional builder. Again, as he spoke to the people of the recent communal troubles from which, in this part of India, the Hindus were the chief sufferers, he warned them that, unless they abandoned their privileged position (most of the land and other property belonged to Hindus), they must expect more trouble in the near future. In other words, he recognised that the Muslim majority had good grounds for demanding better treatment. This was before Pakistan had been agreed to. It was not yet decided that the Muslims would soon become the dominant community politically. But Gandhi saw clearly that their economic grievances were real and in urgent need of attention.

But along with this, he was still fascinated by the problems of personal morality. He showed himself well read in the lives of the early Christian saints. He was impressed by the folk art of Bengal. These things are worth noting, for it is sometimes assumed that he was a narrow-minded ascetic who knew little and cared little about all those aspects of life which were irrelevant to his main concerns.

Gandhi had arrived in the Noakhali district in late October 1946; he remained there till March 1947. For the first two months he lived in one village, Srirampur, whilst he sent his colleagues, Pyarelal, Sushila Nayyar, Sucheta Kripalani, and others, to work from other village centres. Then, from the beginning of January 1947, he began his daily pilgrimage from village to village. Most of this time he walked barefoot, in spite of the fact that the opposition, meaning presumably men who were backing the Muslim League point of view that friendship between Muslim and Hindu was neither possible nor desirable, deliberately fouled the paths or spread briars and thorns along them. His devoted helpers went out early, even earlier than he himself started, to clear and clean the path.

Finally, after two months of this, on 2 March, he left for Bihar, promising to return to Bengal if he was needed. Several of his trusted colleagues remained in Noakhali.

When the news of the Bihar massacres first reached him, he had announced that he would immediately start a fast without limit unless he got news that the killing in Bihar had stopped. This threat, and drastic action from the Central Government (Nehru's government, it may now be called), did effect an immediate cessation of the violence; but the after-effects of the holocaust remained, and it was no easy matter to persuade the terrified Muslims to return to their homes. For one thing, the Muslim League did not want them to do so. Its direct action was intended to prove the need for Pakistan; so the more the communities could be kept apart, and the more hostile they showed themselves to each other, the sooner Pakistan would be realised. And the more little pockets of pure Islam, of Muslims unadulterated with Hindus, could be established up and down the country, the better became the argument for a very extensive Pakistan, which should include all these Muslim enclaves. This appeared to be Jinnah's argument. So, although Gandhi's action was primarily humanitarian, it was also true that his aim was political. He believed that India was one nation, not two. Hindus and Muslims had lived in the same villages up and down the country for centuries; they were inextricably mixed up together. And although they lived a distinct social life and scarcely ever intermarried (but they sometimes joined together in festivals, both Muslim and Hindu, not to mention the

Christian Christmas), in the villages they lived together on good terms; communal riots were recent and had been almost confined to large towns. So his argument that the demand for Pakistan was a purely political demand, invented by political leaders, with no genuine popular backing, was based on essential facts. He was determined to win the two communities back to decent neighbourliness or die in the attempt.

In Bihar he was as outspoken as ever. He utterly rejected the Hindu argument that their action was justifiable revenge for the events in Noakhali. He also rejected the Muslim argument that they could not ever again live in safety among a predominantly Hindu population. He was determined to get the Muslims back to their old homes as a result of invitations from the Hindus who had driven them out. He had a considerable measure of success.

Whilst he was thus working at the grassroots, trying still to save India from civil war and from partition, political events were moving slowly forward towards the handing over of power. The Viceroy, Lord Wavell, had induced members of the Muslim League to come into the Central Government. It was hoped that this would pacify the country; but it did not. To men like Nehru, who were longing to get on with the essential problems of development, planning for the economic and social renewal of India, the presence of these Muslim colleagues was a source of constant frustration. As far as I know, only one man in this Central Ministry, Mr Rajagopalachari, had faith that they could ever become a united team.

The administration was running down. The future was uncertain. No one knew what was expected of him or what his position would be in a few months' time; so there was a dangerous lack of initiative in the government; while Jinnah's "direct action" spread from one area to another. All through this year (1946-47), Calcutta was divided into hostile camps. Hindus and Muslims did not dare to cross certain invisible lines in the streets. Episodes of violence and killing recurred week after week. Then Punjab, another province where Hindus and Muslims were almost equal in number, became the scene of direct action.

On 20 February Attlee announced in the House of Commons that the British Government had decided to hand over the government into Indian hands completely, not later than June 1948. They

still hoped that they could hand over power to a single acceptable
government; but if not, it might be necessary to hand over to
independent provinces in some areas. In order to get ahead with
this policy, Lord Mountbatten was replacing Lord Wavell as
Viceroy.

Lord Mountbatten immediately got to work; so did Jinnah.
The latest British plan seemed to indicate that if certain provinces
in India did not want to join the free Indian union, they might
contract out. Already there was a Muslim League ministry in
Bengal. So there was now some reason to hope that all Bengal
might be included in Pakistan. In the north-west, the Punjab was
an important province with a slight Muslim majority. But hitherto
the Unionist Party of Muslims and Hindus had held the government
there, in co-operation with Congress. Jinnah's Muslim League
was still in opposition. If the Punjab ministry could be undermined
and replaced by a League ministry, then the Punjab could become the
solid core of West Pakistan: first, incite communal riots—that would
undermine the prestige of the ministry; then form a League ministry.
All this worked out as planned. The Hindus and Sikhs were attacked
in various places. It was not quite as bad as what had happened
in Bengal; but it was hideous enough. When Gandhi came to
Delhi to meet his colleagues and the next Viceroy, some Sikhs came
to see him with a sad story. They had been attacked by Muslims.
So, remembering that Gandhi was insisting on non-violence, they
had run away instead of hitting back. What were they to do next?
"If you have so misunderstood me that you run away when you are
attacked, there is nothing more for you to do but accept defeat,"
was the purport of his answer.

I believe it was during this visit to Delhi that Gandhi surprised
me one day, as we were walking and talking together after his evening
prayer, by saying: "Do you realise that the cult of violence is
growing?" Presumably I replied that it certainly seemed so.
Reports of violence were coming from many places. It seemed
obvious. But he reiterated what he was saying, and insisted it
was something new to find many Hindus who were committing
themselves to the way of violence as seeming to be the only way to
uphold their position. This was about the time when there came
into prominence the Rashtriya Swayam Sevak Sangh, a body of ardent
young Hindu patriots who were just as determined to turn India

into a land of pure Hinduism—"back to the Vedas"—as the most ardent Muslim Leaguer was to create a land of pure Islam. Neither believed that men of the two faiths could form one nation. So Gandhi was now engaged in a double battle. He still held to his conviction that there were not two nations, but only one. He still believed that if the British would hand over political power to some Indian Government, whatever its composition, the two great religious communities would soon learn to live in peace; the political issues between them could soon be settled. But now he had the second battle to fight. Not only many Muslims, but an important section of Hindus also, were determined to force the issue, and to achieve separation, by violent action against the other community. Such was the position when Lord Mountbatten arrived in India, charged with the job of finding a government or governments to whom authority could be finally handed over within eighteen months or less.

Lady Mountbatten, who was an important part of the new regime, had met Agatha Harrison before leaving London. When she arrived in Delhi, she invited me to come and see her, primarily or ostensibly to discuss some aspects of humanitarian work. One of the first things she said took my breath away. "You know, we think that Gandhi's demands are quite right. Our job is to meet them as quickly as we can." Earlier Viceroys had recognised that Gandhi could not be left out of account. One or two of them had even come to like him personally—at least for a time. But in their hearts, probably, they all regarded him as an infernal nuisance and an impossible man to deal with. For His Majesty's Viceroy (and cousin) to declare that Gandhi's demand was right and proper was new language. It soon became clear that a new era had in fact opened. A few days later, I had the opportunity of attending a meeting called by Lady Mountbatten, attended chiefly by the wives of the British Governors of the several provinces (their husbands were conferring with Lord Mountbatten about the political situation). Lady Mountbatten suggested that steps must be taken to bring all social welfare activity, including those that represented Indian nationalism, into a common effort to tackle some of the big social issues. You could almost hear these experienced women breathing their contempt at such naive talk. Some of them were vocal: "We have tried all that sort of thing again and again,"

they said, "but it never works. The Indians refuse to co-operate."
"Then," replied Lady Mountbatten coolly, "we must try again, and
see to it that it does work." Within a few weeks, she had formed
a co-ordination committee in which all the main humanitarian
agencies did meet together, and it was a most effective agency
during the tragic months after partition. It remained in being,
as a testimony to India's love for this remarkable woman, for some
years after she had left the country.

Even the Mountbattens, however, could not always persuade
Gandhi to do what they wished. The year 1947 was a year of serious
food shortage. The Mountbattens, together with some others,
wanted to issue appeals for aid in the Western press. Gandhi was
against any such action. India must demonstrate her ability to
tackle her own problems: better, he said, that millions should die,
rather than that India should go hat in hand to the outside world.
When the Mountbattens invited Gandhi to come and discuss the
matter, they asked me to come too, imagining, perhaps, that I could
somehow influence him. But he remained adamant. Naturally,
if generous people in the West sent help, it would be appreciated;
but he would not give his name to any appeal.

It was clear to Lord Mountbatten that the sooner the handover
to an Indian Government could take place the better. Uncertainty
was demoralising everyone, especially the officials. In so far as
the need to grow more food depended on official action, for instance,
there would be no more food grown until a new government was
created, which had some authority. But could the unity of India
still be preserved? Was the Cabinet Mission plan still possible?
After his talks with the leaders of the main parties, Lord Mountbatten came to the conclusion that it could not. Partition seemed
to be inevitable. And the main leaders of the Congress Party,
Nehru and Patel especially, were prepared to accept this: Nehru,
perhaps, because he was determined to get on with his programme
of economic reform, and the Muslim League members of the
provisional government seemed to be bent on frustrating all his
efforts; Patel, perhaps, because he was of the view that partition
would end the strife and violence. In 1943, Jinnah had said to me:
"Once we have Pakistan, India and Pakistan will be the best of
friends. They will find a great many things to undertake together."
I expect he was sincere in this conviction. So the decision was

made, though Gandhi, to the end, thought it wrong and disastrous.

Gandhi attended a meeting of the Congress Working Committee on 1 May. He had not wanted to go, but he went under the usual pressure from his old friends and colleagues. He knew already that most of them had come to the conclusion that partition was inevitable. But they still did not convince him. Five days later, he had a long talk with leaders of the Congress socialists. A full report of what he said that day is published in *Mahatma Gandhi— The Last Phase*.[1] Part of this conversation must be quoted, as it shows how Gandhi stuck to his convictions to the end. The socialists said to him: "You think that the British power need not stay on in India for another thirteen months?" (This refers to Attlee's announcement that the British would withdraw not later than June 1948.) Gandhi replied: "Quite so. If their intention is perfectly honest, they should not bother as to what would happen to the country after them. The country is quite capable of taking care of itself. They can quit with a clear conscience." Socialists: "The Congress leaders have said that the British cannot go away without bringing about a settlement between the Congress and the League." Gandhi: "Supposing no agreement can be arrived at between the Congress and the League even after thirteen months, would that be a reason for them to stay on in India even after that date? I, therefore, say: 'Let them quit now, otherwise their going even after thirteen months will be problematical.'" Socialists: "But if they go, to whom are they to hand over power?" Gandhi: "They can hand over power either to the Muslim League or to the Congress, I do not mind which. If they hand it over to the Congress, the Congress will come to a just settlement with the League. But even if they make it over to the League, the Congress has nothing to fear."

In Maulana Azad's book of memories, *India Wins Freedom*, the impression is given that Gandhi did in fact change his mind on the subject of partition and at the end thought it unnecessary. I believe this is not correct. The Maulana, who had handed over the Presidency of the Congress party to Nehru, thought that it might be better for India to postpone the final departure of the British for two or three years, as he believed that by that time the Muslim

[1]Pyarelal Nayar, *Mahatma Gandhi—The Last Phase*, Vol. 2, pp. 161-5.

League would be persuaded to abandon their demand for Pakistan.
The Maulana, being himself a Muslim, was in close touch with
many Muslims, and he was convinced that the great majority even
among those who professed their support for Jinnah's demand did
not really want to see India divided. They were bargaining for the
best possible terms for the Muslim parts of the country. They
might be brought to see that the Cabinet Mission's plan gave them
all that they needed—more, in one sense, than Pakistan. For it
would not leave millions of Muslims in an India that would be
angry about the creation of Pakistan. The Cabinet Mission's
plan would give assurance to all the Muslims. But, whether the
Maulana was right or wrong, postponement was the very last thing
that Gandhi wanted. He wanted the British to quit at once,
whether the result was to jeopardise the Cabinet Mission's plan
or not. As so often, he was thinking in terms that were so remote
even from his nearest colleagues that they failed to understand one
another. It was not on partition that Gandhi disagreed with the
Maulana, as is suggested in his book, but on the date for the British
to quit. The Maulana was prepared to keep the British a little
longer in order to avoid partition. Gandhi wanted them to go
even before the appointed date, but without insisting on partition as
a condition of their withdrawal. In the event, the date was brought
forward, but with partition.

On 3 June, the Viceroy (Lord Mountbatten), after final consulta-
tions with the leaders of the Congress, the League, and the Sikhs,
announced the plan of partition. The Congress leaders had, of
course, made it clear to the end that this was accepted on their side
with the greatest reluctance. They made one condition: as the
League was insisting that all Muslim majority areas must go into
Pakistan without any consideration of the wishes of the minorities
resident in those areas, so too they must accept the logic of this
argument, and must agree to the partition of Bengal and Punjab,
so that west Bengal, where Hindus were in a majority, and east
Punjab, where they and the Sikhs were in a majority, must remain
in India. The British, through the person of Lord Mountbatten,
insisted that Jinnah must accept this; and he did so under protest.
All this was repugnant to Gandhi. But once it was accepted by
the Congress leaders, he insisted that it must be loyally accepted
by all. Once India was divided, it would be the task of all men of

goodwill in both countries to prove to the other community that they were accepted as good citizens of the country in which they found themselves. The majority of the Congress Working Committee had accepted partition; so, when the larger body, the All-India Congress Committee, met where a number of the members might quickly have responded to a strong lead against any such agreement, Gandhi, far from leading the opposition, intervened to urge general support of the decision, even though he made it clear that he personally regretted it.

These Delhi and other political discussions interrupted what Gandhi, all through this last year of the British Raj, regarded as his real work. This was to stem the conflict between Muslim and Hindu wherever he could, not by pronouncements but by persistent effort at the village level. One day that summer I recall a conversation with a high English ecclesiastic, who had been very critical of Gandhi during the time of the Quit India movement, and had agreed with the British official view that he was to blame for the violence that had broken out in the summer of 1942. Now, in 1947, his comment was: "He has never shown himself greater than at this time." The longest time had been spent in east Bengal; but during the spring of 1947 he spent months in Bihar, and from there he went to the Punjab, and up into the North-West Frontier Province and into Kashmir. In all these areas, there was danger of open conflict, because the Muslim League and the forces that still opposed division were striving against one another.

It may be well to insert a few words about the visit to Kashmir. For some years Jawaharlal Nehru had been concerned about the people of Kashmir, and had supported Sheikh Abdullah, leader of the popular movement, in his fight against the autocratic rule of Maharajah Hari Singh. The Maharajah had strongly objected to Nehru's intervention. During the summer of 1947, Nehru planned a further visit. His friend, Abdullah, was in jail, and the Maharajah raised objections to Nehru's visit. So it was proposed that Gandhi should go instead. After much discussion, Gandhi, the Viceroy, Nehru, and Patel all being involved, Gandhi went, having promised to make no public speeches. He had talks with both the Maharajah and his Prime Minister, Pandit Kak. Presumably, these conversations dealt chiefly with matters of civil and democratic liberties. They can hardly have been cordial. He reported on his visit to

the Maharajah in a letter to Nehru. The Maharajah and his son
(who was present) "both admitted that, with the lapse of British
Paramountcy, the true Paramountcy of the people of Kashmir would
commence. However much they might wish to join the Union of
India, they would have to make the choice in accordance with the
wishes of the people. How ... [that] could be determined was
not discussed at this interview.... Bakshi [who was Abdullah's
colleague in the leadership of the popular movement, but was still
at liberty] was most sanguine that the result of the free vote of the
people, whether on adult franchise or on the existing register, would
be in favour of Kashmir joining the Union provided, of course,
that Sheikh Abdullah and his co-prisoners were released, all bans
removed and the present Prime Minister was not in power. Probably
he echoed the general sentiment."

On his way back to Delhi, Gandhi stopped at Jammu, the
southern city of Kashmir State, close to the Punjab border, where
the population contained a much larger proportion of Hindus than
in the Vale of Kashmir. Here some political workers visited him.
"India will be free on the 15th of August, what of Kashmir?" they
asked him. "That will depend on the people of Kashmir," he
answered. "Should Kashmir join India or Pakistan?" they asked.
"That again," he said, "should be decided by the will of the
Kashmiris."

To this I may add a word from a conversation I had with Gandhi
later in the year. By that time India had been divided; so had
Bengal and the Punjab—in the last case with most disastrous
consequences. We were talking about Kashmir, which had then
become the chief bone of contention. He made it clear that,
whatever else might happen, Kashmir should not be divided.
"We have had too many partitions already." Even if preserving
its unity meant that the majority would vote for union with
Pakistan, that would be much better, he said, than a fresh
partition.

Leaving Jammu, he stopped long enough at a refugee camp in
the Punjab to bring what comfort he could to the sufferers who
had been driven from their homes in Rawalpindi, and then hastened
on to Bihar, which he had hoped to return to very much sooner.
He could not stay there for long, as he had solemnly promised to
be in east Bengal, in Noakhali district, by Independence Day, when

the Hindus would find themselves in Pakistan, and feared that fresh trouble might break upon them.

About this time, I had a letter from Gandhi, inviting me to spend some time with him again. I replied that I would like to be with him on Independence Day, wherever he was likely to be. He replied that he intended to be in Noakhali. So it was arranged that I would join him in Bihar, and travel with him through Calcutta to Noakhali before 15 August. When we reached Calcutta, however, plans were changed. Suhrawardy, who was still Chief Minister of Bengal, came to see Gandhi at the Sodepur ashram, where he was staying, and insisted that he would achieve nothing by going to Noakhali, but that, if he would stay in Calcutta, both of them together could bring peace to Bengal. Gandhi pointed out that he had given a firm promise to the Hindus of Noakhali that he would be with them on the day they were fearing—the day when east Bengal was to become East Pakistan, when, as they saw it, they would be absolutely at the mercy of the Muslims. He could not possibly abandon this promise without the firmest assurances and guarantees from leading Muslims in Noakhali that there would be no trouble there. Could such guarantees be given?

One of the peculiar features of the communal trouble that had stricken Bengal during the past year was the fact that the political leaders knew who were the real "rabble rousers." Gandhi knew, and Suhrawardy knew that he knew, who were the men in Noakhali whose word mattered. If certain men said, "there will be no trouble," then it was almost certain that there would be none. What was more, Gandhi knew that Suhrawardy, as one of the local leaders of the Muslim League, and one who knew the rabble rousers well, could probably induce them to desist from further mischief, if he really wished to do so. Calcutta, on the other hand, as it was part of the Hindu majority area of west Bengal, was losing its Muslim League ministry, and the new Chief Minister, who would take office on 15 August, was a Hindu, a Congressman, and, as it happened, an ardent Gandhian (Profulla Ghosh), not a man who could necessarily control the section of Hindus that was planning to start a campaign of vengeance against the Muslims on 15 August. A few days before this I had called on one of the Congress leaders, Kiron Shanker Roy (who, though a Hindu, happened also to be a family friend of the Suhrawardys), and I had asked him what he

expected to happen on 15 August. "There will probably be fresh
trouble," he said. "Do you mean like last year at this time, when
thousands of people were killed in the streets?" "Perhaps not quite
as bad as that," he said, "but I am afraid there will be many
casualties." I have no reason to think that Roy had any of the
young ruffians under his control, or that he was doing more than
guessing what was likely to happen. But I myself had been conscious, as no one in Calcutta could fail to be, that, morning by
morning, for months past young Hindu activists (to use a polite
euphemism) had been drilling—for what? Presumably, for the
next trial of strength. Now the time was coming.

Suhrawardy and his friends, without delay, obtained the necessary
assurances from the Muslim rabble leaders in Noakhali. So
Gandhi could stay in Calcutta, if he was satisfied that this would
achieve what he wanted. There was at least one powerful argument in favour of it. Suhrawardy had hoped that, after losing
his position as Chief Minister of united Bengal, he would now, with
partition, become Chief Minister of East Bengal. But at this
point he was defeated by a man he had ousted a year or two before.
After partition he would be a man without a job. If, for the past
year, he had apparently been working with the forces of division
and conflict, why could he not now suddenly switch round and
become the great man of peace? If he was seen in action with
Gandhi, he might find his way back into political life under happier
auspices.

The motives of all men are often mixed, and in any case they
are hidden from the eyes of others. After the horrors of the previous
August, it was not surprising that the Hindus of Calcutta thought
ill of the motives that led Suhrawardy suddenly to throw in his
lot with Gandhi. But I had been watching their relationship
through the past year, and I do not believe that his "conversion"
was either sudden or wholly selfish.

The plan of campaign agreed upon by Gandhi and Suhrawardy
was this: they would go first to a part of the city from which Muslims
had been driven out, and would work together there until the local
Hindus invited the Muslims to return. Then they would go to a
part of the city from which the Hindus had fled, and would stay
till the Muslims invited them; and so on till all Calcutta was at
peace again. The house where this work was to begin was a large

but horribly dirty mansion in a part of the city called Beliaghata. The house belonged to a Muslim family, but they had left it. Thither Gandhi went on 13 August—two days before Independence Day. Suhrawardy was to have accompanied him, but he actually arrived a few minutes later. Both were given a hostile reception by a number of young Hindus.

A little later, the shouting outside led to an attempt by some of these young men to climb in by the windows. So we tried to shut the windows, but the only result was a shower of stones, and the glass from the windows was scattered all over the room inside. Fortunately, no one was hurt. So then we closed the shutters. It was soon arranged that some of the young men should come in to the building and talk things over with Gandhi. They were very angry with him for having come to terms with Suhrawardy, whom they regarded as the arch enemy. This led to a long and intense argument, Gandhi trying to convince them that his way was the one and only way to true peace and dignity for all the inhabitants of Calcutta. Freedom for India should mean peace and security for all its inhabitants. But the young men were not easily convinced.

The talks went on till after 8 P.M. When at last one of them suggested that it was time to go, Gandhi agreed. It was already late for him; so he urged them to go, to think things over and then come back in the morning. What he had said, obviously, had a profound effect; for by next morning they were in a different mood. Before long they had agreed to support him in his effort to bring peace and goodwill to the harassed city, and they soon supplied from their number volunteers to protect him and the household from any undesirable visitors. So far, police were in attendance, and they insisted on remaining until the day of Independence. This was now only one day away. What would it bring?

That evening (14 August) the daily prayers were held in the garden of the Beliaghata house. It was a large compound, so thousands of people were able to assemble. It was also extremely muddy, following heavy rains. As usual, Gandhi addressed the crowd at the end of the prayers. He said:

From tomorrow we shall be delivered from the bondage of British rule. But from midnight tonight, India will be partitioned

too. While, therefore, tomorrow will be a day of rejoicing, it
will bo a day of sorrow as well. It will throw a heavy burden of
responsibility upon us. Let us pray to God that He may give
us strength to bear it worthily. Let all those Muslims who were
forced to flee return to their homes. If two million of Hindus
and Muslims are at daggers drawn with one another in Calcutta
[referring, of course, to the population of the city—two millions
is an understatement] with what face can I go to Noakhali and
plead the cause of the Hindus with the Muslims there? And if
the flames of communal strife envelop the country, how can our
newborn freedom survive?

When Gandhi went out to the prayer meeting, he had agreed
that it was wiser for Suhrawardy to remain inside the house. Some
of the young Hindus, though they had met Suhrawardy in the
morning, still had very bitter feelings about him. As it happened,
I had also stayed inside, because of the mud outside. A pleasant
young police officer was also in the house. Every one else had
gone out. In the middle of Gandhi's speech, some of the young
men discovered that Suhrawardy was alone in the house. So here
was their moment to attack him. They came shouting for his
blood. The police officer and I closed the shutters. A bombard-
ment of stones followed. Suhrawardy lay on the floor, his hands
behind his head, and in the coolest manner reported the things the
young men outside were shouting about him. Suhrawardy had
always shown himself a man of courage. For my part, I wondered how long the siege might continue before the "enemy" broke
in. But finally, Gandhi and his granddaughters reappeared, and
he immediately settled down to his writing as if nothing was
happening. However, the shouting continued, and so, after a
time, Gandhi beckoned to one of his granddaughters, got up from
his seat, and, with his hand resting on her shoulder (he always
needed a prop if he was expecting to stand for some time) he walked
to the window and threw open one of the shutters. This brought
him, practically, face to face with the young men. He began speaking in his quietest voice. They all wanted to hear him, so within
seconds there was total silence. He began to rebuke them for not
accepting the partnership with Suhrawardy as essential to the peace-
making mission. After a time, he decided that they were in a mood

to listen to Suhrawardy, so he beckoned to him to come to the
window, and he now put his second hand on Suhrawardy's shoulder. But Suhrawardy had not got far before men in the crowd
began to heckle him. "What about last August? Are you not
ashamed of yourself?" they shouted. "Yes," replied Suhrawardy
without hesitation. "I am ashamed of it. We must all be ashamed."
And he continued by pleading that now all should support
the Mahatma in his great mission of peace. Just at this moment
police brought news of fraternising among Hindus and Muslims in
another part of the city. The Hindus were putting up the flag of
free India for the next morning's celebrations. "May we come
across and help you?" called the Muslims from across the road—
the road that neither community had dared to cross in months.
"Come across, brothers," was the reply; and so it began. Suhrawardy reported this incident to the crowd outside the Beliaghata
house, and some of them cheered. Before long, the speeches
ended, Gandhi dismissed the crowd, and peace prevailed.

Immediately after this was over, he called me to sit beside him
and said he particularly wanted me to understand what had just
happened. The turning point, he said, was Suhrawardy's frank
and open confession of his shame for his action a year before.
"Public confession is always good," added Gandhi. "This time
it has changed the hearts of these young men."

He went on to tell me that he would not be taking part in any
public celebrations on the following day, whatever might happen
in the city, whether it was to be peaceful or no; and we still did not
know what was in store. "On occasions like this," he went on to
say, "I like to make it a day of prayer and fasting. You Protes-
tants have forgotten the efficacy of fasting, but it is one of the best
ways of purifying the heart for more effective service. Moreover,
millions of the people in their villages cannot feast tomorrow, even
if they want to. I cannot forget them, even for one day. Tomorrow, especially, we need to remember them; for if the freedom
of India is to mean anything at all, it must mean food for the
hungry. That is the first thing on our agenda of freedom." I did
not record his exact words, but this was the substance of them. He
said nothing about fasting because of the partition of the country.
I think it is safe to say that he would have spent Independence Day
in prayer and fasting even if there had been no partition.

Then, characteristically, he went on: "This means that we shall
be rising half an hour earlier tomorrow, for a longer period of
prayer. And we shall eat no food. We shall only drink water.
But you are my guest. You are not obliged to get up so early,
and I will gladly arrange for you to have the usual food if you want
it." Naturally, I said I wished to do what he was doing. And so
we went to bed.

As far as I know, the night was undisturbed. Perhaps we heard
a few strange explosions. This became a feature of Calcutta nights
during the following week. Apparently, young men who had
been making bombs to throw at "the enemy" now decided to get
rid of them by throwing them into the water tanks that are numerous
in the city of Calcutta.

It was still dark when we gathered together for the early morning
prayer. If ever prayer was real to me, as meaning aspiration after
all that is good, and dedication to the highest, it was so that morning. No better way of greeting the dawn of Independence Day
could have been imagined for a man whose whole life was a witness
to his conviction that no man is in sole charge of his own fate, and
that no nation can live unless it tries to serve ends higher than those
of self-interest—unless, as Gandhi would put it, it tries to serve
God first, which meant to him, striving after justice for the
humble and poor and oppressed. This way of life is so alien to
the modern mind that it is hard for most people to understand how,
at a moment of such decisive significance in the growth of the nation
he had tried all his life to serve, a man in Gandhi's position could
turn away from all political celebrations and celebrate in the one
way which to him was in keeping with his whole life and thought.

While we were still at our prayers, we heard music in the distance,
and soon some girls, singing Rabindranath Tagore's songs of freedom, drew near to the house. They realised that we were engaged in
prayer; so they fell silent and participated. When we had finished,
they sang again, took Gandhi's blessing, and withdrew into the
darkness. Before long, others came with their Bengal benediction
of sweet music. Surely, it seemed, this must be the dawning of a
better day. But, as usual, Gandhi, after his ablutions, settled to
his work; and to the inmates of that house, the day that had
dawned was just one more day for work to be done and duty fulfilled. Rumours came through that the city was quiet; as far as I

was concerned, I knew nothing for certain until friends of mine came and insisted that I must come out with them to see the wonder of a city released from its year of fear and hatred. Even as I write, twenty years later, the emotion of that day returns in force. When you have lived for most of a year in a city that has been given over to violence and hatred and fear, suddenly to find that all the clouds have lifted, and that the sky is blue and serene, gives a sense of what can best be called "miraculous." No wonder that people spoke of "the miracle of Calcutta," and no wonder they associated Gandhi's name with it. Thus did Indian freedom dawn for Gandhi and for those who were privileged to be in Calcutta on that unforgettable day.

9

The Last Months
(1947-1948)

THE BRITISH had handed over authority in Delhi. India was free. In Calcutta and throughout Bengal, on both sides of the border, an almost miraculous peace had come. In east Bengal, now East Pakistan, the Muslim leaders had kept their promise. Noakhali, like Calcutta, was at peace. But Gandhi was not satisfied. He insisted that there was no miracle, and especially that he was no miracle worker. Moreover, in conversation, during those wonderful days of harmony and goodwill, he was constantly warning us all not to jump to conclusions: "The leaders of some important sections have not come near me since I reached Calcutta. They are not satisfied. They may yet try to break the peace," he kept saying. He was not satisfied that what had happened was more than a passing emotion. Time would show. And meanwhile, the news from the north-west, especially parts of the Punjab, was bad. Communal violence there was getting worse.

Three days after Independence Day, on 18 August, was the Muslim festival of Id. In Calcutta, Muslims invited their Hindu and Christian friends to celebrate with them. Hearts were full of thanksgiving. But even on that day there was at least one unhappy incident. However, all continued quiet until the last day of August. Late that evening an excited crowd came to the Beliaghata house, with some story of a man who had been stabbed for refusing to shout, "victory to Pakistan" (when he was later examined, no trace of injury was found). The young men evidently wanted to kill Suhrawardy; but Suhrawardy had gone to his Calcutta home, to get ready for the departure of Gandhi and himself to Noakhali, which was planned for two days later. As the excitement grew, they attacked two young Muslims, they broke a lot of windows, and began throwing the furniture about. Gandhi was in the midst of them, trying to pacify them but without avail. A large stick was thrown which only just missed him. After a time, the police arrived and cleared the house of rowdies. Soon the Chief Minister appeared, and suggested that it might be necessary to arrest leaders of the Hindu Mahasabha. Gandhi suggested that, instead, the Mahasabha leaders should be given the work of controlling and pacifying the young men who were trying to break the peace. The Mahasabha was a communal organisation, which represented, on the Hindu side, the kind of politics that was represented on the other side by the Muslim League. They had been responsible for drilling youth groups for months past. As with other groups, their leadership was not all of one mind. Next day, Gandhi's secretary, Pyarelal, who had only just come to Calcutta, went with a colleague to see Dr Shyama Prasad Mukerjee, one of the leaders of the Mahasabha, a man of distinction in the life of Calcutta who had held responsible positions in the province and indeed in the public life of India as a whole. Whatever his political outlook, he was a level-headed man, who knew very well that the politics of crude violence achieves nothing good. So he was immediately responsive and issued a public statement, saying (in part): "The majority community in Bengal must realise, the senseless oppression of innocent members of the minority community does not pay and creates a vicious circle which one cannot cut through.... The united efforts of leaders of the communities must see to this." But the violence of the night before was followed by a number of fresh outbreaks on 11 September. It seemed clear that someone had planned all this, and it was not necessarily only members of the Hindu Mahasabha. Another section, called the Forward Bloc, which had broken away from the Congress, was led by Sarat Bose, brother of Subhas Bose, who had led the "Indian National Army," which fought with the Japanese against the British. Sarat Bose had also kept away from Gandhi. What was he up to? Or again, how far was it the work of Sikhs? This community included many of the taxi drivers of Calcutta; they were getting terrible news of Muslim attacks on their community in west Punjab, now the dominant state in West Pakistan. They might well try to take revenge in Calcutta. Gandhi advised those who wanted to stop the trouble to go out among the crowds, and offer their lives for peace. He would have liked to go himself, but he realised that if he did, attention would turn to him, not to peace-making; so the one recourse left to him was to fast. His statement issued at the beginning of the fast said: "It is clear to me that if India is to retain her dearly won independence, all men and women must completely forget lynch-law.... The recognition of the golden rule of never taking the law into one's own hands has no exceptions."

At 8.15 on the evening of 1 September, Gandhi began his fast. But the rioting continued. Sarat Bose was among those who came to see him that day. Later in the day, Dr Shyama Prasad Mukerjee was able to report that by the next morning Hindustan National Guards (the young men who had been parading morning by morning for months past, presumably to teach the Muslims a lesson when independence came) would be patrolling the streets along with Muslim National Guards. During the next day a group of twenty-seven young men who had been actively participating in the riots came to beg forgiveness and implored Gandhi to give up his fast. But he made it a condition that they should prove their change of heart by going out among the rioters and doing what they could to stop the trouble. Other groups also came and made confession of their part in the troubles, and they began handing in their weapons to be destroyed.

Finally, leaders of all three main communities, having seen that the city was absolutely quiet, and that all rioting had stopped, signed a document which said: "We the undersigned promise to Gandhiji that now that peace had been restored in Calcutta once again, we shall never allow communal strife in the city and shall strive unto death to preserve it." Three days and an hour after it began, Gandhi was able to break his fast. During this and the following days, further truck loads of weapons were brought to him to be destroyed. This time all sections of the community participated in the peace-making, without reservation. Gandhi was impatient to leave for the Punjab, as the violence there was increasing all the time. He had received urgent messages from Nehru and other leaders of the new Indian Government to come at once, and he even proposed undertaking this thousand-mile train journey the day after he broke his fast. His friends prevailed on him to stay in Calcutta long enough to participate in a meeting of thanksgiving.

It has to be recorded that two Hindus, Sachin Mittra, a Calcutta graduate who had worked with Gandhi and his friends in the peace-making at Noakhali, and another man in his thirties, Smritish Bannerjee, laid down their lives during the days of rioting in attempts to stop the violence started by some of their fellow-Hindus.

Gandhi had promised to be with the Hindus in Noakhali at the coming of independence; but, as we have seen, he was kept in Calcutta, where his presence had in fact served the east Bengal Hindus best. Nor did they suffer when the news of the outbreaks in Calcutta came through. Just before that, Gandhi had fixed a day for going on to Noakhali. By the time he had helped to bring real peace to Calcutta, the claims of the Punjab were so urgent that he had to abandon his hope of going to see his friends in east Bengal. In fact, he was never able to go there again. But he sent his secretary, Pyarelal, and a number of other colleagues back to Noakhali, while he himself went to the Punjab—or rather to Delhi which by this time had been caught up in the frenzy.

Gandhi spent the last four months of 1947 and the first month of 1948, up to the moment of his assassination, in Delhi, trying for the last time to bring harmony between the two communities, and more especially to bring back a sense of security to the large Muslim minority of the capital city, Delhi, itself, and to the areas all round the city. The establishment of Pakistan had made his task much more difficult. Jinnah, the leader of the Muslim League, and the architect of Pakistan, had argued that the two religious communities were two distinct nations. On this ground he had demanded and finally obtained the separation of the Muslim majority areas of India, which had now become the entirely new State of Pakistan. Most of the Muslim electors, all over India, had voted in support of the Muslim League. So many Hindus were now saying to their Muslim neighbours: "You asked for Pakistan; you have got it. So hurry up and go there." Unfortunately, they over-looked the logical consequence of this, namely, that if the Muslims remaining in India were to go to Pakistan, all the Hindus living in what had now become Pakistan would have to migrate to India. Taking East and West Pakistan together, this would have meant the migration of over ten million Hindus. If all the Muslims remaining on the Indian side had migrated, some forty million would have been involved.

Gandhi had refused to accept Jinnah's thesis; he pointed out that the two communities had lived side by side all over India for hundreds of years; their social customs might be different, and there was, admittedly, practically no intermarriage. But in many ways they shared the same life, and in nearly all India the two communities used one language. In Bengal, both communities spoke Bengali; in the Punjab, both spoke Punjabi; in Sind, both spoke Sindhi; in Gujarat, both spoke Gujarati; and so on. Though the common language of north India was Hindi for the Hindus and Urdu for the Muslims, these two languages were closely akin; even so there was much overlapping. In the cities of U.P., for instance, many men of culture belonged to clubs where they composed Urdu verse. These clubs contained men of both communities.

The Gandhi-Suhrawardy partnership, supported, no doubt, by other factors, had prevented the outbreak of general communal conflict in Bengal; but in the north-west, including the whole of West Pakistan, and the new Indian province of East Punjab, violence had broken out in many towns and villages, and it was in danger of spreading to other parts of India. Happily, there were strong officials in key positions in parts of the United Provinces (now Uttar Pradesh) adjoining (east) Punjab; and they were vigorously led by the Governor, Mrs Sarojini Naidu, and her Ministers. But in spite of determined efforts on the part of Nehru and his colleagues of the Central Government, Delhi fell victim to the rioters. Thousands of Muslims were driven from their homes, and had to camp, during the worst monsoon weather, in miserable shelters on desolate stony ground, with no proper water supply and no drainage. The Sikhs, especially, went about the city slaughtering whom they would. For a time the police seemed to be quite paralysed. I was staying at the time in the Y.M.C.A., New Delhi, whose front entrance is just opposite the back entrance to the Parliament Street Police Station. From the front door I watched Sikhs, fully armed with their *kirpans* (though they had been ordered not to wear them), careering along on motor cycles, going from one murder to the next. The police did nothing.

This was the kind of situation which Gandhi found when he reached Delhi on 9 September. Suhrawardy spent most of the autumn in his company, doing what he could to reassure the Muslims, but what Gandhi needed most in Delhi was the co-operation of local Hindu and Sikh leaders who would help to stop the rioting. Local leadership among the remaining Muslims was also needed, for some of them had equipped themselves with fire-arms and were using them as freely as the Hindus and Sikhs. Within a day or two he had to announce: "I find no one in Delhi who can accompany me and control the Muslims. There is no such person amongst the Sikhs or among the Rashtriya Swayam Sevak Sangh either. I do not know what I shall be able to do here. But one thing is clear. I cannot leave this place until Delhi is peaceful again." In other words, it was again a case of "do or die." And this time the whole of this came true; it was "do *and* die." The Rashtriya Swayam Sevak Sangh, as we have seen, was a body of militant Hindus, who had been organised all over India, with the deliberate purpose of purifying India of all non-Hindu influences, by terrorism or other forms of violence if necessary. In the end they, or those who thought like them, provided the assassin for Gandhi himself. His effort to win them back from their creed of violence failed.

During his first few days, he visited refugee camps, chiefly of local Muslims, and received many deputations from Muslims telling their tales of woe. But he did not forget the Hindu and Sikh sufferers. By the middle of September, already many refugees of these two communities had reached Delhi from Pakistan, with terrible tales of sufferings. Many of them were determined to avenge their sufferings on the Muslims remaining in India. Pyarelal has described Gandhi's visit during these first days to one of the Hindu and Sikh refugee camps:

Their wounds were fresh and bleeding; revenge seemed sweet to many. One of them was heard to say that they had yet avenged only half an anna in the rupee [5 per cent], but, now that "the old man" had come, they would not be able to square up their account. Yet they clung to him. There was something in him which drew them to him in spite of themselves. They might be angry with him [for his determination to protect the Muslims], even quarrel with him, yet in their heart of hearts they knew that he was the friend of all and the enemy of none; he loved them and theirs with a love greater than they themselves were, perhaps,

capable of. They wanted him to guide them even when they
were not prepared to follow his advice.[1]

When they urged him to go to the Punjab, to go even to Pakistan,
to save the Hindus there, he explained that this was just what he
wished to do; he would do it just as soon as Delhi was truly peaceful again, when the Muslim citizens of Delhi no longer had anything
to fear.

Week after week he laboured to win the Hindus and Sikhs back
to sanity, often putting himself in danger. All the time his old
friends and colleagues now heading the government, especially
Nehru and Sardar Patel, came to him with their problems, and,
even if he could not always give the answer, at least he would send
them away with fresh strength and confidence in their ability to
win the battle of decency and good government. Burdened as he
was, he was even able to rescue them with the sanity of a brief
laugh. It was his way to be freely available at all time to all his
friends and others. During those days, I was with him again
and again when one of the leaders of the new government looked
in for a word of advice. One would withdraw to the far side of
the room, and observe how he was able to lift the overpowering
burden from their shoulders.

Although they were engaged in a common effort to restore order
and goodwill, Gandhi and his colleagues did not always agree
about details. I may illustrate this from a personal experience.
Before the end of August, Gandhi had received a cable from Delhi,
asking him to persuade my colleagues of the Friends Service Unit
and myself to go to Delhi, from Bengal, to help with the needs of
the refugees. We agreed to do what we could, and several of us
began working in and around Delhi, under instructions from Sardar
Patel. Before long, realising that one of the most urgent needs
would be to see that the Muslims in camps in India and the Hindus
in camps in Pakistan were properly attended to until they could
be transported over the border, Richard Symonds and I concluded
that it would be well to divide our personnel between India and
Pakistan. When we reported this to Sardar Patel, he was indignant:
"Has Pakistan invited you?" he asked. No, they had not. "But

we did invite you." Yes, they had. "Then why do you want to go to Pakistan?" "Because, when there is trouble in two adjacent countries, and people are suffering in both, we Quakers always try to work on both sides." "Both sides? Why not all sides? Are you going to Afghanistan, and everywhere else?" "No, we were not planning to do so." "Oh well, I don't see why you want to go to Pakistan. But if Bapu [Gandhi] agrees, I suppose I must agree." So we went to Gandhi. Of course, said he, even before we had explained the matter fully, we must certainly work on both sides. So we proceeded to get the necessary permits from the Ministers in both East and West Punjab. However, they laid down that our reports on conditions in the camps should be sent to the two governments direct, and should not be published. They were to be "secret." If they are to be secret, commented Gandhi, they will be worthless. What matters is that your reports should be known. He advised us to discuss the matter with Prime Minister Nehru. When Nehru saw the statement of conditions, he laughed. "Governments have their own language," he said. "If they just say, 'this is a secret document,' they mean, do not rush to the press to get it published. If they say, 'very secret,' that means only tell a few of your special friends. If they say, 'top secret,' then you must really begin to be careful." So we went ahead, and in due course we told Gandhi and others specially concerned what we found in the camps, though our reports in full were only sent to the Ministers. And perhaps, after all, that was best. For each knew that his opposite number in the other country knew what we had found, and that it was up to him to put things right, where it was needed, as quickly as possible. Otherwise, the "secret" report might leak out in the other country and then he would be in trouble.

These are details; but they illustrate how closely Gandhi was following every effort to restore decent standards for the unhappy minorities in both countries. He was so little inclined to confine his concern to the new India that again and again he spoke of his hope before long to go to Pakistan, if the Pakistan authorities would agree, even to settle there. But it was not to be.

While he was continuing to do all that he could from Delhi, and conditions began to improve, with fewer reports of any fresh incidents of violence as the weeks went by, late in October a new

crisis arose in Kashmir. The State of Kashmir lies to the extreme
north of India. It is a huge territory, much of it mountainous. A
great part of the State, as it had grown during the nineteenth century,
is too high in elevation for human habitation, and the valley running
through this part, called Ladakh, is sparsely inhabited by people
whose cultural and linguistic links are with Tibet rather than with
India. The north-western and western parts of the State are inhabited by Muslims, who also form the majority of the population in the central area, the Kashmir Valley proper. This beautiful valley, most of it at an elevation of 5,000 feet above sea-level,
is surrounded by magnificent snowy mountains, and has not un-
fairly been called the Asian Switzerland. It is a productive valley,
but the population has remained desperately poor. More people
live in the valley than in the whole of the rest of the State. Up to
this time (1947), it had been ruled by a Hindu Maharajah, and he
had done little to meet the new demand for democratic institutions.
As we have seen in the last chapter, when Gandhi visited Kashmir
in July, the leader of the National Conference, Sheikh Abdullah,
was in jail, though he was released soon after. The State had a
common frontier with both India and Pakistan after partition, but
the economic links were chiefly with Pakistan. Lord Mountbatten,
on behalf of the British Government, had been pressing all the
ruling princes of the Indian States to adhere without delay either
to India or to Pakistan. But the Maharajah of Kashmir was one of
the few who procrastinated. As the great majority of the population was Muslim it was natural that the leaders of Pakistan felt
that the State should join Pakistan. The Hindu ruler might have
felt more inclined to join India. But India now had his "enemy"
Nehru as Prime Minister, so it may well be that he was hoping to
remain independent of both. Gandhi, as we have seen, had at the
time of his visit in July pressed the Maharajah and the political
leaders of Kashmir to let the issue be decided by the will of the
people. Although it is likely that, if they had had this opportunity,
the majority would have voted for Pakistan, this is not certain, for
many of the Muslim supporters of Sheikh Abdullah's National
Conference Party would have voted for India. Communalism
had not raised its ugly head in the Kashmir Valley; and the forces
working for democracy had received much aid from Jawaharlal
Nehru, whose ancestors belonged to Kashmir, and none from

Jinnah. The opportunity of a free vote was never given them.

Just when it seemed as if the communal violence in the Punjab was at an end, news came that the Kashmir Valley had been invaded by armed men from the North-West Frontier, now a part of Pakistan. These poverty-stricken mountaineers, living between India and Afghanistan for generations past, had often raided their more prosperous neighbours in the low countries of the Punjab. One of the major activities of the British in this part of the world had been an attempt to pacify the frontier, both by punitive expeditions—latterly, air raids—against the villages of the raiders and by efforts to improve the economy of the whole area. So large a raid as this, not simply into the adjacent districts of the Punjab but right across it into Kashmir, was something new. It had, in fact, been contrived by certain Pakistani authorities, and the ammunition used in Kashmir was given to the raiders by Pakistani officials.

As soon as the news of this armed invasion was known in Delhi, the Indian Government responded with all speed to the request of the Maharajah to send military aid. It arrived just in time to save the capital city, Srinagar, from the havoc that overtook smaller towns further down the Valley. At the same time, the Maharajah declared that the State of Kashmir was joined to the Union of India.

Gandhi spoke and wrote strongly about the invasion of Kashmir. He declared that, whether the active support of the raiders by the Pakistan Government was proved or not, a government that could not prevent such an invasion was unfit to govern and ought to resign.

He openly supported the action of the Indian Government in sending troops to Kashmir to stop the raiders. Some of his friends, including people in the West who admired his convictions about the power of non-violence, were shocked to read this in the reports sent by press correspondents. Had he been correctly reported? I received a letter from Agatha Harrison in London begging me to get the record straight. So I went to see Gandhi about it. He assured me that he had not been misreported. Of course, he would have been happy if the people of Kashmir had the courage and the discipline to meet the raiders unarmed; this he had made clear from the beginning. But he knew that they were not ready for this difficult venture. The only defence they knew or believed in was armed defence. So this could not be denied them. He had been quick, he said, to speak out, for the Pakistan Government might think that he, as a man of non-violence, might try to dissuade the Indian Government from sending armed assistance to Kashmir. This he could not possibly do. He could not ask other men to act in accordance with principles he knew they did not accept. As non-violent resistance was out of the question, armed resistance was necessary, and he must express his approval of what they were doing.

The fact that Gandhi "blessed the troops that were sent to Kashmir" has been quoted as evidence that, with the coming of independence to India, he had abandoned his conviction that non-violence should always be preferred to the use of armed force. But this is a mistake. To the end of his life he held fast to the conviction that, given the immense courage that such a course required, the way of non-violent resistance was always better than armed resistance. Only, he never allowed that non-violence could be erected as an excuse for doing nothing. It is, no doubt, true that he said on one occasion: "It is better to be a soldier than to be a coward." But he knew that there was still a better alternative, though not many men were yet ready for it.

Gandhi was not content simply to applaud what his friends in the Government of India were doing. He recognised that the Kashmir raid represented an unsolved social problem that affected the whole North-West Frontier people. He urged some of us to investigate this problem, and to find out how the needs of the Pathans (the frontier people) could be legitimately met. What were their real needs? After all, he had learnt much about the Frontier from his long association with Khan Abdul Ghaffar Khan, whose life-long passion was the conquest of poverty among his people. Nor was Gandhi content that the Maharajah should alone decide the destiny of Kashmir. He still believed that the choice between union with India or with Pakistan must be made by the people of Kashmir, and that they must do it as one unit.

If Gandhi's advice had been followed, the Kashmir quarrel between India and Pakistan might well have been settled quickly. He did not like the reference to the United Nations. He told me that he believed it would only lead to confusion and delay. He would have preferred that, if the matter could not be settled by direct negotiation, some Englishman, if one could be found who would be impartial and who would have a background of knowledge, might be brought in to help. Indeed, he took the view that if the British had done their job properly, the whole matter would have been settled before Independence. It was still not too late for them to do their duty in the matter. But his friend, Nehru, who always had the strongest feelings about Kashmir, would not listen to him on this. The English had gone; they must not be brought back on any account at any point. Accordingly, at the end of the year, India appealed to the Security Council of the United Nations to stop the Pakistan invasion, and so to open the way for a free decision by the Kashmiris about their own destiny. What followed is a matter of history, which takes us far past the end of Gandhi's life.

The Kashmir affair may seem to a later generation to be the main political event of the closing weeks of the year of India's independence; but to Gandhi himself the daily need for more effective protection for the Muslims remaining in India, first and foremost those who were in Delhi, remained paramount. This was his constant preoccupation. For weeks at a time, Delhi seemed to be peaceful; then fresh trouble would break out. Hindu and Sikh refugees from West Pakistan kept pouring into the city. Try as they would, the authorities could not prevent this great influx. Many refugees, of course, settled in other cities and in rural areas. Efforts were made to fit them in where they could most quickly find some appropriate employment. Considering the extent of the upheaval, it was amazing what full statistics were kept of those who left for Pakistan, and of those who came in; but, of course, the two armies of refugees, those going to Pakistan and those coming to India, did not fit. In particular, a great number of those who came to India were small shopkeepers, who naturally believed that a great capital city would give them an opportunity for a new livelihood. There was at least one occasion when a train was filled with refugees who were being evacuated from one of the big transit camps in East Punjab. Before the train left, the refugees learnt that they were being taken to some other part of the Punjab to settle, not to Delhi; whereupon, they all left the train. Hundreds and thousands did in fact set up little booths along the main highways in Delhi, in spite of objections from the city authorities. And in the first place, they lived in most unhygienic cramped quarters on top of their new shops. Soon they were making some sort of a living. But there were others determined to have better living quarters than these, who turned on the Muslims still in Delhi and tried to drive them from their homes.

The position of the Muslims who had stayed in Delhi and other towns and cities of northern India was tragic. Many of them had supported the Muslim League in its demand for Pakistan. Pakistan had been duly achieved, but they were not in it. Were they loyal to India or were they not? It was not surprising that many Hindus doubted their patriotism. If they were at heart friends of Pakistan, had they not better go there? If they hesitated they must be driven out. Many of them came to Gandhi in their distress. He did his best to help them, and did not fail to point out to them that they could not expect to be trusted by their Hindu neighbours unless they showed clearly that they were no longer hankering after a bigger Pakistan, but were prepared to be loyal citizens of India. At the same time, he denounced the action of the refugees who were trying to steal their homes from them (Muslims) and he continued to press his friend and colleague, Sardar Patel, who as Home Minister was responsible, to control the police who were often as communally minded as the refugees themselves. Sometimes, indeed, refugees might be members of the families of the police, and their stories of sufferings in Pakistan inflamed the police to act against the Muslims in Delhi. Many of the Hindu and Sikh refugees also came to Gandhi with their tales of woe. Right into the winter, many of them had to remain in tents on the outskirts of the city, while better accommodation was being arranged. It seemed wrong to Gandhi that he was living in the comfort of a room in Birla House while these refugees, who were suffering for the sins of their leaders, were exposed to all the misery of camp life through the winter. Again and again he did, in fact, achieve some reform or amelioration of their lot, but the madness still continued, and he confessed that he could hardly go on living under these circumstances. Had freedom come too soon, he asked? Clearly there was far more violence in the hearts of the people in India than even he had seen. The non-violence that had been employed in the struggle against the British was the non-violence of the weak, not of the strong. Violence and hatred had now taken possession of multitudes. What more could be done to stop it?

I had been in Delhi during the first days of January 1948, and had seen Gandhi several times and talked about some of the problems of the refugees. On 11 January, I went to tell him that I was planning to go to Calcutta next day. He asked me to come in to see him again on my way to the train the next morning, as he was writing a letter to a common friend Richard Symonds in Calcutta, and he would like me to take it by hand. So, next morning about eight o'clock, I came to collect the letter. I was a little earlier than he had anticipated, and he was still writing the letter.

It was a Monday, which meant that it was his day of silence. For some years, Gandhi, in order to protect himself from the constant pressure of visitors, had kept one day in the week (as far as I know it was always Monday) as a day of complete silence. He did not speak a word to anyone, unless, I suppose, there was some very urgent need to do so. People could still come and see him if they wished, and they were free to speak to him; but if any reply was needed, he would write a brief note on some scrap of paper. It would be interesting to know how many of these scraps are treasured by his friends.

On this particular Monday, whilst he finished writing the letter, his secretary, Pyarelal, called me to him and said: "Here is a snapshot that someone took the other day, which may amuse you." The snapshot showed Gandhi sitting on his mat, writing, while Pyarelal's young niece, aged five or six, had gone up to him and poked her nose into his cheek. As I saw this photograph, naturally I laughed. Gandhi looked up from his writing to discover what the fun was. So we handed him the snapshot. He looked at it, and then beckoned to the little girl, who was running around a little way off. She ran to his side; in dumb show the old man and the little girl admired the picture of the two of them together. They had their little laugh together (laughter was permitted on the silent day as on every other day); then Gandhi handed me the letter, and I said "good-bye." It was the last time that I saw him.

The train from Delhi to Calcutta takes over twenty-four hours. Early on Tuesday morning, we stopped at a station where I could buy the morning's paper. "Gandhi begins a fast" was the bold headline. I was incredulous. The picture of the old man happily laughing with the little girl was still in my mind. But I soon saw the truth. As so often, Gandhi had succeeded in showing an outward serenity and cheerfulness when his inner mind was seething with unhappiness. All through these four months he had been battling to the best of his ability with the madness all around. Whereas the rest of us just went on from day to day trying to do the day's work, hoping against hope that in course of time the two countries would settle down, and the fever would pass, he was not content with this. Rather than see free India cursed with this virulent disease of communalism, he must turn inward, see where he had failed, and try to purify himself for a more effective challenge to the communal frenzy. Fasting was to him the final resort, when every other kind of action seemed to have failed. He might die in his attempt to bring the country to its senses. Or he might in some measure succeed in his shock tactics. In any case, he believed that a fast, if entered upon with pure, selfless motives, would cleanse his own heart and mind, and might help him to see what more could be done that had not been attempted already. This fast, which he had declared when he broke his silence that Monday evening to address the crowd assembled for his prayers, was to be without limit of time. It could be broken if all the leaders of the main communities in Delhi—Hindu, Sikh, Muslim—agreed to defend one another from further molestation. He was repeating his Calcutta demand.

The fast began on 13 January 1948. Five days later he was able to break it. Leaders of all the main communities in Delhi undertook a solemn pledge that they would protect the minority community with their lives. They knew that if they failed to do this, Gandhi would fast himself to death. He was unwilling to be a living witness to a free India in which the Muslims could not live in safety.

The fast made a great impression in Pakistan. For many years the supporters of the Muslim League had been fed on the belief that Gandhi was an enemy of Islam. Jinnah, in particular, had no use for the Mahatma, and took every opportunity to speak against him. But this fast was too much for his prejudice. Moreover, in response to the Mahatma's appeals, the Indian Government agreed to pay to Pakistan a sum of forty-four million pounds, which were due as part of the assets of undivided India, and which the government had been withholding because of the Kashmir conflict.

Gandhi began to look forward to fresh efforts. He hoped soon to go to West Pakistan, to persuade the people there to invite their Hindu and Sikh neighbours to return to their homes. He was determined if possible to reverse the refugee movement on both sides, to restore communal harmony by the deliberate act of the people as a whole. But this was not to be.

One section of the Indian population was still wholly unreconciled. This was the Rashtriya Swayam Sevak Sangh, and those who shared their passion to purify India of every non-Hindu influence. Their organisation was based chiefly in Maharashtra, round Bombay and Poona, with no organised group in Delhi, so they had not been among the leaders who had promised to protect the Muslims. They saw now that they could never drive every Muslim out of India so long as Gandhi lived. Two days after Gandhi broke his fast, a bomb was thrown during the evening prayers. It exploded some distance from him and he ignored it. Next day, referring to this incident, he declared that the congratulations he had received at his escape would only be deserved "if I fall as a result of such an explosion and yet retain a smile on my face and no malice against the assailant." He pleaded with the police not to molest the youth who had thrown the bomb, but to convert him with love and persuasion.

The authorities were anxious to give him better protection, but he would not tolerate their plan to have a police search of those who came evening by evening to the prayer meeting. It was twelve days later that Nathuram Godse, a journalist from Poona, came forward to greet him as he came walking to the prayers between his two granddaughters, and shot him at point-blank range. He was heard to utter the words, "He Rama" (Oh, God), as he fell.

A few weeks later, when I was in Pakistan, I met people who believed that the Hindus as a whole had rejoiced when they heard of Gandhi's death. Presumably, a few did so. But the vast mass was profoundly shocked. Many who had been angry with him for his defence of the Muslims were now shocked into penitence for their own short-sightedness. I was in the great city of Calcutta when the news of his death came through from Delhi. It seemed as if the whole city was stunned. Within an hour or two of his death, many thousands were walking towards the river to bathe, this being the orthodox Hindu response to the news of the death of a great saint or leader. Every voice seemed to be hushed. It was a city bound together in a common emotion of overwhelming sorrow. And so, no doubt, it was in the towns and villages throughout the country. Was ever one man loved so deeply and so personally in his lifetime by so many?

For months, the Muslim minority throughout India was safe from molestation. The Rashtriya Sevak Sangh, by destroying the Mahatma, had given the country the shock it needed. Those who had been angrily criticising him now saw the tragic consequence of their own short-sighted anger. They knew that he had been right. After a time, Indo-Pakistan relations deteriorated again, and the struggle for sanity had to begin all over again. Even as I write this, nearly twenty years later, the fundamental problem of Hindu-Muslim relations in the two countries has not found its settlement. But Gandhi's legacy remains, and all those who genuinely accepted his leadership know that they must keep on working for the healing of the breach.

10

Epilogue

In October 1949, the Indian Council of World Affairs published a pamphlet entitled *Political Ideas of Mahatma Gandhi*. There were five essays by five different authors. I was one of them. The other four were all Indians. I had written my essay a few months before Independence and, of course, before Gandhi's death. Reading it again nearly twenty years later, I find it still expresses my impression of Gandhi's political ideas; so, with slight modification and addition, I append it here.

What follows is an attempt to restate Gandhi's political philosophy (though I rather hesitate to use such a high-sounding word) and to suggest some of the things in his teaching that the world should pay special attention to. I must add that this was written, not in the light of any systematic re-reading of his own writings, but rather as the personal reflections of an Englishman who had read most of his weekly writings during the last twenty years of his life, and who had a good many opportunities of drinking from the fountain-source.

Let us, in the first place, try to assign Gandhi to his appropriate political grouping. Was he a conservative, or a liberal, or a socialist, or a radical, or a communist, or an anarchist? My reply would be, he was all those things. I seem to hear some impatient critic, who is an ardent adherent of one or other of these political doctrines, say: "Then he must have been a muddle-headed fool, from whom we have nothing to learn." Be patient, and let me explain why such a summary dismissal of his political teaching is not justified. I believe that in every human being who is not seriously limited in his personality there is in fact some element of most, if not all, of these seemingly contradictory attitudes to life. I have noted again and again that men who are extremely radical in politics may be ultra-conservative in their ideas of art or in some aspects of personal life; and the conservative in politics may be strongly socialistic in some of his local activities. Sincere and devoted communists can be thorough-going liberal individualists in some departments of life, and so on. Now, the great merit of Gandhi is that he was such a complete man that he could recognise the need for some element of every one of these principles in the life of the community. Without being woolly, he could and did strike a balance among them all.

Let us look at the matter a little more closely. In what sense was Gandhi a conservative? Surely, in his recognition of the value of the human heritage, both in religion and in social life. In his attitude to the religious heritage, he was constantly reminding us that what has given vitality to millions of human beings, including many of the world's great sages and seers, cannot wisely be rejected as mere superstition. By all means submit the ancient teachings to intelligent scrutiny, so as to distinguish the essential religious inspiration from superstitious accretions, but show a healthy respect for the wisdom of past ages. So, too, in social life. He saw that the ancient civilisations of India and China have endured through the ages, surviving shock after shock of invasion, exploitation, and massacre, because the common people have held fast to a social tradition, based on the local production of the necessities of food, clothing, and shelter, held together by a tradition of family interdependence and of village self-government. Although his passion for the well-being of the Indian villager was at least equal to that of the most radical reformer of the younger generation, he was still able to see that the traditional life of India's villages contains values that must be preserved. To use the homely metaphor, he warns us against the danger of throwing out the baby with the bath-water.

Gandhi the liberal. For those who think of his life chiefly in terms of the movements of civil disobedience that he led against the British Government, it might seem that he was a believer in direct action, rather than in the art of persuasion by reason, which, I take it, is the essence of the liberal creed. But this is a mistaken view. There can be very few men of his political eminence who have spent so many hours of their lives trying patiently to reason with their political opponents. His daily prayer talks were always quiet appeals to reason. In all his public speaking, he shunned the arts of the orator. He spoke to a crowd of thousands in the same quiet and restrained tone of voice that he used if talking to one or two intimate friends. He never tried to stir the emotions of his audience, still less the dangerous passions. "Be reasonable, be restrained, be patient, think the best of your adversary, try to win him instead of coercing him"—this was his constant theme. In private, what endless hours he spent in patient reasoning with his adversaries, whether they were critics among his own friends and colleagues, or political adversaries, Indian or British. He could be shatteringly frank, both with his intimate friends and with his critics. But this frankness was always courteous, often shot through with humour. His was so far from the temper that tries to kick the opponent when he is down that he would rather rush to offer him a helping hand, so that his enemy may stand up again. "I am a born co-operator," he was fond of saying. Surely all this is of the essence of the liberal spirit.

Was Gandhi a socialist? I have always felt some hesitation in giving an affirmative answer to this question. But he himself at certain times so emphatically declared himself to be one that it seems impossible to deny it. But what did he mean by being a "socialist"? As far as I know, he never committed himself to any rigid socialist doctrine, such as the State ownership of the means of production, but it has been noted by other commentators that his writings have a strongly socialistic flavour. He was at least a convinced socialiser. He would not exempt any capitalist from the drastic doctrine that a man who consumes more than he needs is robbing the poor. One of his guiding principles in politics was that the needs of the community and the service of the poor should always override every selfish or individual interest. In this sense he was a socialist indeed. His friendship with certain wealthy capitalists was no more a denial of his socialistic principles than his friendship with soldiers denied his pacifist convictions.

Gandhi the radical. Perhaps, it is enough to observe that whenever he became convinced that an existing institution was evil, whether, for instance, British rule in India or the social system of untouchability, he immediately became the advocate of radical measures. The evil must be cut out from the root, and no palliative or half-measure would satisfy him. He saw that, if an institution was radically evil, minor reforms may be even dangerous, since they delude people into thinking that the evil has been cured, when in fact only the visible growth has been cut down, and the evil root remains in the soil, ready to spring up again suddenly and un-expectedly as soon as the next rains come.

Was Gandhi a communist? Again, as with his socialism, if the question means, did he accept certain doctrines, such as class war, dictatorship of the proletariat, the necessity of violent revolution as the only means to a classless society, dialectical materialism or any other materialistic interpretation of history, then he is no communist. But if practice matters more than theory, then Gandhi was much more truly a communist than most of those who subscribe to communist theory. Those who lived with him even for short periods had real experience of a commonwealth in which the principle of "from each according to his ability, to each according to his need" was the practice of daily life.

A rather closer analysis is needed of Gandhi the anarchist. One is often tempted to believe, when reading his comments on public affairs, that he believed that that country was happiest which had the least government. His ideal was a land of self-governing villages, knit together by the minimum of central control. His deep faith in the common man—or rather, in common men, for it was one of his most singular characteristics that, in an age that tends to deal with human beings in the mass, he still saw every single villager, however humble and anonymous, as a soul to be respected and treated as an individual—this deep faith led him to believe that decentralisation of authority accords best with the dignity of man. It is here, perhaps, that his political outlook seemed to differ most from that of normal socialism. To the socialist, it seems essential that the State should be given authority in order to prevent the masses from being exploited by the power of individual wealth. The anarchist doubts whether the cure will be much better than the disease. Will the citizen whose actions are being checked at every point by an army of bureaucrats really have much more freedom, more scope for living a full life, than the citizen who is a wage-slave? Community control, says the anarchist, does not mean necessarily State control. Let the State, or today even the world unit, the United Nations, have necessary powers of co-ordination, let it have adequate powers to prevent undue concentra-tion of wealth in private hands. But this should be combined with the least possible central direction of effort, with the minimum control over the daily life of the citizen.

Gandhi held views which were much closer to the anarchist than to the socialist in these matters. But, here again, he was not to be identified with the whole anarchist philosophy; for, alongside of his preference for the minimum of essential government, he fully recognised the necessity for every happy community to accept the rule of law. No conservative or constitutionalist could express himself more strongly on this. As a man who was driven by his conscience to defy the law of the lands in which he was living, first in South Africa, and later in India, he again and again insisted that such a man must be scrupulously careful to obey every law that his conscience does not reject. He must not get into the habit of assuming that because some laws are intolerably evil, therefore, the citizen is free to resist or evade every law which he finds onerous or disagreeable, or all laws enacted by a questionable authority. Gandhi believed in "going the second mile" even with an alien government, whose whole system of government he was challenging. Disobedience must be reserved for those occasions when you are prepared to die rather than to obey.

Of course, for Gandhi, as for other men, the rule of law in which he believed was primarily home-made law, or perhaps it would be better to call it home-grown law; that is to say, the rule of community behaviour which has been found through long practice to accord best with the needs of the society involved: a law, a custom which can be modified by general consent, or by regular legislative procedure, as the pattern of life changes. Yet, so important is respect for law as cement to the life of a people that it is better, except on the rarest occasions, to obey a law fastened on a country by an alien ruler than to allow a general tendency towards lawlessness to develop.

Thus, we may see in Gandhi's political outlook elements that are characteristic of conservatism, elements also of liberalism, of radicalism, of socialism, of communism, of anarchism, but also a high regard for the rule of law. Where is all this leading us?

In the first place, it is not surprising that a great original thinker, as Gandhi's whole life and character proclaim him, should refuse to fit into the conventional categories. But this does not get us far. What we need to understand is the nature of his originality. It

surely consists in this, that in an age when people seem to be
exceptionally ready to use any means that provide a short cut to
the political goal of their desire—when, in other words, the goal,
the end, is everything, so that any means of reaching it are held
to be justified—Gandhi was far more concerned about means than
about ends. This emphasis he justified on several grounds. The
means we use, he pointed out, can be controlled, for these are
the weapons we actually use today. The end always remains
uncertain. It depends on many uncertain factors, some of them
quite beyond our control. Moreover, it may be doubted whether
ends and means can be separated entirely. The means we use will
in a large measure control our ends. Thus, in particular, if we
resort to violent means to achieve our goal, it is likely that violence
will persist as an ingredient of the new political framework we are
striving to create. Can a moral end be achieved by immoral means?
Can freedom be won by coercion? Can a peaceful national life be
built through a violent revolution?

Truth and non-violence have been the watchwords emblazoned
on the Gandhian banner throughout his public career. This is
hardly the place to discuss the full significance of his insistence on
truth. That carries us beyond the rather restricted political field
of this discussion. It is fundamental to the whole of his moral
outlook. But to the world as a whole, Gandhi stands as the
prophetic voice of his generation, indeed of this century, who
consistently advocated non-violent action as the right means to
use in combating every injustice, for righting every wrong.

Yet, in spite of his own insistence that it is a principle of universal
application, it has been widely regarded as no more than a technique
for the use of colonial peoples in their struggle to free themselves
from alien rule. Many have seen it as an ingenious method for
undermining the authority of a powerful government in an age
when armed revolt is almost impossible, as the armed strength
that is at the disposal of the modern State is so overwhelmingly
strong in contrast to anything the rebels may be able to acquire.
It is very clear now, as it was to Gandhi himself before his death,
that most of his Indian followers were adopting non-violent forms
of action as a useful technique for undermining British authority,
and that they had not become non-violent in their minds. He
himself was recorded as saying, not long before his death: "The

non-violence that was offered during the past thirty years was that of the weak. ... India has no experience of the non-violence of the strong." What, then, is this non-violence of the strong? Has it any relevance to the world's plight today?

Gandhi's non-violence challenges the whole tendency to concen- trate power in the hands of the State. It is not only in socialist or fascist countries that the State today takes more and more power into its hands. This is an almost universal tendency. It is seen at its most intense form wherever the large modern State is built on the conscription of youth for defence. Military conscription of the whole youth of any country is a new phenomenon, which grew up in the nineteenth century. Napoleon was, perhaps, its originator. Nowadays, it is customary for the State to force every young man to spend a year or more of training to defend his country, in other words, training to kill. Thus, at the most formative period of a man's life, he and his fellows are put into a machine, out of which most of them come so moulded as to be slaves of the State. They may resent and actively dislike the training; but it does things to them in spite of their dislike. They come to assume that it is the natural duty of all men to be ready to defend their country by fighting and killing; they also come to assume that the nation State has absolute authority over them, body and soul, and can at any time command them to absolute obedience. Such doctrines, whether advanced by a socialist State or a capitalist State or a so-called democratic State, are absolutely abhorrent to the follower of Gandhi, both because they are blasphemy against human personality and because they give a distorted view of the duty a man owes to the community. Gandhi is not demanding the freedom of the unmitigated individualist, but he claims that each man should find his own way to perform his appropriate duty to the community; the performance of intelligent and useful work for the community is quite different from servile duty to the State. (In passing, it should be noted that it is absurd to identify the State with the community.) There is a great deal to be said for enacting general obligations for all young men, and probably women too, to give service to the community. But in most cases such service can best be planned in consultation with local authorities—or in some cases with a church or with some world association for service. Some may give a year's service by working on roads or railways, some in mines, some in the mercantile marine or as dock labourers, some in the fields or in hospitals. As far as possible each should give the service that fits him most, or for which he has the best aptitude. Universal service thus organised would help every man to become a good citizen of the world and it should help to break down class distinctions. It will make men healthy in body and mind, but it will not make them slaves of the State, nor will it make them enemies of any people.

Complete renunciation of war and military training is only possible for a community whose citizens accept and rejoice in the rich variety of human types, and who have learnt the true principle of toleration.

Gandhi suggests that it is high time to apply this principle and method of mutual toleration to the relations of States, even when they find themselves in conflict. Armament of one State against another, as if the barbarous foreigners could not be expected to respect any argument except the threat of force, really suggests not that the foreigners are barbarous but that we are. A civilised man treats his fellowmen with openness and confidence, knowing from looking into his own heart that the way to evoke goodwill is to display goodwill. None of us cares to surrender to threats. Why should we assume that the "enemy" will behave in exactly the opposite way? The surest way to perpetuate hostility is to arm against him and to display distrust of him. The way to win him to fruitful co-operation is to act as if we expect him to behave as we should behave. As I understand the Gandhian view of international relations, it is something like this: just as the world needs men of conservative mind, men of liberal mind, radicals, socialists, communists, anarchists, in order to ensure the right balance between the different forces that must interact for the fruitful and harmonious development of the whole community, so the world needs the varied contributions of Russians, Chinese, Africans, Arabs, Europeans, Americans, and all the rest; if they would but learn to treat one another with mutual respect, the whole world would be enriched by the variety of their contributions. But there will be quarrels. What then? First, as rational, civilised beings, we must try to settle such quarrels by rational methods, by direct conversations, by diplomacy. If such negotiations fail, let some disinterested party be called in to advise, or let the dispute be referred to third party judgment.

And if the worst comes to the worst, and some country falls under the rule of bad men who are determined to overrun and conquer their neighbours by violence, let the civilised people show their superior civilisation by resisting, not with counter-measures of violence, but with disciplined refusal to co-operate with the aggressor. In Gandhian words, that is the time to "do or die," which does not mean "kill or be killed." It means: resist with your life, but commit no violence.

Today, most thoughtful people will agree with all this except the last. All nations in a world community: good. Negotiation and arbitration instead of war: good. But non-violence in response to aggression: no. Sadly they turn away, saying either, "that is unrealistic," or "it is too hard for us." They may frankly declare: "Yes, that is the non-violence of the strong; but we are too weak to endure such agonies without hitting back."

The most obvious argument in support of the Gandhian alternative is that the opposite method, meeting force with force, has been tried all through human history, and it has finally brought mankind to the very brink of world destruction. Whatever may be said about the comparatively mild wars of the past, when nations even in war time tried to follow some restraint, today war has become so frightful, inflicting such inconceivable suffering on the masses of civilians, men, women, and children together, and it leaves behind such bitterness, hatred, and debasement of the moral coinage that, even at the risk of enduring injustice for a longer time, more civilised and manly means must be found to resist injustice, domination, and even armed aggression.

Mahatma Gandhi spent his whole life trying to evolve just such alternative means of peaceful struggle. Have they any real validity for the modern age?

The sceptic will, no doubt, point out that no form of mass civil disobedience can have the smallest effect against atom bombs—or even ordinary bombs. The bombs will drop equally on the pacifist and the militarist. But, true though this is, it remains true also that an unarmed State is less likely to be the victim of aggression in the modern world than a heavily armed State. Under the circumstances that now prevail, a government can only get the blind support of their citizens for attacking another country if their propaganda has been able to suggest that the "enemy" is getting ready to attack. It would be difficult for any press, however much under government control, to convince the public that a neighbouring country was about to attack if in fact it was disarmed. It may well be that today, especially for the greater States, disarmament is the safest policy. A State that has no armament at all is evidently prepared to rely on justice and honourable dealing, rather than on threats and bomb-boasting.

The conclusion each of us will reach at the end of an argument of this kind will depend on our conviction as to the nature of man. Is he at heart a moral being, capable of living on good terms with his neighbours, fit to become part of a great world society? Is man fundamentally trustworthy? Or is he an untamable wild beast, whose greed and selfishness will sooner or later get the better of him, and who must, therefore, be kept under restraint? In each of us, no doubt, there is not only something of the beast, which will always be, but also something of the angel. When we think of ourselves and our friends, or our fellow-nationals, we are fairly confident of the angelic qualities, sure that we and they are fit to be free citizens of a free State. We never harbour thoughts of aggression against other nations—no, not even to increase our trade and profits. But the other fellows are different. That is the trouble. As we read our newspapers and shudder with horror at the frightful deeds recorded from distant (sometimes not so distant) places, we feel that we could not sleep securely in our beds at night if the government did not provide for our security against these dangerous foreigners. But we should remember that that is exactly what the dangerous foreigners think about us.

It was surely one of Gandhi's greatest qualities that he always believed that other men could be, and at heart really wished to be, as good and moral as he. Perhaps this is the foundation of faith for the man of peace or of non-violence. We must trust other nations, said Gandhi, expecting them to behave as well as we expect our own nation to behave.

There is, indeed, one great difficulty about extending the sphere of non-violence from the individual to the community. Whereas in the sphere of non-violent resistance to injustice within a country, one man alone, or even a few, can start such a resistance, and so demonstrate its value, the disarmed State, which has resolved to live courageously in a world of armed States, can only come into being when there is a very widespread conviction among its people that such disarmament is good and right. The whole level of public morale must be raised to something far above what any nation has yet reached, before the great majority of a nation will be courageous enough to risk all and face the world unarmed. Such action of large multitudes is, no doubt, always the result of mixed motives. Some might be moved by what they take to be common prudence, not to mention the great economies that would follow. But without the ingredient of a very powerful moral conviction, a sense of a great crusade on behalf of the welfare of man, such a break from the habits of human societies over thousands of years is hardly conceivable. All the more reason, surely, for all men of goodwill, for all who care for peace and harmony (and who does not?) to give the matter the most thorough attention. Nothing is stranger in human behaviour today than the almost universal tendency of reasonable men to say (in effect): "Of course, we will take all reasonable steps to ensure peace; only, for God's sake, don't ask us to turn pacifist and throw away our armed protection." But today these final moral challenges cannot be evaded. The world must choose life or death. The old way will take us surely to death. The Gandhian way, the courageous way, seeking moral means to achieve the great end of "One World," may bring life to mankind.

Let us listen to Gandhi's own voice on this: "Tit for tat," he wrote a few months before his death, "is the law of the brute or unregenerate man. Such men have had their day. The world is sick of the application of the law of the jungle. It is thirsting for the brave law of love for hate, truth for untruth, tolerance for intolerance. If this law of regenerate man is not to rule the world, it is thrice doomed." Which of you, Gandhi asks every man and woman, is willing to dare the new way of life and hope with me?

Appendix

BETWEEN 1927 and his death, Mahatma Gandhi wrote some thirty or forty letters and notes to me. From those that I have preserved, I am here giving a selection, in some cases because of the intrinsic importance of their content; but in most cases because they illustrate the endless variety of the man, and his ways of looking at things and people. He was a most voluminous correspondent. It is hardly credible that a man who carried such heavy responsibilities as he did, and was at the beck and call of so many, found time to write in his own hand (or rather, his two hands) such quantities of letters. They were never perfunctory. Everyone of his innumerable friends was to him a single identifiable man or woman. He did not sit down to write the same letter to several different people. Even if he was asking his friends to uphold him through a fast, he would still make each letter special for the friend he was addressing. It will be noted that in the earlier letters I was either "friend" or "Mr Alexander"; after the Round Table Conference in London I became "Horace" to him, and he then began to sign himself as "Bapu," the name he was called by his closest circle of friends at the ashram and in the Congress leadership. It really means just simply "father"; but in India this term is used more widely beyond the immediate family circle than in the West.

I first visited Gandhi's ashram near Ahmedabad in March 1928, where I stayed for a week. On the day I left, he said that as I had spent some days with them, I might have noticed things that seemed to need improvement; if so, he hoped I should write to him about them, for he was always glad to have suggestions for improvement. Then he pointed to a tap, under which the members of the ashram washed their hands after meals. There was no drainage under the tap, so the water ran down into the earth, and made a muddy patch. This, he said, was hygienically bad, so an Englishman, such as I was, would very likely notice this failure of hygiene and might suggest that it should be put right.   In fact he hoped to put it right soon, but the ashram was rather short of money.

I think I wrote on my return to England; and having first said, apparently, that I would not feel inclined to bother to write about small matters of hygiene, I did nevertheless wonder whether he might find it a good plan to introduce a period of silence into the daily prayers.   Here is his reply:

(This first letter is typed, and is dated 22-6-28, on printed paper of the Satyagrahashram, Sabarmati, B.B.C.I. Ry.)

Dear Friend,

I have long delayed replying to your letter, as I have hoped to send you a fairly lengthy reply.   But I see that I am not likely to get sufficient leisure for attempting a very full reply in the near future.

What you say about silent prayer and congregational silence I understand and I appreciate also in theory.   When I was in South Africa, I attended several such meetings.   But I was not much struck with the performance.   In India, it will fall flat.   After all, there are many ways of worship and it is not necessary to graft new ways, if old ones will answer.   I am myself not satisfied with what we are able to do in the Ashram, I cannot procure a devotional mood all of a sudden or in an artificial manner.   If some of us in the Ashram really have that mood whilst at prayer, it is bound to have its effect in due course.   It is because of the belief that there are earnest souls in the Ashram who approach the prayer time in a proper devotional mood, that I have persisted in retaining the congregational prayer meetings in spite of odds and sometimes even severe disappoint-ments.   I may be partial, but my own experience is that our prayer meetings are very slowly but surely growing in dignity and strength.   But I am painfully aware of the fact that we are far away from what we want to achieve.   Nevertheless, I shall bear your suggestions in mind.   I have already discussed them with friends.

You seem to think lightly of my having invited suggestions with reference to sanitary matters. In my own humble opinion, we needlessly divide life into watertight compartments, religious and other. Whereas if a man has true religion in him, it must show itself in the smallest detail of life. To me sanitation in a community such as ours is based upon common spiritual effort. The slightest irregularity in sanitary, social and political life is a sign of spiritual poverty. It is a sign of inattention and neglect of duty. Anyway, the Ashram life is based upon this conception of fundamental unity of life.

Yours sincerely,

M.K. Gandhi

Nearly a year later, C. F. Andrews, who was then in England, showed me a book by a woman doctor, Dr Vaughan, who had investigated the medical effects of the purdah restriction on the life of women in India and, I believe, other Asian countries. He asked me to send this book to Gandhi when I had read it, and this I did. From his reply it is clear that I had said that I hoped he would not feel that this was another book of defamation of India, like the then notorious book, *Mother India* by Katherine Mayo. Also, I had evidently sent him some Quaker books. As far as I recall, when I was at the ashram, Mahadev Desai, Gandhi's secretary, had told me that they would like to know more about Quakers, and in particular they would like to have books telling about William Penn and his *Holy Experiment* of establishing an un-armed state (Pennsylvania) in North America, and about John Woolman and his pioneering efforts to emancipate slaves and to treat them as social equals. Finally, it is clear that I had told him in the same letter that went with Dr Vaughan's book that I had found a passage in his Autobiography, which I had recently read, where his reference to his wife had bothered me (years later, when I tried to identify this passage in the Autobiography, I was no longer able even to find it).

(This letter, also typed, comes from the Ashram at Sabarmati, and is dated 7-3-1929.)

Dear Friend,

I have your letter as also Dr Vaughan's book. I have gone through the booklet. There is no comparison between Miss Mayo's production and Dr Vaughan's essay. It is a very serious contribution to a thorny subject. I propose to make use of it in the pages of *Young India*.

I do not know whether I have already written to you telling you that the Quaker books you referred to were duly received by me some months after the receipt of your letter. I was grateful for the gift. You have now learnt why I had to give up the idea of going to Europe.

I have not seen the reference to my wife. But I can tell you that the relations between us are of the happiest kind. It is quite true if the writings gave you the impression that I do not carry my wife with me through her intellect. Her loyalty is amazing and she has followed me through all the transformations that my life has undergone. My own conviction is that most probably the reverence felt by the Indian men towards India's women is quite equal to that felt in the West; but it is of a different type. The Western form of reverence yielding the first place to women and many such other things, seems to me to be highly artificial and sometimes even hypocritical. All the same, there is much to criticise in our treatment of women. Some laws are bad, some husbands are monsters, some parents are heartless towards their daughters. In these matters toleration is, in my opinion, the key to mutual understanding. Every social institution however admirable it may be has its own shortcomings. I know you are too generous to take this paragraph for special pleading in our treatment of women where it falls short of the standard that justice demands. I have simply told you as I have felt.

Yours sincerely,
M.K. Gandhi

During the next year, brief letters passed between us in relation to Reginald Reynolds, whom I had introduced to Gandhi as a young Englishman and Quaker who wanted to live at his Ashram for some time. These notes do not need to be reprinted here. Then, in 1930, while he was in jail during the time of civil disobedience, I spent a few months in India, sent by C.F. Andrews with the support of the Society of Friends in England, and Lord Irwin allowed me to see Gandhi in jail. However, nothing came of my own or other efforts to get him out of jail in time to attend the first Round Table Conference, which met in London in the autumn of 1930. I was able to watch this Conference at fairly close quarters, through the eyes of some of its Indian members, so I ventured to send Gandhi a favourable report of the progress being made. From his reply it is clear that I specially referred to the queries that were being raised in London as to the attitude of the Indian National Congress to the debts incurred by the Government of India. Would the Congress honour them? Here is his reply:

(It is written in his own hand from Y.C.P., meaning Yeravda Central Prison, at Poona, dated 23-12-1930, and the envelope is addressed to "Friend Horace Alexander," which he perhaps took to be the habitual mode of address of the members of the Society of Friends to one another).

Dear Friend,

I was glad to hear from you. If the R.T.C. results in doing something worthy of the great sacrifice of the nation and therefore of acceptance, I should be delighted. But as I have told you, having been filled with distrust [this refers to our conversation three months earlier in the jail] nothing but an accomplished result will reassure me. The question of debts is incredibly simple. The Lahore resolution [of the Congress a year earlier] has an explicit condition about reference to an impartial tribunal. But you have my assurance that no congressman has ever enunciated the doctrine of total repudiation. What congressmen including myself demand is that the nation's representatives should have the right of having any portion of the so-called national debt, concessions and the like being referred to an independent tribunal whose decision should be final and binding on both the parties.

I feel I am quite safe in saying this even for Pandit Jawaharlal Nehru. Not to adopt the course above indicated would be disloyal to the nation as total repudiation without just cause would undoubtedly be dishonourable. Whatever Maulana Muhammad Ali may think of me, I have nothing but kindly feelings about him. And I feel that time will remove misunderstandings. Having no feeling either against Islam or Mussulmans, I feel absolutely at ease [I had told him of a visit I had paid with C.F. Andrews to the sick bed of the younger of the two famous "Ali brothers," at one time close associates of Gandhi but now his critics. Muhammad Ali had come to the Round Table Conference, but he took to his bed and died a few weeks later. I recall the warm embrace with which he greeted Andrews, rising up in his bed to do so]. My love to Reginald. I know Charlie Andrews is no longer with you.

Yours sincerely,
M.K. Gandhi

Between this and the next letter, there is a long gap, which included Gandhi's visit to the Round Table Conference in London, when I was closely associated with him; my colleagues at the Quaker College at Birmingham (Woodbrooke) had generously made it possible for me to spend a couple of days each week in London assisting Charlie Andrews to cope with the innumerable demands made on Gandhi while he was in London. Thus I became a member of the household, and got into the habit of calling Gandhi "Bapu." As soon as he returned to India after the Conference he was arrested, and started a long residence in the Yeravda Central Prison at Poona.

Yeravda Central Prison,
25th March 1932

My dear Horace,

You will have no difficulty in recognising this handwriting. Mahadev was just sent to me when I had again to fall back on the left hand. I was glad to have your note. Agatha [Harrison] has been keeping me informed to the extent that she can of your activities and the papers that I am allowed to receive do also now and then mention something of the activities of all the many friends who have interested themselves in this struggle and Hoyland [J.S. Hoyland, my colleague at Woodbrooke] has been telling me of the silent prayers. I know that they are all precious and not one prayer of the heart is without an adequate response. What though one does not see tangible results of all the heartfelt prayers?

You are quite right in being happy for me to have this enforced rest. If it had not come to me there would have been in all probability a breakdown. The time here does not hang heavy. There is the spinning wheel, and there are the silent companions the books and I need some time for doing a little writing. And then I have Sardar Vallabhbhai Patel with me who last time was not kept with me but just a wall separated him from me. And now I have Mahadev.

Yes, I wanted that special message from Olive. I was sorry that I could not come into closer touch with her during those precious days at Selly Oak, but I have imagination enough to understand what her beautiful life must be like. Our love to you and Olive and all the friends.

Bapu

Three months later came this letter. The first paragraph refers to a young English woman who had helped Charlie Andrews with his writings and had met Gandhi in London. It had now become clear that her cancer was incurable.

Y.C.P.,
23-6-32

My dear Horace,

I have your two letters. It was just like you to remind me about Lauri. I remember her quite well. She appealed to me at once as a beautiful character. And then it was Charlie who, I think, brought her to me. I wrote to her at once and sent my letter by air mail. At least I asked the authorities to send it so and wrote it in time for the air mail. I know that she is brave enough to face all the illnesses that may be in store for her and also death.

We are all three keeping well and quite fit. Mahadev and I pass the time spinning, reading, writing; Sardar in reading and envelope-making out of scraps of paper that come to us by chance. I call this healthy wealth-production in the name of and for the sake of all.

I wanted to write to you earlier but somehow or other it escaped me. You will be pleased to learn that at the Ashram the minute of silence has been increased to *five* minutes. From the letters I was getting from the Ashram I saw that the concentrated labours of the inmates made them highstrung and therefore I felt that it was likely that those who were not used to such concentrated work might not be able to follow the prayer with required serenity. If therefore they had five minutes unbreakable silence to compose themselves and put themselves in tune with the Infinite the prayer would be more fruitful. This was introduced now nearly a month ago or a little longer. And Narandas tells me that the silence has done much good.

I have not yet got Charlie's book. I expect it every week. We constantly think of you as the Settlement [Woodbrooke in those days called itself a "settlement" rather than a college]. It was a happy time you gave me at Selly Oak. Olive is a great reminder to us all in faithful devotion and utter cheerfulness in spite of frail condition. Mahadev says he does remember the conversation she had with him and many other sweet things at Woodbrooke. We both wish her many more years of loving service.

With love from us all to the whole family.

> Yours,
> Bapu

In September of that year came his fast against the MacDonald Award which would have given the Untouchables wholly separate political constituencies from the Caste Hindus. Gandhi had always declared that he could not live to see such a political vivisection of India. After the fast he wrote:

Y.C.P.,
4-10-32

My dear Horace,

I have your letter. I have written so much to so many friends about the fast that I don't feel like saying anything in this letter. No doubt you will see some of the letters that are going by this week's mail. This however I will say: God was never nearer to me than during the fast. And I felt the love of you all although I had not then any letter from England. My love to you and Olive.

Bapu

Although he was not released from jail, Gandhi was given permission to carry on work and correspondence on behalf of the Untouchables, from henceforth to be known by him and many others as Harijans (Children of God). His relationship with Dr Ambedkar, himself a Harijan and leader of an important section of Harijans in western India, had always been a delicate and difficult one. Dr Ambedkar strongly disapproved of Gandhi's approach to the problems of untouchability. At the time of the Round Table Conference, with Gandhi's encouragement, I had made personal contact with Dr Ambedkar, with whose standpoint I had a measure of sympathy. From the two letters (typed) that follow, it is clear that I had written to Gandhi about Dr Ambedkar in the period immediately after the fast. He had visited England, where I had seen him.

Yeravda Central Prison,
5 January 1933

My dear Horace,

I am overdue in acknowledging your and other love letters, but the work before me has to take precedence over everything else.

I am glad you were able to see Dr Ansari and other friends, and gladder still that you were able to have that long conversation with Dr Ambedkar. Of course he has still got that over-sensi-

tiveness and terrible suspicion, but there is to me nothing
unnatural in it. As I used to say so often in London, he had
every excuse for the bitterness with which only he could speak
whenever he spoke about untouchability, or of those touchable
Hindus who had anything to do with it. He has not only
witnessed the inhuman wrongs done to the social pariahs of
Hinduism, but in spite of all his culture, all the honours he has
received, he has, when he is in India, still to suffer many insults
to which untouchables are exposed. The wonder is that he is so
tolerant and forbearing as he showed himself, for instance, at the
time when the Yeravda pact was being hammered into shape.
It was perfectly open to him to withstand all pressure and remain
defiant, but he allowed himself to be moved by friendly pressure.
He will soften if the terms of the Yeravda Pact are carried out
in full by the caste Hindus, but though things are shaping well
on the whole, I am experiencing new difficulties from day to day.
They do not dismay me. I was prepared for them. I knew
that that little fast was not enough penance for moving to right
action the great mass of Hindu humanity. Many lives might
have to be given before the last remnant of untouchability is gone.
But no sacrifice will be too great to remove a wrong which lies
like a dead weight, not only on Hindu society, but on all who
surround it. I get now and then piteous letters from Christian
Indians who, being born of untouchable parents, are isolated
from the rest of their fellows. Such is the contagious nature of
this dreadful disease.

    With our love to you and Olive.

                                                    Yours,
                                                    Bapu

Another typed letter on similar topics, from the Prison, 31st
March, 1933.

My dear Horace,

    Your long letter pleased me immensely. You should repeat
the performance whenever the spirit moves you.

    You will see that I have made use in the current *Harijan* of
one important portion of your letter. The other important part
is with reference to reproducing in the *Harijan* the views of Dr

Ambedkar and those of the Sanatanists [the orthodox Hindus who were opposing Gandhi's reforms]. This is not always possible. I gave much thought to it. To make the paper self-supporting, to refuse all advertisements as the initiator of the movement to give my views as exhaustively as possible on the current happenings about Harijans, to combine all these things in one paper became an almost impossible task. And then, the reproduction of Sanatani views and those of the Ambedkar school was unnecessary for the vast majority of readers, because they knew all the sides of the question, and they had been published in the daily press. It could then be of use only to the foreign readers, of whom there are naturally but a select few. Whether few or many they could not be neglected, and I knew that they were being well supplied with the literature outside what could be handled by the *Harijan*. And this extra reading they had to do, whether through the *Harijan* or through the original sources, and I came to the conclusion that I must leave them to gather the different viewpoints through the original sources. And because I have done so, it has been possible for me, even from almost the beginning, to make the *Harijan* self-supporting. I have certainly taken extraordinary precautions not to give any colouring to the views of the other side, whenever it has been necessary for me to give them. More than this, I must not say.

Thus, though I am not able to give effect, as you would wish it, to this part of your letter, you know that everything you say must produce its invisible effect upon my mind, and therefore whatever you think is worth passing on to me you should do unhesitatingly. The freer and fuller the criticism of friends and associates like you, the lighter and better will my work be, and such criticism will itself be an important part of your contribution to the Harijan cause.

Please share this letter with C.F. Andrews, Jack Hoyland and others.

I hope you are now so well that there is no occasion even to make enquiry about your health. Love to you all from us all,

Bapu

There was a brief note written on 7-5-33 from Yeravda, asking for "the prayers of all of you" for the fast he undertook for self-purification at that time. Then the following, written on 15-12-33; this is written entirely in his own hand. During these years I rarely troubled him with a letter, since Agatha Harrison, who was acting as secretary of the India Conciliation Group, and for whose full-time support Gandhi had made himself responsible, was in regular correspondence with him, and I saw her letters from him. The occasion of this letter is that I had found that people in England were still under the influence of the "Rome interview" of two years earlier; now that Gandhi was free, it seemed important to get a specific statement about it from him.

My dear Horace,

Agatha has sent me your letter to her about that imaginary interview in Rome. It is wonderful how journalism has become degraded. Thank God the bulk of mankind remains unaffected even by the most widely read newspapers. But this reflection in no way absolves me from having to deal with the particular allegation. If Agatha can trace the two statements of the Rome journalists, I can deal with the matter at once. I hope both you and Olive are keeping well. Love to you all.

Bapu

[As far as I know, Agatha did this and further elucidation followed, Miraben giving a very detailed account of what had really happened in Rome.]

Next year (1934) there was a move from some quarters to try to bring Gandhi to England again. I was doubtful of the wisdom of this, believing that Gandhi was most effective in India and that the Indian nationalist case would be better presented to the English people by Jawaharlal Nehru than by Gandhi himself. I wrote to him in this sense, and received the following reply, dated 27-9-34.

My dear Horace,

I love you all the more, if more was possible, for your frank letter. You will be surprised to know that long before I received your letter I had expressed the opinion that Jawaharlal could present the Indian case more convincingly than I before English audiences. What you have said therefore is not new to me. But even apart from that I am quite sure that I must not leave India for the present at any rate. I can speak to you all more effectively from here. Nor do I think that any purpose can be served by sending Mrs G. there alone. I am sure that both she and I must be dismissed from the minds of English friends in so far as our visit is concerned. I want every minute I can have for the things I have said in my recent statement. Love to you and Olive.

Bapu

[This statement was, I think, mainly a new call for more effective work for the destruction of untouchability.]

For several years, either short notes on personal matters came from Gandhi himself or he commissioned one or other of his personal assistants to write on his behalf: Mahadev Desai, Miraben, Rajkumari Amrit Kaur, Pyarelal Nayar. No doubt in every case they were reporting Gandhi himself very exactly, but none of these letters is sufficiently significant to demand quotation in whole or even in part. So we come right down to April 1942, when the war had been proceeding for many months, and Gandhi was finding himself torn between his grief at the suffering incurred by the British and other belligerents, and his increasing dislike of British official policies towards India. My wife (Olive) had died at the beginning of the year. He had at that time cabled a message of sympathy. A little later came the visit of Sir Stafford Cripps to India with proposals from the British Government which he had hoped might prove acceptable to the leaders of the Indian Congress as well as to the Muslim League and other Indian parties. As we have seen, the proposals were very nearly accepted, but Gandhi was dissatisfied with them. He decided to open his heart to me, and accordingly wrote the following letter, dated 22-4-41, (an error for '42) written in his own hand from Sevagram, Wardha, C.P.

My dear Horace,

I have been wanting to write to you and Agatha all this time but my preoccupations have been in the way. But more than that, the reluctance to send you a cheerless letter has been the cause. It is still there, greater than ever. Nevertheless I must write what I feel. I hope you had my wire about Olive. How well I remember her radiant face in spite of her permanent disability. God gave and He has taken away. I know it is well with her, for she walked in His light.

Sir Stafford has come and gone. How nice it would have been, if he had not come with that dismal mission. He of all people should never have [come] without having at least ascertained Jawaharlal's wishes. How could the British Government at this stage have behaved as they did? Why should they have sent proposals without discussing them with the principal parties? Not one single party was satisfied. In trying to please all, the proposals pleased none.

I talked to him frankly but as a friend if for nothing else, for Andrews' sake. [C.F. Andrews had died a few months before this, and Gandhi had said that the best memorial of Andrews would be for the best Indians and the best Englishmen to meet and never adjourn till they had come to an agreement] I told him that I was speaking to him with Andrews' spirit as my witness. I made suggestions but all to no avail. As usual they were not practical. I had not wanted to go. I had nothing to say being anti all wars. I went because he was anxious to see me. All this I mention in order to give you the background. I was not present throughout the negotiations with the WC [Working Committee]. I had come away. You know the result. It was inevitable. The whole thing has left a bad taste in the mouth.

My firm opinion is that the British should leave India now in an orderly manner and not run the risk that they did in Singapore, Malaya and Burma. That act would mean courage of a high order, confession of human limitations and right doing by India. Britain cannot defend India, much less herself on Indian soil with any strength. The best thing she can do is to leave India to her fate. I feel somehow that India will not do badly then. I must not argue this point if it is not obvious to you.

I am sending a copy of this to Agatha. Of course you are at liberty to share this with anybody else. Love.

Yours,

Bapu

This was all written in his own handwriting, but copies were kept; I first saw it at the ashram early in June 1942, when I reached India to participate in civil defence work undertaken by the Friends Ambulance Unit in India. Before we started our work, Richard Symonds and I visited Gandhi at Sevagram, and talked with him, not only about the work we hoped to do in Bengal, but also about his relations with the Government in Delhi. We were somewhat reassured by our talks, but events were moving steadily towards a new conflict, as the next letter shows. The originals of this and the next are missing, but copies were made while they were still in my possession.

The first is a letter written soon after our first visit to him.

Sevagram, Wardha, C.P.

My dear Horace,

I have your dear letter, of course you will do as the spirit moves you. You will come when you like and so will Symonds. But when you find anything to criticise you will do so as frankly and fearlessly as Charlie [Andrews] used to do. Of course your primary mission is ambulance work and if you found avoiding me or Sevagram necessary you will unhesitatingly avoid me. I shall not misunderstand you in any way whatever. Love.

Bapu

A few weeks later came the decision of the Congress Working Committee proposing a new movement of civil disobedience. I went at once to Sevagram to talk this over with Gandhi, and I was reassured by his assurance that he still wanted to find a way of agreement, and that he had confidence that he could have friendly talks with the Viceroy. Then I also went to see Nehru at Allahabad, to tell him about the work our Ambulance Unit was planning and

to get his interpretation of the latest moves. At the end of July
came the decision to go ahead with civil disobedience. This led me
to send a strong plea to Gandhi, and this in return brought replies
from him. In this case I think it appropriate to publish here my
letter to him as well as his reply, both of which he had planned to
publish in *Harijan*. But before he could do this he was arrested,
and the letters were only published in the south Indian paper,
The Hindu. He also wrote me a personal letter, which may come
first.

> Birla House, Bombay,
> 3 August 1942

My dear Horace,

I read your touching letter for the second time in the train.
And I decided to print it without giving your name and without
the prefatory part. If possible I shall enclose a copy of my note
on it. I wrote it then and there in the train. I could not do
better than that. Often I have found that silence is more eloquent
than speech and action the best of all. But as I have been writing
and explaining, I thought I must not make an exception in this
case. Moreover your letter has invited an answer.

If there is anything more I should do, I am ever ready. Do
tell me fully and frankly; no stone should be left unturned to
remove misunderstandings. My grave misgiving is that those
who are in authority do not want to part with India. With
them it seems that to lose India is to lose the battle. It is terrible
if it is true. In my opinion to keep India as a possession is to
lose the battle. Help me to solve the doubt which I have expressed
in the columns of *Harijan*. Love.

> Bapu

This is what I had written:

Jawaharlal Nehru helped me to get a clear picture of the
background of the Congress resolution. But I do not believe
even he can truly imagine the emotional background in England
today, any more than the Editor of the *New Statesman*, let us

say, can understand the background here. One of the strongest reasons, it always seems to me, for renouncing war utterly is that a war atmosphere is always so demoralising to the nations participating in war. The debasement of moral standards takes all manner of subtle forms. Now, England has been at war for about three years. During one of those years she was facing the greatest ordeal that her population has ever known, and she was practically bearing it alone. And in spite of the comparative lack of air raids in recent months, the ordeal of battle goes on unabated, with the final outcome as dark as ever. *You* may feel sure that England and her Allies will win. But I do not see what proof you or anyone else can have of that until it happens. Anyhow, everyone in England realises that they are still 'up against it,' as they have never been; that when Hitler speaks of annihilating England if he wins, he means just what he says. Now, quite frankly, it seems to me just inevitable that English people, whatever their attitude to Indian freedom, should see in the Congress proposal today a most cruel stab in the back. I don't for a moment doubt that those men and women in Bow or Lancashire who were your friends in 1930, and who have always been friends of Indian freedom, are saying hard things about you today for apparently giving them still one more blow in a vital spot just when they are in mortal danger from relentless foes. And they are not saying those hard things because Churchill or even Cripps tells them to, but because it looks just like that to them. Much as I deplore Cripps' broadcast, I have to confess that if I were in England today, lacking the insight that you and Nehru and other friends have been giving me, I might think as he thinks. If this conflict must be—it must be. But I would beg you to say something before it begins that will show your English friends (you know you have many) why you have felt driven to open this way to their possible annihilation. I want them to realise that it is for you, as it is for them, a terribly painful step to take—a real agony. I hate to think that your friends in England, with their minds all warped, it may be, by their ordeal, should think that you are blind to what this step may mean to them, and, of course, to the Chinese and the Russians. Please forgive this outpouring. I just feel I must share this burden with you.

Gandhi's comment, intended for publication in *Harijan* was as follows:

> This is a letter from a well-known English friend, who is also one of the best English friends India has. It demands as gentle and genuine an answer as his letter is gentle and genuine. I believe every word of what he says about British emotion. Agatha Harrison sends me cable after cable revealing her deep pain over what I am doing and the Congress is doing. And Agatha Harrison, weak in body though she is, is wearing herself out in removing the cobwebs of misunderstanding. She sees every responsible English statesman who will see her (and let me admit that they all see her) and pleads for India's cause. But she is up against a blind wall. I seem to have lost the credit that I thought I used to enjoy in those circles. It is most difficult to repair a loss for which there is no accountable reason that the loser can see. For the moment I must content myself with repetition of assurances and protestations of good faith. I would not lose credit even for entrance into heaven. But there are moments when it becomes necessary to risk (not to incur) the loss of credit for the sake of the creditor himself.
>
> I began my experiments in non-cooperation with the members of my family. I had no occasion to regret the adventure, for the risks were run for their sake as they themselves discovered—some soon and some late. Love and truth are as gentle as they are sometimes hard beyond endurance.
>
> I have passed many sleepless nights to discover the various ways of ending the struggle with the least commotion. But I saw that some form of conflict was inevitable to bring home the truth to the British mind. I have no doubt that events would show that I was right, that I acted in the spirit of pure friendship. British authority would deal summarily with the movement. The sufferings will be all on the side of the people. True, but in the end Britain will lose in the moral fibre. But to let her continue as she is doing is to make her bankrupt, and, perhaps, lose the battle, whereas the movement, which I have advised the Congress to take up, is designed to prevent bankruptcy and enable Great Britain to acquire a moral height which must secure victory for her and her Allies. There is no claim here for philanthropy.

The fact stands and nobody has ever denied it, that by this movement India stands to gain her goal of independence. But this is irrelevant here. What is relevant is the fundamental fact that the movement is designed to help Britain in spite of herself. This is a very big, almost arrogant claim. I am not ashamed to advance it because it comes from an agonised heart. Time alone will show the truth or falsehood of the claim. I have no doubt as to the verdict. For the testimony of reason may be wrong, but of the heart never.

Gandhi was in jail by the time I received these letters. In 1943 I returned to England, so I had no further correspondence with him until he was released in 1944. When I heard that he was going to Bengal, I felt it right to send him some of my impressions of what had happened in Bengal at the time of the arrests of the Congress leaders in July and August, 1942. From what I had seen and heard during that time, it seemed evident that there had in fact been a lot of violence and sabotage on the side of the nationalists, in addition to the violence from the Government side in the effort to suppress the movement. The following reply reached me in England (the original has disappeared).

12 June 1944

My dear Horace,

I have your long letter—long for the time and the way in which it had to be sent, not for the subject-matter. Some of what you tell me I had known already after coming out, and some of it is startling. All of it is good as coming from you, even the part that I know to be wrong. But that which is wrong does not diminish the importance of what you have said. The defects of your narrative arise from your good nature. I would rather have the latter than have the defects removed at the sacrifice of it. I need not thus have qualified my appreciation of your letter but for the fear of misleading you into the belief that I accept the whole of your version without any deduction. To discuss the deduction is not germane to what I want to say. You know the other side of the picture. The popular fury was pardon-

able; the vindictive and inhuman retribution wholly indefensible.
But I will not take your time over this.

Your anxiety that I should offer co-operation at least for the
alleviation of hunger I fully understand. My difficulty is that
I cannot, for the reason that the alleviation is only apparent.
The Viceroy's good intentions in the matter are not to be doubted.
His promptness in rushing to Bengal on arrival was worthy of
the soldier that he is. The agency through which he had and
has to work is not designed to carry out the work of alleviation.
You are entitled to put your noble work and experience against
what I am saying. That only shows that evil by itself and in
itself has no life. It requires the prop of good for its sustenance.
Hospitals, roads, railways are probably good in themselves but
when they are instruments of evil they are to be shunned. They
become snares. You will now realise somewhat my meaning.
Sufficient to say that at no time has India been so bound down
as now. The remedy is liberty consistent with the movements of
Allied troops. But there is deep mutual distrust. Authority
distrusts the Congress and every public body including the Muslim
League. Public opinion is flouted at almost every turn. In this
state of things voluntary co-operation becomes impossible. I have
tried in vain to see the Viceroy or be permitted to see the Working
Committee members. Now, tell me what to do. I know what
not to do. I am praying to God to tell me what to do. You
can assist.

I had a pleasant visit with James Vail [an American Quaker
who had visited India to see how American aid could be brought
to the Bengal famine victims]. Love to all who think of me.

Bapu

I was able to return to India in January, 1946. Agatha Harrison
arrived there a few weeks before me. On my arrival I found this
letter from Gandhi.

Madras,
31-1-46

My dear Horace,
   Welcome. You will meet me when and where you can. Agatha
knows my movement. Love.

Bapu

Apart from brief notes, I only received one long letter during
the next year, as we were meeting from time to time. This letter
needs to be recorded in full, as it shows his mind actively at work
on a number of matters. The first part deals with a plan for a
world conference or meeting of convinced pacifists. As soon as
the war was over, the Friends Peace Committee in London had
begun working on a plan by which it was hoped that a limited
number of active pacifists from the West might visit India and
meet Gandhi and a few of his fellow-workers, to get from him
immediately the inspiration that his experiments in non-violence
were already giving to many who read about his work. Gandhi
accepted the plan, and I was responsible for acting as liaison
between the Quakers in London and elsewhere and Gandhi himself.
The latter part of this letter is concerned with the story of an experiment with truth that he had undertaken whilst on the march in the
Noakhali District of East Bengal. I have given some account of this
beginning on page 141.
   This is a typed letter dictated from Patna, 25 March 1947.

My dear Horace,
   Gladys [Owen] has given me your letter and I had a fairly long
discussion with her as a result of which she has written to you a
letter which I enclose herewith. She has gone to see the Friends
Unit [some Quaker relief workers were in Bihar, some distance
from Patna, helping the victims of communal strife] and she is
expected to return tonight. I think her presentation of my position is fairly correct. But let me put it in my own language.
   What I feel is that however much detached we may want to be
from our surroundings and the unseen atmosphere about us we
cannot but be affected by it. Hence I am not sure whether,

whilst the British military forces are in India, we can possibly
be in real Indian atmosphere of peace and tranquillity, if these
are ever to be her lot during our generation. The present dis-
temper may continue beyond January next [the date suggested for
the conference] and if it does not I am afraid it won't be because
of sanity regained by the communities but because of the fear of
the military. What is the use of our meeting under the protection
of the bayonet, whether it is British or Indian? May it not be
wise therefore for sincere peace-lovers to pray in their homes
every day if you like, even for five minutes at the same time throughout the world? It will be easy enough for everyone to find out
the hour which should correspond with the time, say, in Calcutta
or any place in India. We can even make the calculations and
publish the different times for the different centres. The value
would lie in finding the exact time. [In his own handwriting
Gandhi then wrote the following sentence.] If you still think
that a meeting should take place here, I suggest postponement
till after the withdrawal of British arms.

These are my random thoughts, not for you to act upon unless
they fully appeal to you, because in this matter I have yielded to
your judgement. If you propose to go on with your idea and
want to have the meeting at the time you have conceived, send me
the thirty names (of suggested Indian participants) and I shall
send you my suggestions as to whether I want to add to the list.

With reference to milk distribution in Madras you have another
ministry there now. I wonder if it will make any difference.
I hold on to my suggestion. [I do not now recall what this was
referring to.]

About my own private affair I have done and am doing all
I can. I suppose you already know that Manu no longer sleeps
in the same bed with me. This departure was made by her with
my full approval in order to please Bapa [A.P. Thakkar] who,
though he saw nothing absolutely wrong, would appeal to her not
to continue whilst I was in Bihar and whilst I was engaged in this
important work. I do not agree with the conclusion. But I did
not wish to argue and therefore I promptly agreed.

Whilst I am dictating this letter I see that you could not know
this because the decision was made on the last day of my stay in
Himechar. What, however, is the subject of examination is my

mental attitude, whether it is correct or whether as Kishorelal and some other Indian friends consider, it is a remnant of my sexuality however unconscious it might be. My whole mental outlook will be changed immediately I saw this defect in me. Only then the weakness was coeval with the time when I took the vow of Brahmacharya [chastity] which was probably in 1902. It may be that their definition of Brahmacharya is different from mine. Love.

Yours,
Bapu

The last note that seems worth publishing is a brief letter of a very different character. Gandhi had told me he was coming to Delhi at the beginning of May 1947, and that he was expecting to meet me as soon as he arrived. The day before he was due, I fell ill with some stomach upset, and I had to go into hospital for a few days. There came this characteristic note in his own handwriting:

N.D.
2.5.47

My dear Horace,

Naughty of you to be ill. I must make a desperate effort to see you in your bed and make you laugh. Love.

Bapu

I knew that there were many urgent political matters awaiting his attention on his arrival in Delhi. Nevertheless, that same evening he turned up, just after his normal bedtime, and spent some twenty minutes with me and made me laugh.

That was the way he always treated his innumerable friends.

Index

Additional copies of this book are available.
Please send us $8.95 plus $1.50 postage &
handling (Pennsylvania residents please add 54¢ tax).
Make checks payable to:
Gandhi Through Western Eyes
249 Bortondale Road
Media, Pennsylvania 19063

FROM
NEW SOCIETY
PUBLISHERS